D1600908

HERBERT E. BOLTON AND THE HISTORIOGRAPHY OF THE AMERICAS

The Americas

Compiled by Joanna Barr.

HERBERT E. BOLTON AND THE HISTORIOGRAPHY OF THE AMERICAS

RUSSELL M. MAGNAGHI

Studies in Historiography, Number 5
John David Smith, *Series Editor*

GREENWOOD PRESS
Westport, Connecticut • London

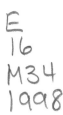

E
16
M34
1998

Library of Congress Cataloging-in-Publication Data

Magnaghi, Russell M.
   Herbert E. Bolton and the historiography of the Americas / Russell
M. Magnaghi.
     p. cm.—(Studies in historiography, ISSN 1046–526X ; no. 5)
   Includes bibliographical references and index.
   ISBN 0–313–29895–5 (alk. paper)
   1. America—Historiography. 2. Bolton, Herbert Eugene,
1870–1953. 3. Western Hemisphere—Historiography. I. Bolton,
Herbert Eugene, 1870–1953. II. Title. III. Series.
E16.M34   1998
970'.0072—DC21   97–38566

British Library Cataloguing in Publication Data is available.

Library of Congress Catalog Card Number: 97–38566
ISBN: 0–313–29895–5
ISSN: 1046–526X

First published in 1998

Greenwood Press, 88 Post Road West, Westport, CT 06881
An imprint of Greenwood Publishing Group, Inc.

Printed in the United States of America

The paper used in this book complies with the
Permanent Paper Standard issued by the National
Information Standards Organization (Z39.48–1984).

10 9 8 7 6 5 4 3 2 1

Copyright Acknowledgments

The author and publisher gratefully acknowledge permission for use of the following material:

Excerpts from the Bolton Correspondence from the Bancroft Library. Courtesy of the Bolton family.

Excerpts from the Herbert Eugene Bolton Papers (BANC MSS C-B 840), The Bancroft Library, University of California, Berkeley. Courtesy of the Bancroft Library.

Excerpts from the Henry Morse Stephens Papers (BANC MSS C-B 926), The Bancroft Library, University of California, Berkeley. Courtesy of the Bancroft Library.

Excerpts from the Mary Letitia Ross Papers, accession number ac 73-163. Courtesy of the Georgia Department of Archives and History.

Excerpts from the Magnaghi Papers (University Series 47), NMU Archives. Courtesy of NMU Archives (Central Upper Peninsula and Northern Michigan University Archives), Dr. Donald Cutter, W. J. Eccles, J. Manuel Espinosa, Henry May, Engel Sluiter, Donald Worcester, Woodrow Borah, the Estate of Ursula Lamb, Hereward Senior, Osvaldo Holguin Callo, Augusto Montenegro González, Amber H. Moss Jr., the Estate of Raymond H. Fisher, and Elizabeth J. Barnwell.

Excerpts from the Smith College History Department Minutes for February 22, 1935 and "The Committee on the Departmental Offering Submits . . ." from February 13, 1935. Courtesy of Smith College.

Excerpts from John Bannon's "A Bit of Autobio." Courtesy of St. Louis University and Midwest Jesuit Archives.

Every reasonable effort has been made to trace the owners of copyright materials in this book, but in some instances this has proven impossible. The author and publisher will be glad to receive information leading to more complete acknowledgments in subsequent printings of the book and in the meantime extend their apologies for any omissions.

For Grace and Mario Magnaghi:
parents with an appreciation of history

Contents

Photo essay follows page 81.

Preface

Within American historiography, Herbert Eugene Bolton (1870-1953) holds a unique position because of the various directions his studies took. On one level he is listed among "sectional historians" of the United States—a Western historian who stressed Spain's contribution to North American history.[1] He stressed the colonial history of the underbelly of the United States from Florida to California. He coined a term and developed a school called the Spanish Borderlands. However, despite errors in interpretation, Bolton was more than a sectional historian. Going beyond traditional notions of United States history and beyond his mentors, John Bach McMaster and Frederick Jackson Turner, he stressed both the comparative nature of United States colonial history and, his crowning achievement, the history of the Americas concept. Bolton conceived a "Universal American History, that is the history of the Americas from the North Pole to the South Pole and from Columbus to Now." If Western civilization could be studied as a unit, then why not the Western Hemisphere?

In 1919, early in the development of the history of the Americas concept, Bolton described this new form of synthetic history. He based the concept on certain aspects of Frederick Jackson Turner's frontier theory. Bolton saw the importance of the coming of European civilization into the New World. It entered the Americas, developed within the new environment, and eventually created the various independent nations and experiences of the nineteenth century. Thus Bolton's history of the Americas started with the general European background, and the cultural and institutional premises of American history, followed by the occupation of the American continents and the transmission of European civilization in the particular national variations (Dutch, English, French, Portuguese, Russian, Spanish, and Swedish), and ended with colonial expansion and international rivalries. After this first stage of the history, the English and Spanish colonies won independence, and eventually independence for the Brazilians and Canadians evolved. Bolton's progression began with a concentration on national development and the interrelations and relations with the outside world, and ended with a look at the contemporary Americas.[2] Bolton believed that the individual should first view the history of the Americas in this broader context to better appreciate and understand the whole; individual national histories could then be studied within this context.

Bolton never saw this synthetic history as a thesis;[3] rather, as his biographer John Francis Bannon has written, "the Americas device was a technique, an approach which sought to highlight similarities and dissimilarities to heighten appreciation and understanding of the human experience in the Western Hemisphere."[4] However, disciples of this approach, like Lewis Hanke, labeled it the "Bolton theory," and there were others who thought likewise. The commonality of this new approach—as seen in the questioning title of conference sessions and books, "Do the Americas have a common history?"—also caused negative reactions from many historians who ultimately ignored the debate and the value of this new form of comparative history.

Unfortunately, Bolton never thoroughly analyzed the concept to the satisfaction of the historical community. Although he had given the concept considerable thought, he was not a particularly philosophical or analytical historian. He narrated the story adequately but seemed unable to realize his broader concept. He promised his publishers a textbook, followed by an interpretative study of the Americas, but his many other projects intervened and these two were either never undertaken or never completed. The only tangible items from all of Bolton's voluminous correspondence concerning the concept are a few articles, introductions, and his class syllabus, *History of the Americas*.

Bolton never stressed the concept of comparative history. At the same time as Bolton, the Belgian historian Henri Pirenne and the French historian Marc Bloch were pioneering this new field of historical interpretation.

The historiography of the Americas approach has been limited. Articles, usually biographical in nature, highlighted Bolton throughout his lifetime. At the time of his death, a plethora of obituaries merely mentioned the Americas concept.[5] In 1924, in an attempt to answer the many requests sent to him seeking advice about his new approach, Bolton wrote the first published work to discuss his approach.[6] His 1928 syllabus provides some additional insights into the scope and significance of American history, especially in the introduction.[7] Four years later, Bolton presented his famous speech, "The Epic of Greater America," at the Toronto meeting of the American Historical Association. This speech comes closest to an analysis of the Americas concept. Over the years this address has been reprinted in a number of publications.[8] In 1936, his former student J. Manuel Espinosa (Ph.D. 1934) took on the task of explaining the Bolton approach in a short article published in a rather obscure journal, *The Historical Bulletin*.[9]

In 1939 Edmundo O'Gorman first raised the critical discussion of the Americas concept in an article published in *Universidad de la Habana* and later translated.[10] In 1941, William Binkley, George W. Brown, Edmundo O'Gorman, and Germán Arciniegas presented various hemispheric positions on the question in a session of the American Historical Association.[11] Years later, Lewis Hanke would use this theme for his edited work *Do the Americas Have a Common History?*, published in 1964.

After Bolton's death, a number of studies appeared that dealt with Bolton and the Americas. José de Onís discussed the matter in an article in *The Americas*, and in 1958, one of Hanke's students, Charles L. Eastlack, wrote an analysis of Bolton's work as a master's thesis at the University of Texas.[12] Bannon's biography in the late 1970s provides some basic observations on the Americas concept but does little more.[13]

Historiographically, historians give Bolton's role in the development of the Americas concept sporadic attention. General surveys of United States, Canadian, and Latin American historiography mention the man and the Americas concept.[14] However, in 1964, John Francis Bannon, S.J., one of the early proponents of the concept, diminished the importance of Bolton's Americas focus by stressing his work as a Borderlands historian.[15] Furthermore, over the years, myth and legend developed about the concept.

Today, the value of Bolton's concept of hemispheric history is immanent. In 1932 Bolton said such an approach would achieve the following goals: (1) to go beyond limiting national histories; (2) to get a better understanding of the history and culture of the entire region, which, due to expanding importance of inter-American relations, was imperative; (3) to gain more meaning for national histories when they are understood in light of the other histories; and (4) to show that "it is quite desirable from the standpoint of correct historiography."[16] In the contemporary world, many of these reasons are still valid. We are concerned with the multicultural nature of each of our national societies. The North American Free Trade Agreement (NAFTA) is bringing the United States, Canada, and Mexico closer together on economic and eventually on social and cultural levels. This will expand when other Western Hemisphere nations are signatories to the agreement. And as it was true in the past, it is true today; it is still sound historiography.

The purpose of this study is to look at the forces that shaped Bolton's thinking and brought about the development of the Americas concept. In the process, many of the myths connected with the development and exposition of the concept will be examined. For instance, Bolton's idea to study the history of the Western Hemisphere as a entity can be traced back to the sixteenth century. Historians and their ideas do not develop in a vacuum, and this was true of Bolton. In many ways, Bolton built on the work of others and developed a new approach to an old concept. While Bolton went to college and eventually developed his concept, there were forces at work that had direct and indirect influence on him. His interest in the Americas concept developed gradually from his days at the University of Wisconsin, where he studied under Frederick Jackson Turner and was introduced to the frontier thesis. These ideas gained new meaning when Bolton encountered the Spanish story of Texas and the rich documentation in the Mexican archives. His view further expanded as he encountered multi-national colonial expansion and rivalry in the Caribbean and then saw the larger role of the Spanish not only in Texas but also in the Southwest and throughout the Spanish Borderlands. If there was a multi-national story in the Caribbean, what about North America? This led to the 1920 publication *The Colonization of North America*, written by Bolton and his former student Thomas M. Marshall, a comparative approach to United States history.

Simultaneously, the United States was becoming a world power, seeking commercial advantage in Latin America, fighting against the Spanish in 1898, acquiring former Spanish possessions, and then entering World War I. At this time historians were looking at regional history in a broader perspective, and many of them were appalled by the lack of world knowledge that Americans possessed. The opening of the Panama Canal in 1914 caused many historians to focus on the history of the Pacific Ocean and its link with European expansion as regional history with which Americans should be familiar.

Bolton was influenced not only by academe but by world events as well. When he published his syllabus in 1928, president-elect Herbert Hoover traveled to Latin America and initiated what became Franklin Roosevelt's Good Neighbor policy. This policy and subsequent hemispheric solidarity during World War II closely parallel Bolton's work on the Americas. By the early 1940s the State Department viewed Bolton as one of the leading specialists on inter-American relations, and officials utilized his expertise and that of his students, many of whom joined the State Department's Latin American desk during the war.

Bolton lived to see his concept of hemispheric history taught in colleges and universities throughout North America. Although he never published his textbook on the history of the Americas, he did see his student John F. Bannon produce a version. By the time of his death in 1953, he could look with pride at the development of the concept of hemispheric history, "from pole to pole and from Columbus to the present."

NOTES

1. Michael Krause and Davis D. Joyce, *The Writing of American History*, rev. ed. (Norman: University of Oklahoma Press, 1985), 277-281.
2. Herbert E. Bolton to Arthur Schlesinger, 11/26/1919, Bolton Papers, Out, Bancroft Library, University of California, Berkeley. (Bolton Papers, part 2, Correspondence, is divided into categories In and Out. Hereafter cited as Bolton Papers In or Out.)
3. The only time he used the term "thesis" was in a letter to Verner W. Crane in 1919.
4. John F. Bannon, *Herbert Eugene Bolton: The Historian and the Man, 1870-1953* (Tucson: University of Arizona Press, 1978), 255-256.
5. For a rather complete listing of these articles, see ibid., 264-265.
6. Herbert E. Bolton, "An Introductory Course in American History," *Historical Outlook* 15.1 (1924): 17-20.
7. Herbert E. Bolton, *History of the Americas: A Syllabus with Maps* (Boston: Ginn, 1928).
8. Herbert E. Bolton, "The Epic of Greater America," *American Historical Review* 38 (1933): 448-474; *La epopeya de la máxima América*, trans. Carmen Alessio Robles, Publication no. 30 (México, DF: Instituto Panamericano de Geografía e Historia, 1937); *Wider Horizons of American History* (New York: Appleton-Century, 1939); John F. Bannon, ed., *Bolton and the Spanish Borderlands* (Norman: University of Oklahoma Press, 1963) 301-332; Lewis Hanke, ed., *Do the Americas Have a Common History? A Critique of the Bolton Theory* (New York: Knopf, 1964), 67-102.
9. J. Manuel Espinosa, "Bolton: History of the Americas," *Historical Bulletin* 14 (1936): 81-82.
10. Edmundo O'Gorman, *Do the Americas Have A Common History?* trans. Angel Flores, Points of View no. 3 (Washington, DC: Pan-American Union, Division of Intellectual Cooperation, 1941).
11. William C. Binkley, "Have the Americas a Common History?: A United States View," *Canadian Historical Review* 23 (1942): 125-132; George W. Brown, "Have the Americas a Common History?: A Canadian View," *Canadian Historical Review* 23 (1942): 132-138; O'Gorman; "Have the Americas a Common History?: A Mexican View," *Canadian Historican Review* 23 (1942): 139-148; Germán Arciniegas, "Have the Americas a Common History? A South American View," *Canadian Historical Review* 23 (1942): 148-156.
12. José de Onís, "The Americas of Herbert E. Bolton," *The Americas* 12 (1955): 157-168; Charles L. Eastlack, "Herbert Eugene Bolton (1870-1953): His Ideas and Practice as a Historian of the Americas" (thesis, University of Texas, Austin, 1958).
13. Bannon, *Herbert Eugene Bolton*, 255-256.
14. Krause and Joyce, *Writing of American History*, 277-281; Carl Berger, *The Writing of Canadian History: Aspects of English-Canadian Historical Writing Since 1900*, 2nd ed. (Toronto: University of Toronto Press, 1986); Héctor José Tanzi, "Historiografía americana," *Revista de historia de América* 104 (1987): 65-112.
15. Bannon, *Spanish Borderlands*, 301.
16. Bolton, "Epic of Greater America," 448-449.

Acknowledgments

Over the years this study has been aided by numerous Boltonians, colleagues from throughout the Americas, and students of history. Discussions with and the lectures of John Francis Bannon, S.J., provided a foundation for the project. Lawrence Kinnaird once asked why I did not focus on the developmental forces behind Bolton's concepts. At other times Lewis Hanke and, later, Silvio A. Zavala provided the written support that pushed the project forward. Letters to Mary Callaghan, J. Manuel Espinosa, and Donald Worcester elicited timely, informative, and enthusiastic responses. In November 1992 I was able to meet with Dr. Espinosa in Washington, DC, and discuss Bolton and the concept at length. At the University of California, Berkeley, the following emeritus faculty — Woodrow Borah, Henry May, Engel Sluiter, and Kenneth Stampp — were extremely helpful. The late professors Raymond H. Fisher of the University of California at Los Angeles, Ursula Lamb of the University of Arizona, and Stephen Barnwell of Northern Michigan University provided me with personal insights. Richard Greenleaf at Tulane University was helpful in explaining the present state of his course on the subject. Bolton scholar Alberto Hurtado of Arizona State University provided direction to the study. Gerald Cardoso of Washington, DC, served as a translator of Brazilian documents. Ambler H. Moss, Jr., director of the North-South Center, University of Miami, provided useful information on the Center.

Professors Felipe Castro and Elias Margolis Schweber of the National Autonomous University of Mexico; Rita Maria Lino of Mackenzie University, São Paulo, Brazil; Luis Celis Muñoz of the Catholic Pontifical University of Chile, Santiago; Augusto Montenegro González and Rosa Elena Gómez Hurtado of the Pontifical Javerian University in Bogotá, Colombia; Nikita L. Harwich of Andrés Bello Catholic University, Caracas, Venezuela; and Oswaldo Holguín Callo of the Catholic Pontifical University of Peru, Lima, provided important information and insights into the development of academic programs taking an Americas orientation in their respective countries. Retired professor Guillermo Morón of Simón Bolivas University of Caracas and dean of the National Academy of History updated the publication history of the *General History of Americas* series. From Canada came assistance from W. J. Eccles, emeritus professor of the University of Toronto; Paul W. Bennett of Upper Canada College in Toronto; Phebe Chartrand, archivist, and Bruce Dolphin, McGill University Archives; Hereward Senior of McGill University, Montreal; and Elisabeth Karner of the Canadian Foundation for the Americas.

The library staffs at Northern Michigan University, the William Clements Library at the University of Michigan, Michigan State University, the James Bell Collection at the University of Minnesota, the Newberry Library in Chicago, the University of Texas, Tulane University, Smith College Archives, Queen's University's College Archives in Kingston, Ontario, and the Universidad de las Américas, and Bonnie Hardwick of the Bancroft Library, University of California, Berkeley, provided me with timely assistance in my ongoing research.

Over the years many others, both on and off Northern Michigan University's campus, have provided me with assistance, criticism, and encouragement. My colleagues Judith DeMark, Martin Dolan, Eugene A. Whitehouse, and J. Manuel Espinoza read and critiqued the manuscript. The students in the Junior-Senior Seminars, coming from a generation unfamiliar with the Boltonian concept, provided me with important insights and criticisms. Troy Huggett, while studying at Northern, spent a semester assisting me with portions of this study. Karen Wallingford provided invaluable editorial assistance, as did Sue Ann Salo and Madonna Marsden. My designation as a Peter White Scholar of Northern Michigan University provided the financial assistance necessary to complete the research for this project.

Finally I would like to thank my mother, Grace Mendiara Magnaghi, who first brought the Spanish history of California to my attention and in many ways made this work possible. My wife, Diane Kordich, who listened on our morning trips to work, encouraged me to complete the final revisions. To all of these people I extend my sincerest thanks and appreciation.

1

Pre-Bolton Formulations of the History of the Americas

To understand and appreciate Herbert E. Bolton's position and interest in the history of the Americas, it is paramount to understand the development of the concept in the centuries prior to Bolton. Historians first viewed the Western Hemisphere as Spanish real estate whose story could be told as a unit. Later, as other European nations entered the hemisphere and created colonies, historians focused on these experiences. After independence created individual nations, each nation had its own history; however, the broader picture was still distorted. Throughout these developments, few historians had the foresight to focus on the broader history of the Americas rather than on individual histories.

The idea of taking a broad approach to history—a universal history both sacred and profane—had been a favorite approach in the Middle Ages. Then, during the Renaissance, nationalism and large geographical divisions emerged, destroying the old paradigms. European historiography shifted its focus from sacred models to national, regional, and local themes.

This was not the case in Spain. After the discovery of America and the Magellan expedition (1519-1522), which was the first to circumnavigate the globe, Spain clearly possessed claim on a world of immense proportions—from Labrador on the north to Tierra del Fuego on the south. When Spanish historians like Peter Martyr, Antonio de Herrera, Gonzalo Fernández de Oviedo, and José de Acosta wrote of the New World, they had to deal with a mass of data and a new variety of physical and human types spread over a continental empire.[1]

Over the centuries, other European scholars took a broad approach to their studies of the Americas. In 1553, German historian Sebastian Münster included South America, "the Cod Kingdom" of Newfoundland, and

Florida in his work.[2] A Frenchman, Andrewe Thevet, published *The New Found Worlde or Antarctike* in 1568 and took a position similar to Münster's.[3] The French Huguenot historian Lancelot du Voisin, Sieur de La Popelinière (1541-1608), in his *Les Trois Mondes* [4] forwarded the merit of French and other non-Spanish claims. Richard Hakluyt, seeking to get England involved in colonization, not only published English accounts but also translated French and Spanish chronicles of New World activities, creating a large English-language library on the subject.[5] Samuel Purchas, a compiler of travel books, continued Hakluyt's work, taking a broad historical approach in his published manuscripts.

In eighteenth-century Europe, historians and general scientists continued this trend. In Spain, Colonel Antonio de Alcedo of the Spanish Army produced a five-volume work, *El diccionario geográfico histórico de las Indias Occidentales o América* (1786-1789), using personal diaries and family correspondence.[6] This dictionary follows a gazetteer format, and although the content provides no analysis, it covers topics throughout the hemisphere. The French *philosophes* were interested in various aspects of the moral, natural, and philosophical histories of the New World. When the famous *Encyclopédie*, the great gathering of Enlightenment knowledge, was published in 1751, "America" was allotted a scant fifty lines, but as the years passed, a pro-French view of the Americas presented some nineteen pages of text.[7]

At this time a number of English historians began to focus on an approach exclusive to a history of the Americas. The earliest result of this focus, *An Account of the European Settlements in America*, was published in 1757.[8] Although it was written chiefly by Will Burke, the book is usually associated with Will's more famous partner, Edmund Burke, who collaborated in the piece. Edmund Burke later wrote that he "had some small hand" in its development. He was probably referring to the revisions that he made in the manuscript. Whatever Edmund's exact involvement in the work, this writing experience provided him with important insights into European colonization and shaped his attitudes toward the thirteen colonies during their struggle for independence.[9]

The *Account* was written because "the recent trouble there" (referring to the Seven Years War) had stimulated interest in the subject. The Burkes tried to present a balanced picture in their history. However, some critics complain of *Account's* inherent weakness because of the use of available secondary sources rather than original documentation; others point out that in larger matters the authors demonstrated an overall breadth of vision. Despite the anti-Spanish view held by many English, the Burkes sympathized with the humanitarian efforts of the Catholic clergy to lessen the suffering of the Indians and African slaves. Although Edmund Burke disliked New England Puritanism, he took pride in the political liberty that the English colonists had developed in the New World.[10]

The volumes vary in their content from narrative history to gazetteer reporting. Content analysis reveals the following emphasis on the different colonial experiences: English in North America (27.5%) and the Caribbean (11.7%); the grand story of discovery and conquest (26.2%); Spanish America (15%); French, Dutch, and Danes (7.7%); Native Americans (5.5%); and the Portuguese in Brazil (3.7%).

When these accounts were written, one of the primary concerns was to promote the development of national trade and commerce or strategic interests. This was true in the eighteenth century as well as in the twentieth century. Despite its style and emphasis, the work proved to be so popular with readers that it went through eight British editions by 1801. The first American edition was published at Boston in 1835.

W. A. Young's *The History of North and South America*, published in 1776, followed the Burkes' work. Young noted that many previously published books tended to emphasize one area and proved to be too voluminous and expensive for many readers. His two small volumes were written to help the average reader "understand properly the present state of our American affairs" on the eve of the American War of Independence.[11] He took a broad perspective that included the rest of the Americas: Canada, Latin America, and the Caribbean. Young even discussed the European character in New World settlement.[12] Unfortunately, he drew too heavily from the Burkes' history. Although he sought to cover the problem with a different table of contents, a close study shows the Burkes' material had been inserted unchanged throughout the two volumes.[13]

The next person to write an Americas history was the Scottish historian William Robertson (1721-1793). Trained at the University of Edinburgh, he followed the new eighteenth-century mode that championed a more scientific approach.[14] This previously little-known Presbyterian clergyman changed his life when he published *History of Scotland during the Reigns of Queen Mary and King James VI* in 1759. This work was read throughout Britain and was viewed as a major contribution to eighteenth-century historiography. Robertson's research on his first historical study introduced him to the sixteenth century, which he concluded was the period when "the powers of Europe were formed into one great political system."[15] He believed it was a pivotal era when the Renaissance and the Reformation were blended with the discovery and exploration of America. Because the ruler in the midst of all of these developments was Emperor Charles V (King Charles I of Spain), Robertson thought it was important to write a history of the emperor's reign. By the summer of 1761, Robertson's work had progressed well, but it would take him another seven years to complete the work.

While he was engaged in writing this opus, Robertson attracted the literary attention of the Tory Prime Minister, the Earl of Bute (1761-1763), and of King George III, both of whom encouraged him to work on a history of England once he finished with Charles V. In order to provide Robertson with enough free time to work on his projected history, Bute secured him the principalship of the University of Edinburgh and, soon after, the post of royal historiographer of Scotland. Fortunately for the *History of America*, Bute's fortunes declined; he resigned in 1763 and disappeared from political life two years later. Because no one else was as enthusiastic about the history of England, Robertson now had the financial security to work undisturbed on his projected history of the Spanish Empire.[16]

In the preface to the detailed history of Charles's reign, Robertson reveals his plans. Since the Spanish conquest and colonization of the New World were so important in the history of the world and impacted Europe, Robertson did not want to treat the subject superficially. He reserved this "for a separate history" that would take him approximately eight years to complete.

In the spirit of the Enlightenment, Robertson sought only the most complete sources for his study, aspiring to obtain historically accurate and authentic information. Through his interested and obliging friend Lord Grantham, who was appointed ambassador to the court of Madrid, Robertson gained access to Spanish documents. Grantham engaged Reverend Robert Waddilove, chaplain of the embassy, to conduct the necessary research. For five years Waddilove worked diligently and provided Robertson with rare and valuable sixteenth-century editions of books along with copies of priceless manuscripts.[17]

Robertson also compiled convoluted oral histories by sending Reverend Waddilove a series of questions to be asked in such a fashion that they could be answered "without disclosing any thing that was improper to be communicated to a foreigner." These were translated into Spanish and given to various persons who had lived in the New World. The responses he received proved to be invaluable to his research.

Robertson was able to mine European archives through the help of his associates. The archives of Simancas in Spain proved to be invaluable. Through other ambassadors, Robertson obtained information and documents from government libraries and archives in Vienna and St. Petersburg. Catherine the Great, through her personal physician, Dr. Rogerson, personally arranged to make previously unavailable information about the Russian exploration of coastal Alaska available to Robertson. He also obtained data from Portuguese and French sources, and Governor Thomas Hutchinson of Massachusetts and others provided him with information on the Indians of the Americas. Finally, on the advice of Edward Gibbon, Robertson included an extensive bibliography.

Originally, Robertson contemplated a history of the Americas that would include the Spanish, Portuguese, and English experiences.[18] Once the individual stories were written, the entire study was to be published as a set of volumes. In 1775 the advent of the American War of Independence changed his plans. "It is lucky," he wrote, "that my American History was not finished before this event. How many plausible theories, that I should have been entitled to form, are contradicted by what has now happened!"[19] As a result, he waited "with the solicitude of a good citizen, until the ferment subside, and regular government be re-established." He added that only then could he return to the work.[20] Unfortunately, the struggle continued, and Robertson did not return to his opus. By 1784 he had written a manuscript of several hundred pages dealing with the British colonies. However, he put it aside with the advent of United States independence, explaining, "what would have been a good introduction to the settlement of British Colonies, will suit very ill the establishment of Independent States."[21]

His energy ran out before histories of Brazil and the Caribbean could be started. These were eventually written by Bryan Edwards and Robert Southey, respectively. Although Robertson destroyed many of his manuscripts prior to his death, his histories of Virginia and Massachusetts survived. In 1796, Robertson's son published these as books IX and X of the *History*.

Robertson felt that the Spanish story was "not only the most splendid portion of the American story but so much detached, as, by itself, to form a perfect whole, remarkable for the unity of the subject." For him, the Spanish history was significant because it was the Spanish who set colonial patterns that the other imperial powers followed, and he hoped to show this development in his projected volumes on the Americas.[22]

Robertson took new directions in these volumes. First, he went to the roots of the history of the Americas—the Indian civilizations. Using the limited materials available at the time, Robertson presented the indigenous cultures of Mexico and Peru and "the manners and policy of its most uncivilized inhabitants." He had no sympathy with the legend of the "noble savage" but showed an unusual awareness of the relationship between geography and history.[23] Since discovery was so important to the development of this work, Robertson traced its history from antiquity to the fifteenth-century Portuguese voyages. In another unique development, he included a remarkable chapter in Book VII that analyzed the nature and effects of Spanish colonization in the New World and discussed contemporary Bourbon Reform.

Historians have declared Robertson's work both classic and scholarly. He used his enormous number of sources critically and with "great fidelity," as historian Justin Winsor noted. The result was a clearly written history based on sound judgment and views sympathetic to the Spanish. His work was seen as the first history of the Western Hemisphere. Other historians have considered him equal or superior to his friends David Hume (1711-1776) and Edward Gibbon (1737-1794).[24]

Spanish scholars were impressed with Robertson's work. The distinguished statesman, economist, historian, and president of the Royal Academy of History at Madrid, Pedro Rodríguez de Campomanes (1723-1803), read the work with admiration. In August 1802, the Academy unanimously elected Robertson a corresponding member. Members were so impressed with the work that a translation was authorized, and by the end of the year it was nearly completed. Campomanes had warned Robertson to expect that the government might take offense at such a translation and prohibit it. Research had barely begun on enhancing the work when officials assailed it as offensive to Spanish honor, a *precursor de fatalidades* (precursor of trouble), and a source of corruption to the "youth of Spain" and the "unwary reader" everywhere. Government officials forbade the translated publication, and by a royal decree of December 23, 1778, its introduction into Spanish America and the Philippines was prohibited.[25] In an attempt to refute the errors that it believed were inherent in the work, the Spanish government gave Juan Bautista Muñoz the official charge to write a correct history. Muñoz published his *Historia del Nuevo Mundo* in 1793 at Madrid, but it did not replace Robertson's work.

British interest in a broad Americas approach did not end with Robertson. In 1795, William Winterbotham published his four-volume *American Historical, Geographical, Commercial and Philosophical Views of the American United States and of the European Settlements in America and the West-Indies*; the monumental *A General History of North and South America* which was anonymously published at London in 1834, ran over one thousand pages.[26]

European historians and others used an Americas approach throughout the nineteenth century, and the historiographical tradition continued. In many cases, historians developed these works for European or United States commercial advantage in the New World. Between 1826 and 1844, David Baille Warden (1772-1845) developed his ten-volume chronology entitled *Chronologie historique de l'Amérique*.[27] The International Congress of Americanists traces its roots back to the mid-nineteenth century with the establishment of the *Société Américaine de France*. The members developed a publication program in 1858, and seventeen years later held the Society's first international congress at Nancy, France. Since that time, meetings have been held every other year in both Europe and the Americas, except during war years.[28] The scholarly presentations of these congresses, which cover Americas topics, fill large volumes. In 1895, a group of predominantly French scholars joined together to organize the *Société des Américanistes de Paris*, which is dedicated to the historical and scientific study of the American continent and its inhabitants from the pre-Columbian era to the present. The organization continues to meet and to publish scholarly articles in *Journal de la Société des Américanistes de Paris*.[29]

In Britain in 1808, John MacGregor, the secretary of the Board of Trade in London, published a two-volume work entitled *The Progress of America: From the Discovery by Columbus to the Year 1846*. The first volume was a statistical history of the Americas, with the intrusion of an anti-Spanish bias; the second volume was devoted solely to the United States and commercial information.[30] British historian Robert Mackenzie (1823-81) wrote a number of works on United States history and the nineteenth-century world.[31] His last work, posthumously published in 1882, was *America: A History*, which took a hemispheric approach but with a late-nineteenth century imperialist focus toward native peoples, French Canada, and Latin America that was critical of Spanish settlement in the New World. In 1894 the publishers updated and reissued the book, and included a "Summary of Recent Events" and an afterword written by Prime Minister William E. Gladstone titled "The Future of the English-Speaking Races," which is jingoism at its worst.[32]

Nations with a colonial heritage in the Americas were more interested in the broader approach to hemispheric history than in nationalistic histories. In the nineteenth century, the Italians, with their long but indirect connection with the Americas, took a broad approach. Between 1820 and 1822, Giuseppe Compagnoni published twenty-eight small volumes entitled *Storia dell'America*, a continuation of the Count of Segur's larger history.[33] Even in the landlocked German states, historians, geographers, and scientists were interested in the New World. The most famous German explorer, natural philosopher, and scientist to study portions of Latin America was Alexander von Humboldt (1769-1859).[34] Between 1799 and 1804, he visited Cuba, Venezuela, Colombia, Ecuador, Peru, and Mexico, gathering thousands of specimens and data. Although he planned to continue his research in North America, his plan to visit Canada and the United States was never realized. But the multi-volume work on the material he did gather was of near-hemispheric proportions. As the century passed, other Germans developed histories of the Americas.[35] A native of Bremen, Johann Georg Kohl, was interested in exploration, geography, research and traveling and spent many years in North America although he never visited South America.[36] He published much of his research under the title, *Codex Americanus Geographicus*.

The development of the Americas approach in Europe saw a parallel development in the New World and the emergence of a new phase in its historiography. As the Latin American nations gained their independence, national histories followed. America, which could be studied during the colonial era as a single entity, now broke down into sixteen separate nation-states, a change that was evidenced by the developing historiography. Soon after, however, educators in some of the nations urged the teaching of a broader Americas approach, thus creating a paradox. Much as Bolton would later stress, it was hoped that citizens would come to see the interconnectedness of hemispheric history. Discussions progressed, but the results were as varied as the number of nations.

Following the European tradition, in 1856 the French-born Benedictine priest and director of Rio de Janeiro's National Library, Frei Camilo de Monserrate, proposed that the history of all of the American nations be taught in Brazilian schools. He contended that "the teaching of the national history cannot be complete except as parallel to the history of other American nations." Only through a comparative approach would Brazilians be able to understand many problems in their history.[37]

Unfortunately, Brazil did not heed Frei Camilo's call. Thirty years later B. F. Ramiz Galvão complained of the strong French influence in Brazilian textbooks and maintained that the books should meet "the needs of an American people."[38]

Across the continent, on the shores of the Pacific, the famed Chilean historian and educator Diego Barros Arana stressed the importance of an Americas approach.[39] This was done soon after a review of the national curriculum in the late 1850s.[40] On December 31, 1863, he became rector of the National Institute, and soon after, he undertook the development of a work on the Americas.[41] Between July and August 1864 he completed the first volume of his *Compendio de historia de América*, which dealt with indigenous America and the conquest. Volume II of the *Compendio*, dealing with the colonial and revolutionary eras, was completed by the end of the year, and the entire work was published in March 1865. This was quickly followed by *Compendio elemental de historia de América*, a one-volume summary of the larger work.[42]

Due to the hectic writing and production schedule, the history contained numerous errors. But Barros Arana thought that it was more important to get these publications into the hands of students and that revisions could be incorporated into the text in later editions. The faculty at the University of Chile gave their immediate and unanimous approval for both the incorporation of the Americas approach into the Chilean educational system and the utilization of Barros Arana's texts.

Beginning at the National College of Buenos Aires in 1863, educators in Argentina also saw the value in teaching the Americas as a unit. Eventually this broad approach entered the secondary, vocational, and college curricula throughout the country. In the 1880s, the Minister of Public Instruction mandated that primary and secondary teachers use Barros Arana's *Compendio elemental de historia de América*.[43]

The value of such an approach to the history of the hemisphere continued to be debated in Brazil. The leading opponent was Eduardo Prado. In 1893 he contended that an American fraternity was an illusion, and the fact that the United States and Brazil were on the same continent was merely a geographical accident "to which it would be puerile to attribute an exaggerated importance...for we find ourselves separated not solely by great distance, but by race, by religion, by character, by language, and by the traditions of our people."[44] Prado's opinions on the rest of Latin America were similarly hostile. He pointed out that the hatred among these nations was worse than that among European nations, and condemned their chaotic governments and finances.[45]

In the passing years Brazil often reasserted this exclusive view of itself vis-à-vis Latin America and the United States. In many ways, Brazil's attitude toward its immediate and distant neighbors served as a solid reason for the development of an Americas concept. It could possibly make people understand the larger history and developments, and appreciate their differences. A series of conversations between the Brazilian Foreign Minister, Baron Rio Branco, and the head of the United States legation (soon to be appointed ambassador), David E. Thompson, provides some interesting Brazilian views of South America. In 1905, Thompson wrote to the State Department that Baron Rio Branco "has no little ill-feeling for Argentina, Perú, and Bolivia, and no liking for any of the South American countries other than his own, unless it may be Chile...." During a dispute between Brazil and Perú, Rio Branco told Thompson, "No Spanish speaking country is good and no person of Spanish blood can be believed."[46] Later Rio Branco called for Latin American solidarity against the "Monroism" of the United States,[47] yet he continued to rail against neighboring Argentina for her attitude toward South American neighbors: "in all the world she [Argentina] thinks she has no peer except in numbers, not even excepting your own great country [the United States]; in South America she wishes to pose as dictator."[48] Fortunately, the Brazilian newspaper *A Notícia* was also calling for peace and understanding in South America.

With the exchange of ambassadors in March 1905, some Brazilian newspapers praised the action and the role of the United States. However, in the *Jornal do Comércio*, an editorial expressed fear that the United States embassy would be a Trojan horse which the northern nation would use to infiltrate and dominate Brazil. The editor concluded that the "international police" were on patrol![49]

Brazil gradually modified its critical attitude toward the United States. In 1908 the first Brazilian ambassador to the United States, Joaquim Nabuco, writing under the pen name of J. Penn, published an article, "The United States, Brazil, and Monroism," which had some kind things to say about the Monroe Doctrine. In 1914, Manuel de Oliveira Lima wrote his pioneer work, *The Evolution of Brazil Compared with That of Anglo-Saxon America*. Although it took a comparative approach, it did not lead to a consideration of hemispheric history as a whole. Brazil's attitude toward its neighbors is a fine example of the type of ultranationalism that the history of the Americas sought to modify and alter.[50]

Beginning in the late eighteenth century and continuing through the nineteenth century, the perception of a common history among the emerging nations of the hemisphere slowly developed in the United States. This slow development of a comparative historical approach was caused by the narrow perspective and historical nationalism many American historians were accused of having. However, there were some individuals and historians who took a broader historical view.[51]

While in Paris between 1785 and 1788, Thomas Jefferson wrote a series of letters stressing the importance of the Spanish language and the role Spain played in the Americas. He emphasized the importance of knowing the Spanish language because Americans already had close connections with Spain, which Jefferson believed would grow as the years passed and new relations with Spanish America developed. Furthermore, Jefferson noted that the early history of America was a Spanish story, and in the eighteenth century most of the history of America was written in Spanish. Jefferson concluded his argument for a sound knowledge of the Spanish language by noting that such knowledge would be invaluable for a political candidate seeking public office and that it "should be known to every inhabitant who means to look beyond the limits of his farm."[52]

United States citizens had mixed emotions about and views of their Latin American neighbors. A limited knowledge and understanding of the region plus anti-Spanish prejudice based on sixteenth-century English attitudes (sometimes referred to as the Black Legend), old religious prejudices such as anti-Catholicism, and growing Anglo-Saxon racism influenced Americans' attitudes.[53] The belief that Latin America was different from Anglo America due to "vicious institutions," culture, heritage, violence, and language were shared by most Americans, including President Monroe, and was directed toward Mexicans prior to and through the Mexican-American War.[54] These unicultural attitudes would influence future generations of Americans. In the mid-nineteenth century, many American writers tended to be xenophobic and hispanophobic in their presentations.[55]

While these prejudicial attitudes flourished, changes were developing as American interest in Latin America expanded. In the first half of the nineteenth century, business interests, diplomats, naval officers, scholars, scientists, and others helped acquaint Americans with Latin America. During this time the United States acquired portions of Spain's colonial empire: Florida and Louisiana, later Texas, then from Mexico and after the Mexican-American War, the entire Southwest. As a result, some Americans began to appreciate the importance of understanding this non-Anglo history of the United States.

During the 1840s and 1850s a number of books that took a broad approach to the history of the New World were published. In 1844, Samuel G. Goodrich (1793-1860), a prolific writer and compiler of school books and children's books, published one of the first juvenile books dealing with the history of the Americas. This was rather unusual because at this time hispanophobia was widespread. His book, *A Pictorial History of America; Embracing Both the Northern and Southern Portions of the New World,* concentrated on the United States but included the history of all other parts of the Americas as well.[56] The book went through ten editions between 1844 and 1858. Goodrich published other works using a similar approach.[57]

Historians and others were taking a wider view of hemispheric history. Previously narrow, Anglo-centered history gave way to the inclusion of the history of the Spanish Empire. In the 1850s Buckingham Smith tried to make Americans conscious of Spain's colonization in the United States. He proposed the publication of a large "Documentary History of that part of the United States once under Spanish domination," which unfortunately, was never realized.[58] John Russell Bartlett, whose broad interests were founded in his French Canadian education, served as the United States Commissioner (1850-1853) determining the United States-Mexican boundary. During his stay in Mexico, the people and society impressed Bartlett. After visiting the Spanish archives in San Antonio, he wrote that while Northern states had spent money copying documents from European archives, "Texas possesses in her own records voluminous documents of equal value...."[59]

While former Spanish colonies like Texas had old and valuable records, bibliophiles like John Carter Brown sought to create their own libraries. On the advice of his friend Bartlett, Brown developed a magnificent collection of books and housed them in a library in Providence, Rhode Island. After visiting the library, the Argentine scholar Domingo Sarmiento praised the library for its "most complete, abundant, and instructive collection of Spanish authors, above all, those who have written upon South America." Brown had books that even the library of the British Museum lacked.[60]

During the last quarter of the nineteenth century, the United States underwent fundamental changes on a number of levels; nationalism, in particular, was more strident. In 1884 the first president of the American Historical Association, Andrew D. White, noted that because of this nationalistic outlook, it was impossible for a scholar to specialize in any history but that of Britain or the United States.[61] Later Bolton, who was educated during this time, wrote that he was taught an "orthodox history" of the United States between the Rio Grande and the 49th parallel.

Along with the historical tenor of the times, the country was simultaneously developing into an industrial nation with global commercial ties. Thus, it is not surprising to find a number of historians throughout the United States taking tentative steps toward a new comprehensive and comparative approach to American history. These historians were beginning to recognize that non-Anglo experiences were significant to the history of the United States. Other historians began exploring the little-known recesses of Latin American history, believing that knowledge and under-standing could be useful to the merchant dealing with commerce south of the Rio Grande.

In San Francisco, Hubert Howe Bancroft (1832-1918) collected Spanish documents relating to the history of the Far West. His History Company also produced significant volumes on the history of the West that dis-cussed the Spanish, Mexican, and Russian developments in great detail. His collection formed the core of the Bancroft Library at the University of California at Berkeley, with its excellent resources on the history of the American West and the Americas.[62]

Phineas C. Headley led the way with an edited history of the Americas titled *The History of the Two Americas*, published in 1878. He noted the importance of the Americas approach in his introduction. Headley con-cluded that the day was coming when Americans would look to Europe merely for inspiration, but would look for meaning in the wonders of the Americas.[63]

The "Fathers of American History" were brought together in a massive compilation of works including Jeremy Belknap's *Biographies of the Early Discoverers*, William Robertson's *The History of South America*, James Grahame's *The History of North America*, David Ramsay's *History of the United States*, and William Hubbard's *History of the Indian Wars of New England*. With the addition of an appendix that brought the story to 1878, Headley's work became an easily accessible information source that was available to the average citizen. Benson J. Lossing commented on the value of the volume and wrote that the early history of the Americas paralleled each section, and that due to travel and communication, North and South America "are daily becoming more and more intimately associated." As a result, "a more intimate knowledge" of Latin America is "essential to our well-informed people, especially the portion engaged in traffic."[64]

A series of nineteenth-century historians who worked in either the Bor-derlands or comparative colonial history followed with a focus in these fields. It is possible that these historians were influential in the develop-ment of Bolton's concepts.

Justin Winsor, who, according to Edward Channing, was unrivaled for his knowledge of American history, developed a work taking a broader approach to United States history.[65] This approach is best demonstrated in his eight-volume *Narrative and Critical History of America* (1884-1889), which presents colonial history in its broadest terms, discussing not only the English story but the French, Spanish, and Portuguese stories as well.[66] Students utilizing Winsor's volumes were presented with a nontraditional approach to American history.[67]

Three other historians, Frank W. Blackmar, John Fiske, and Reuben Gold Thwaites, also published more inclusive histories in the early 1890s. In 1891 Frank W. Blackmar published *Spanish Institutions of the Southwest*. He conceived the idea for the work while he was a graduate student at Johns Hopkins University. Ray Allen Billington wrote: "The holy temple of the Teutonists was the Johns Hopkins University, and its high priest was Herbert Baxter Adams," who was Blackmar's professor. This Teutonic orientation served as the basis of mainstream American historical thought beginning in the 1880s.[68] Blackmar had been influenced by a California resident who was familiar with the Spanish legacy in the state, and despite his training, he thought that Spanish-American institutions were valuable to study and could be used for comparative purposes when set against the Anglo-American story.[69]

For Blackmar, who was breaking the Teutonic focus of his generation in his work, the Southwest was "a comparatively new field for the study of the colonial history of institutions." Because of this it figured in neither the colonial nor the national development of the United States, and as a result "its contributions to our national life have necessarily been meagre." Due to the growing importance of the Southwest, "a component part of the great American Commonwealth," Blackmar felt that it was not merely local history but part of the national story as well. He also stressed the comparative nature of Spanish and English colonial history and institutions within the present limits of the United States.[70]

Around the same time, John Fiske was writing his two-volume history, *The Discovery of America*.[71] Fiske opened with Columbus's discovery of the New World and included the non-Spanish discoveries and explorations of the Americas. Although he took a broad approach, he ended with a pro-English view of colonization that was typical of many historians and atypical of the Americas approach.[72]

Reuben Gold Thwaites developed a comparative history of the United States colonies.[73] Although the bulk of the study concentrated on the English story, Thwaites took an international approach. This is evident from his discussion of the imperial policies, exploration, and Euro-Indian relations. Thwaites included a chapter on New France from 1608 to 1750 and ended with a brief review of the effects of French colonization. Broadly expanded, this approach would be incorporated in Bolton and Marshall's 1920 pioneer intercolonial study.

In 1901, Woodbury Lowery took what later became the Boltonian position stressing the role of the Spanish Borderlands. In the Preface of *The Spanish Settlements Within the Present Limits of the United States, 1513-1561*, he stressed the supracolonial nature of United States colonial history. He then focused on the Spanish and went on to note: "no one has thus far attempted a synthetic treatment of her [Spain's] policy in her North American possessions, the reasons for her preliminary success, her later apathy, and her final decadence." He further noted that his work would concentrate on "the outlying, neglected and half-forgotten provinces of the Viceroyalty of Mexico." Predating Bolton's later work, Lowery noted the defensive nature of the Spanish frontier.[74]

Although Lowery was pioneering a new approach to United States history, he took a pro-Anglo-Saxon view when he wrote that even in the newly obtained former Spanish possessions, "There may be traced many of those elements of weakness which rendered them incapable of a successful opposition to the inroad of the Anglo-Saxon."

After noting his objective position in regard to the Spanish, Lowery introduced an early Americanist position: "The ideal history of a nation should contain in parallel columns the history of the actions of her sister nations in like circumstances and under similar impulses." Using the comparative approach, scholars could study the expulsion of the Jews from Spain in the fifteenth century and from Russia in the nineteenth, or the exclusion of foreigners from Spanish colonies and of the Chinese from the United States.[75]

Although Lowery believed the historical record and chronicles were important, he maintained the importance of the efforts of the Smithsonian Institution through the Bureau of Ethnology, which "had accumulated in its publications an inexhaustible store of ethnographic and historical material indispensable to all writers on American history." Lowery expressed his "indebtedness" to Justin Winsor's *Narrative and Critical History of America* and to the works of Hubert Howe Bancroft, and the manuscripts of John G. Shea. A year and a half later, in the fall of 1902, University of Texas professor Bolton had become familiar with Lowery's historiographic views and was using the above mentioned works in his course on "European Expansion."

Between 1904 and 1908, Albert Bushnell Hart edited and published a series of twenty-seven volumes titled "The American Nation: A History," which would be utilized by mainstream educators. The series focused on non-English aspects of colonial history, including the Dutch, French, and Swedes. Edward G. Bourne's monograph, *Spain in America, 1450-1580*, was one of the earliest volumes to develop a non-Anglo approach, and was considered "one of the best volumes in the series."[76] Hart wrote in the Preface that it showed "the existence of a Spanish culture in the colonies of an extent and degree not realized by previous writers." Bourne noted that his work filled the gap between Columbus and the beginnings of English colonization that past historians had omitted because they believed the information did "not prepar[e] the way for future Anglo-Saxon occupation." Bourne also showed that the Spanish experience was actually the first stage of the transmission of European culture into the Americas, a position that Bolton later adopted. In his concluding introductory remarks, Bourne wrote that his study would be important for American students because more than half of the United States territory had once been under Spanish control, because the United States had recently acquired lands and several million people whose European culture was derived from Spain, and finally, because growing contacts with Spanish America made it essential for Americans to have a better knowledge and understanding of that region.[77]

The International Congress of Arts and Sciences convened on the morning of September 24, 1904, at the St. Louis World's Fair; the main speakers were Edward G. Bourne and Frederick Jackson Turner. In his speech, "The Relation of American History to Other Fields of Historical Study," Bourne advocated a broader and comparative treatment of the history of European colonization in the New World and called for historians to concentrate on Spain's role in the story of colonization.

Turner, who is best known for his thesis on frontier American history and had presented it eleven years earlier, now stressed the value of using a comparative approach in relationship to frontier history:

A comparative study of the process of settlement of the United States would be another important contribution [after immigration history]. If, with our own methods of the occupation of the frontier, we should compare those of other countries which have dealt with similar problems, — such as Russia, Germany, and the English colonies in Canada, Australia, and Africa, — we should undoubtedly find most fruitful results.[78]

Turner was a proponent, but not a practitioner, of comparative history, and would offer encouragement to his student, Bolton, in the years when Bolton developed his ideas.

Adolph Bandelier, a Swiss-born archaeologist of the Southwest, presented another view of the Americas. He wrote an article titled "America" that appeared in the 1907 edition of the *Catholic Encyclopedia* and brought forth the theme of the Americas centered around Christianity.[79] The article opens with a lengthy discussion of the American Indians; it discusses Spanish, Portuguese, French, and English colonization; and it ends with a broad application of the American independence movement. Strong Catholic ties with the history of colonization made this encyclopedic presentation of Americas history possible.

Simultaneous with these developments, professors began taking a broader approach to hemispheric history in the classroom. In 1884 at Columbia University, Daniel de Leon began offering courses on inter-American relations. In the 1890s, University of California professor Bernard Moses was an early advocate of the history of the Americas, pioneering the study and the publishing of Spanish American history so that by the time he retired in 1911, he was an eminently known Latin American historian. In 1898, as the war with Spain was unwinding, he published *The Establishment of Spanish Rule in America: An Introduction to the History and Politics of Spanish America*, which has been described as the "first scholarly history of colonial Hispanic America by a professor of the subject with a student following, to be published in the United States."[80] In the Preface he stated that the book "aims...to suggest that American history is not all told in the history of the United States, and, by making accessible in a concise form a general account of the Spanish colonies in their earlier decades, to offer an introduction to the neglected half of American history." In the final chapter Moses presents a lengthy analysis contrasting Spanish and English institutions.[81]

At this time Moses also gave an important pro-Americas talk to the Southern California Teachers' Association, laying the foundation for Bolton's work.[82] Moses pointed out that students in the United States and elsewhere were being taught a narrow and nationalistic history of their respective nations. However, he noted "American history, in its proper sense, embraces all attempts to found and develop civilized society on this continent, whether these attempts were made by the English, the French, the Portuguese, or the Spanish." European history was studied because of our cultural and political heritage; however, "there is no external event comparable with the discovery and settlement of the American continent; no other event so full of suggestions and positive instruction concerning the nature and growth of society." For Moses it was essential that students see American history in its true light, knowing the similarities and differences of the colonies and subsequent independent nations.

In his talk he pointed out that it was the teacher's task to keep in check the tendency toward narrowness and provincialism that would ultimately lead to social bigotry: "It is high time, therefore, that we should adopt a more comprehensive view of American history, and consider our institutions and achievements in relation to the institutions and achievements of other nations that began as we began on the virgin soil of a new world." Speaking on the eve of the Spanish-American War, Moses noted that this broader approach would eliminate the lies taught "for the sake of patriotic results," and that "patriotism will take care of itself" as a result of a better understanding by a more broadly educated and intelligent citizenry. Moses concluded that it was not unpatriotic to study the institutions of other nations, because such a comparative study would actually provide "our patriotism a broad and rational basis and it is especially needful for the sake of the emphasis of contrast which it lays on our own history and institutions."

In 1904 William R. Shepherd, who was on the history faculty at Columbia University, began to teach a course on Spanish American history. A decade later he published *Latin America*, which proved to be popular both with the public and within academic circles, and which many considered the single best volume on the subject at the time. In 1909, at a session of the American Historical Association annual meeting, Shepherd stressed the importance of studying not only English, but French, Dutch, Spanish, and Portuguese colonial history as well.[83] He noted that non-English colonial activities were presented merely "as a series of detached episodes possessing a sort of picturesque interest quite unimportant in character."

However, he also stressed the importance of investigating the French, Spanish, and other experiences not only for their own sakes but also for an increased understanding of their relations with each other, their rich cultural survivals and influences, and their relationship to the history of the United States. Shepherd emphasized the importance of the role of the French in Canada as an important ingredient in the history of the hemisphere. Shepherd concluded by stating that only through the use of comparative colonial history could a historical balance be reestablished; as a result, the whole story would be known and appreciated as part of a rich national history. These enlightened early Americanists who called for a comparative and multi-cultural approach to United States history were laying the foundation for the development of Bolton's concepts.

While historians focused on these scholarly endeavors, the reality of peace, trade, commerce, and hemispheric defense was on the minds of other Americans. Secretary of State James G. Blaine (1830-1893) was at the forefront of this movement. He served briefly under President James Garfield in 1881 and then under President Benjamin Harrison (1889-1892). Blaine was concerned about the state of American trade and its competition from European, especially English, sources. He proposed reciprocity treaties as a potential solution, but found little support in Congress. Blaine also tried to mediate recurring Latin American disputes.

Blaine is best known for Pan-Americanism, which Secretary of State Henry Clay had promoted during the presidency of John Quincy Adams. However, little has been done since. In 1881, with President Garfield's approval, Blaine invited the nations of the hemisphere to Washington for a meeting the following year to consider "methods of preventing war between the nations of America." However, after Garfield's assassination and Blaine's resignation, the invitation was withdrawn. In 1888, Congress authorized a conference to consider a plan for peace by arbitration and the removal of commercial barriers between nations in the hemisphere. When the conference met a year later, Blaine was once again Secretary of State. Although many common problems were discussed during the conference (1889-1890), the most memorable result was Andrew Carnegie's financial backing for the creation of the Pan-American Union, headquartered in Washington, DC.[84] The conference and the establishment of the complex placed the United States in closer association with Latin American affairs and concerns.

During the regime of Porfírio Díaz (1876-1911), United States investments in Mexico commercially bound the two nations together. After the Spanish-American War (1898), the United States took a more active role vis-à-vis Latin America. The United States maintained political control over Cuba, created a commonwealth of the Philippines, and acquired Guam and Puerto Rico. The subsequent acquisition of the Panama Canal Zone in 1903 and the completion of the Canal eleven years later created new American commercial and strategic interests in the Caribbean region. In 1928, historian Clarence Haring wrote: "the United States has become the principal Caribbean power, and in a sense a Spanish-American power as well."[85]

American commercial interests in Latin America reverted to the early days of the nineteenth century. Over the years, several hemispheric commercial conferences were held in the United States. In June 1897, President William McKinley attended the Pan-American Commercial Congress in Philadelphia. As a result of the Spanish-American War, the United States was considered a world power and took on an imperialistic attitude. This attitude enhanced American desire to acquire Latin American markets. This led to the creation of the Pan-American Exposition at Buffalo; its objective was "to promote commercial and social interests among the States and countries of the Western Hemisphere."[86] The exposition ran through the summer of 1901 and attracted representatives of nations from throughout the hemisphere.[87] When President McKinley attended the exposition, he stressed that industrial growth promoted progress and that true success would be achieved through "reciprocal" commercial relations with Pan-American nations.[88] The official guidebook concluded that, due to the efforts of the fair's management, a "vast interest in Pan-Americanism has been created."

At the same time the United States became involved in Caribbean affairs, Spanish Americans began to suspect Anglo-Saxon intentions. The expansionist experience of the Mexican-American War culminated in the Treaty of Guadalupe Hidalgo (1848) and resulted in Mexico's loss of some 20 percent of its national domain. In response to this suspicion, United States statesmen sought to allay Spanish-American fears. In 1905 some Brazilians feared that the exchange of ambassadors with the United States might lead to the United States trying to dominate Brazil. But in 1906 Secretary of State Elihu Root, who was attending the Third International Conference of American States at Rio de Janeiro, stated that all nations in the Americas were equal, and the United States would respect their independence and sovereignty. For the Secretary of State, it would be through the expansion of trade in cooperation with other nations that all nations of the hemisphere would benefit, and the United States would "grow in wealth, in wisdom, and in spirit." He concluded, "We may all become greater and stronger together."[89]

President Woodrow Wilson expressed similar sentiments in an address to the Fifth Annual Meeting of the Southern Commercial Congress at Mobile, Alabama, on October 27, 1913. This was the origin of the "Wilson Doctrine," which sought to block the threat of European economic expansion into Latin America.[90] Wilson further enunciated this in a message to Congress on December 7, 1915, and in a memorable address to the Second Pan-American Scientific Congress at Washington in January 1916. Wilson ignored any idea of "political suzerainty or selfish control," and declared "that the states of America are not hostile rivals but cooperating friends...in a very true and deep sense a unit in world affairs, spiritual partners, standing together, quick with common sympathies and common ideals."[91]

These and other disclaimers "of imperialistic aims on the part of the United States made a deep and lasting impression in many sections of Latin America, especially in the larger states of the southern continent."[92] President Wilson's subsequent statements helped cement friendship ties between Anglo and Latin America and strengthened the Pan-American spirit. Simultaneously, better journalistic ties and the opening of news agency offices further contributed to a better understanding between the two sections of the hemisphere. The motion picture industry's promotion of mutual understanding also made a profound impact on the two regions.

With the opening of the Panama Canal, steamship travel between North and South America expanded, allowing citizens from both areas to visit and experience one another's cultures. By 1925, thousands of Latin American students were studying in the United States; however, their studies were directed primarily toward scientific and technical subjects rather than the liberal arts.[93] At the same time, the influx of millions of European immigrants caused highly xenophobic, Anglo-Protestant tendencies to redevelop and manifest themselves in history textbooks. Once again history books stressed the English colonial story to the near exclusion of the Dutch, French, and Spanish.[94]

Although the concept of the history of the Americas had been around since the sixteenth century, historians did not lay the foundation on which Bolton would build until the late nineteenth century. The concept existed and was appreciated when it was understood, but it needed a leader to promulgate it.

NOTES

1. Angel Delgado-Gómez, *Spanish Historical Writing about the New World, 1493-1700* (Providence, RI: John Carter Brown Library, 1992).

2. Sebastian Münster, *A Treatyse of the Newe India*, trans. Richard Eden (London: Edward Sutton, 1553).

3. André Thevet, *The New Found Worlde or Antarctike* (London: Henry Bynneman, 1568), 102-36.

4. Lancelot du Voisin, Sieur de La Popelinière, *Les Trois Mondes* (Paris: Pierre L'Huillier, 1582).

5. George Bruner Parks, *Richard Hakluyt and the English Voyages*, ed. James A. Williamson (1928; 2nd ed. New York: Frederick Ungar, 1961) — for Hakluyt's publications, see 262-269; Henry S. Burrage, ed., *Early English and French Voyages, Chiefly from Hakluyt, 1534-1608* (New York: Charles Scribner's Sons, 1906).

6. J. R. Páez, "Don Antonio de Alcedo y su biblioteca americana," *Boletín de la*

Academia Nacional de la Historia (Quito) 37 (1937): 90-91; Antonio de Alcedo, *El diccionario geográfico histórico de las Indias Occidentales o América*, 5 vols. (Madrid: Imprenta de B. Cano, 1786-1789), and *The Geographical and Historical Dictionary of America and the West Indies...*, trans. G. A. Thompson, 5 vols. (1812-1815; repr. New York: Burt Franklin, 1970).

7. Beulah H. Swigart, "The Americas as Revealed in the *Encyclopédie*" (diss., University of Illinois, Urbana, 1939).

8. Edmund Burke, *An Account of the European Settlements in America*, 2 vols. (London: R. & J. Dodsley, 1757).

9. The actual relationship is unclear. Some say they were cousins, and others are unsure. See Gerald W. Chapman, *Edmund Burke: The Practical Imagination* (Cambridge, MA: Harvard University Press, 1967), 18, 283; Russell Kirk, *Edmund Burke: A Genius Reconsidered* (Peru, IL: Sherwood Sugden, 1988), 36; Nicholas K. Robinson, *Edmund Burke: A Life in Caricature* (New Haven: Yale University Press, 1996).

10. Carl B. Cone, *Burke and the Nature of Politics*, 2 vols. (1957; 2nd ed. Lexington: University of Kentucky Press, 1964), 1: 29.

11. W. A. Young, *The History of North and South America, with an Account of the First Discovery of the New World, the Customs, Genius, and Persons of the Original Inhabitants, and a Particular Description [of] Air, Soil, Natural Products, Manufactures and Commerce of Each Settlement Including a Geographical, Commercial and Historical Survey of the British Settlements, from the Earliest Times to the Present Period, with an Account of the West Indies and American Islands, to Which Is Added an Impartial Enquiry into the Present American Dispute*, 2 vols. (London: for J. Whitaker, 1776).

12. Ibid., 1: A2.

13. For an example of this plagiarism see Young, 1: 122, and Burke, *An Account* 2: 247; and Young, 1: 127, and Burke, 2: 253. The portion *An Impartial Enquiry into the Present American Dispute* is Young's own work.

14. "William Robertson," in *The Dictionary of National Biography*, 1311-1316. This article provides a fine overview of Robertson. Much of what follows is drawn from R. A. Humphreys, *William Robertson and His "History of America"* (London: Hispanic and Luso-Brazilian Councils, 1954).

15. Preface to *The History of the Reign of the Emperor Charles the Fifth* and *The History of Scotland*, in *The Works of William Robertson*, 8 vols. (Oxford: Talboys and Wheeler, 1825), 1: 70-73.

16. Humphreys, *William Robertson*, 11.

17. Preface to William Roberton, *History of America*, 2 vols. (Philadelphia: Johnson & Warner, 1812).

18. Ibid., 1:iii.

19. Dugald Stewart, *Biographical Memoir, of Adam Smith, L.L.D., of William Robertson, D.D., and of Thomas Reid, D.D.* (Edinburgh: G. Ramsay & Co., 1811), 246.

20. Preface to *History of America*.

21. William Robertson to [?], March 8, 1784, British Museum, Add. MSS. 35350, fols. 70 ff., in Humphreys, *William Robertson*, 14.

22. Robertson, *History of America*, 1:iii and iv.

23. John B. Black, *The Art of History: A Study of Four Great Historians of the Eighteenth Century* (1926, New York: Russell & Russell, 1965), 137-138.

24. A. Curtis Wilgus, *The Historiography of Latin America: A Guide to Historical Writing, 1500-1800* (Metuchen, NJ: Scarecrow Press, 1975), 214.

25. "Examen de la historia de América, escrita por el Doctor Guillermo Robertson...traducida del Yngles por dn. Ramon de Guebara...Y conclusión de este asunto, prohibiendo S. M. la impresión y publicación de este obra en España y sus dominios," British Museum, Add. MSS. 17633, in Humphreys, *William Robertson*, 26-27. Interest in Robertson's work persisted, as indicated by the reprintings and translations.

26. William Winterbotham, *American Historical, Geographical, Commercial and Philosophical Views of the American United States and of the European Settlements in America and the West-Indies*, 4 vols. (London: J. Ridgway, 1795); and Anonymous, *A General History of North and South America* (London: Mayhew Isaac and Co., 1834).

27. David Bailie Warden, *Chronologie historique de l'Amérique*, 10 vols. (Paris: A. Dupont et Roret, 1826-1844).

28. Juan Comas, *Cien años de congresos internacionales de americanistas: Ensayo histórico-crítico y bibliográfico* (México, DF: Instituto de Investigaciones Históricas, 1974).

29. "Règlement de la Société des Américanistes de Paris," *Journal de la Société de Américanistes de Paris* 1 (1895-1896): 1-2; Pascal Rivale, "L'Américanisme français à la veille de la fondation de la Société des Américanistes," *Journal de la Société des Américanistes de Paris* 81 (1995): 207-231.

30. John MacGregor, *The Progress of America: From the Discovery by Columbus to the Year 1846*, 2 vols. (London: Whittaker and Co., 1847).

31. Mackenzie's works include *America and Her Army* (London: Thomas Nelson, 1865); *The United States of America: A History* (London: Thomas Nelson, 1870); *The Nineteenth Century* (1880; London: Thomas Nelson, 1895); *America: A History* (1882; London: Thomas Nelson, 1894).

32. Mackenzie, *America: A History* (1894), 558-565.

33. Giuseppe Compagnoni, *Storia dell'America, in continuazione del compendio della storia universale del Sig. conte di Segur...*, 28 vols. (Milan: Fusi, Stella e Com., 1820-1822).

34. Among the numerous biographies and studies of Humboldt are Douglas Botting, *Humboldt and the Cosmos* (New York: Harper, 1973); Helmut De Terra, *Humboldt: The Life and Times of Alexander von Humboldt, 1769-1859* (New York: Knopf, 1955); Lotte Kellner, *Alexander von Humboldt* (New York: Oxford University Press, 1963).

35. Franz Justus Kottenkamp, *Geschichte der Colonisation Amerika's*, 2 vols. (Frankfurt: Literarische Anstalt, 1850); Albert Scobel, *Nordamerika, Mexico, Mittelamerika und Westindien, kommerziell, politisch und statistich* (Leipzig: Metzger & Wittig, 1882).

36. Two recent studies on Kohl are *The Articulate Traveler: Johann Georg Kohl: Chronicler of the American Continents*, Washington, DC, Library of Congress Exhibition, Madison Building Foyer, March 24-June 27, 1993; Hans-Albrecht Koch, Margrit B. Knewson, and John A. Wolter, eds., *Progress of Discovery: Johann Georg Kohl* (Graz, Austria: Akademisch Druck, 1993).

37. Hélio Vianna, *Estudios de história colonial* (São Paulo: Compania Editora Nacional, 1948), 17. Frei Camilo's paper was prepared in French and was pub-

lished in the *Anais da Biblioteca Nacional do Rio de Janeiro* 12 (1884-1885): 391-394. All of Vianna's "Ensino e conceito de história de América" (15-31) is worth reading.

38. Vianna, *Estudios*, 18.

39. Ricardo Donoso, *Diego Barros Arana* (México, DF: Instituto Panamericano de Geografía e Historia, 1967), 64-66.

40. Allen Woll, *A Functional Past: The Uses of History in Nineteenth-Century Chile* (Baton Rouge: Louisiana State University Press, 1982), 158.

41. Barros Arana, Diego, *Compendio de historia de América.* 2 vols. Santiago, Chile: Imprenta de Ferrocarril, 1865. Besides these volumes, Barros Arana also wrote works on rhetoric, grammar, literary history, literary composition, and geography. He spent his later years writing a massive multi-volume history of Chile.

42. "Compendio de la historia de América, por don Diego Barros Arana. Noticia sobre esta obra," *Anales de la Universidad* 22 (Mayo 1865): 634.

43. Juan E. Cassani, "Disertación del director del Instituto de Didáctica," in *II° Congreso Internacional de Historia de América* (Buenos Aires: Academia Nacional de la Historia, 1938), 193-207. The *Compendio* was published at Buenos Aires in 1881 and again in 1887. A revised third edition was published at Santiago in 1894, and in 1887 a "new edition" was released. It was reissued in 1907, 1918, 1921, 1924, 1926, and 1932 at Paris. The last date of publication coincided with Bolton's presidential address, "The Epic of Greater America" at Toronto. See Donoso, *Barros Arana*, 376.

44. Eduardo Prado, *A ilusão americana*, 2nd ed. (Paris: A. Collins, 1895), 7. The first edition was published at Rio de Janeiro in 1893, during the Naval Revolt, and was suppressed by the government. In 1953 a facsimile edition was reprinted.

45. Ibid., 12.

46. David E. Thompson to John Hay (Petrópolis, Brazil, 01/15/1905), Dispatches from United States Ministers to Brazil, microcopy 0121, reel 73 (01/03-08/31/1905), National Archives, Record Group 59, (hereafter, Dispatches).

47. *A Notícia*, 01/16/1905; *Jornal do Comercio*, 01/17/1905, 03/04/1905; *A Nacão*, 03/03/1905; *Tribuna de Petrópolis*, 03/09/1905.

48. Thompson to Hay, (Petrópolis, 03/18/1905), Dispatches.

49. *Jornal do Comercio*, 03/19/1905.

50. Manuel de Oliveira Lima, *The Evolution of Brazil Compared with That of Spanish and Anglo-Saxon America* (Stanford, CA: Stanford University Press, 1914).

51. C. Vann Woodward, "The Comparability of American History," in *The Comparative Approach to American History*, C. Vann Woodward, ed. (New York: Basic Books, 1968), 3-17.

52. Thomas Jefferson to Peter Carr (Paris, 08/19/1785, 08/10/1787, 08/06/1788); to Thomas Mann Randolph (07/06/1787), in Julian P. Boyd, et al, eds. *The Papers of Thomas Jefferson* (Princeton: Princeton University Press, 1955-1956), 8: 408, 11: 558, 12: 14, 13: 470.

53. Arthur P. Whitaker, *The United States and the Independence of Latin America, 1800-1830* (Baltimore: Johns Hopkins University Press, 1941); William S. Maltby, *The Black Legend in England: The Development of Anti-Spanish Sentiment, 1558-1660* (Durham, NC: Duke University Press, 1971); Gregorio Funes, review of *Ensayo de la historia civil del Paraguay, Buenos Aires y Tucumán*, *North American Review and Miscellaneous Journal* 3 (1821): 432-443; S. K. Padover, ed., *The Complete Madison*

(New York: Harper, 1953), 322; Alexander H. Everett, *America: Or a General Survey of the Political Situation of the Several Powers of the Western Continent* (Philadelphia: H. C. Carey & I. Lea, 1827), 240-241; Edward Everett, *The Discovery and Colonization of America, and Immigration to the United States* (Boston: Little, Brown, 1853), 10-11.

54. Reginald Horsman, *Race and Manifest Destiny: The Origins of American Racial Anglo-Saxonism* (Cambridge, MA: Harvard University Press, 1981).

55. Marie Léonone Fell, *The Foundations of Nativism in American Textbooks, 1783-1860* (Washington, DC: Catholic University of America Press, 1941), 20.

56. Samuel G. Goodrich, *A Pictorial History of America: Embracing Both the Northern and Southern Portions of the New World* (Hartford, CT: House and Brown, 1852).

57. Other works by Goodrich include: *North America: Or the United States and the Adjacent Countries* (Louisville, KY: Morton and Griswold, 1847) and his juvenile works *Peter Parley's Tales About South America* (Baltimore: J. Jewett, 1832) and *Peter Parley's Pictorial History of North and South America* (Hartford, CT: Peter Parley Publishing, 1858).

58. Harry Bernstein, *Making an Inter-American Mind* (Gainesville: University of Florida Press, 1961), 153-156.

59. Lewis Hanke, ed., *Do the Americas Have a Common History? A Critique of the Bolton Theory* (New York: Knopf, 1964), 8.

60. Domingo Sarmiento, *North and South America: Discourse Delivered Before the Rhode Island Historical Society, December 27, 1865* (Providence: Rhode Island Historical Society, 1865), 4-5.

61. Herman Ausubel, *Historians and Their Craft: A Study of the Presidential Addresses of the American Historical Association, 1884-1945* (New York: Columbia University Press, 1950), 19.

62. Michael Krause and Davis D. Joyce, *The Writing of American History*, rev. ed. (Norman: University of Oklahoma Press, 1985), 272-274; John W. Caughey, "Hubert Howe Bancroft, Historian of Western America," *American Historical Review* 50 (1945): 461-470; W. A. Morris, "The Origin and Authorship of the Bancroft Pacific States Publications: A History of a History," *Oregon Historical Society Quarterly* 4 (1903): 287-364; H. H. Bancroft, "My Method of Writing History," in his *Literary Industries: A Memoir* (New York: Harper, 1891), 330-348.

63. Phineas C. Headley, ed., *The History of Two Americas* (Chicago: A. S. L. Coburn, 1878), xv.

64. Ibid., frontispiece.

65. See Krause and Joyce, *Writing of American History*, 197-199.

66. The history of North and South America to the eighteenth century appears in volumes 1-5. The last volume deals with the later history of British, Spanish, and Portuguese America. The history of the United States from 1763 to 1850 is covered in subsequent volumes.

67. Krause and Joyce, *Writing of American History*, 198.

68. Ray Allen Billington, *Frederick Jackson Turner: Historian, Scholar, Teacher* (New York: Oxford University Press, 1973), 65.

69. Frank W. Blackmar, *Spanish Institutions of the Southwest* (Baltimore: Johns Hopkins University Press, 1891), v.

70. Ibid., 1-13.

71. Milton Berman, *John Fiske: The Evolution of a Popularizer* (Cambridge, MA:

Harvard University Press, 1961). See pages 226-231 for comments on *The Discovery of America*.

72. John Spencer Clark, *The Life and Letters of John Fiske*, 2 vols. (Boston: Houghton Mifflin, 1917), 2: 417-437.

73. Reuben G. Thwaites, *The Colonies, 1492-1750* (New York: Longman's, Green, 1897). For information on Thwaites, see Krause and Joyce, *Writing of American History*, 274-275; Frederick Jackson Turner. *Reuben Gold Thwaites, Memorial Address* (Madison: Wisconsin State Historical Society, 1914); C. W. Alvord, "A Critical Analysis of the Works of Reuben Gold Thwaites," in Mississippi Valley Historical Association, *Proceedings for the Year 1913-1914* 7 (1914): 321-333.

74. Woodbury Lowery, *The Spanish Settlements Within the Present Limits of the United States, 1513-1561* (New York: G. P. Putnam's, 1901), vi-vii.

75. Ibid., vii-viii.

76. John Higham, *History: Professional Scholarship in America* (1965; Baltimore: Johns Hopkins University Press, 1983), 40-41.

77. Edward G. Bourne, *Spain in America, 1450-1580* (New York: Harper, 1904), xix-xx.

78. Edward G. Bourne, "The Relation of American History to Other Fields of Historical Study," and Frederick Jackson Turner, "Problems in American History," in *Congress of Arts and Science, Universal Exposition, St. Louis, 1904*, ed. Howard J. Rogers, 2 vols. (Boston: Houghton Mifflin, 1906), 2: 172-182.

79. Adolph Bandelier, "America," in *The Catholic Encyclopedia* (1907): 409-416.

80. James E. Watson, "Bernard Moses: Pioneer in Latin American Scholarship," *Hispanic American Historical Review* 42 (1962): 213.

81. Bernard Moses, *The Establishment of Spanish Rule in America: An Introduction to the History and Politics of Spanish America* (New York: G. P. Putnam's, 1898), iii, 293-312.

82. This section is based on Bernard Moses, "The Neglected Half of American History," *University Chronicle* (Berkeley), 1 (1898): 120-126; Hanke, *Do the Americas*, 53-59.

83. William R. Shepherd, "The Contribution of the Romance Nations to the History of the Americas, in *Annual Report of the American Historical Association for the Year 1909* (Washington, DC: Government Printing Office, 1910), 221-227; Hanke, *Do the Americas*, 60-63.

84. Arthur P. Whitaker, *The Western Hemisphere Idea* (Ithaca, NY: Cornell University Press, 1954), 61-85; Alonso Aguilar, *Pan-Americanism from Monroe to the Present: A View from the Other Side*, trans. Asa Zatz (New York: Monthly Review Press, 1968), 36-42.

85. Clarence H. Haring, *South America Looks at the United States* (New York: Macmillan, 1928), 2.

86. *Official Catalogue and Guide Book to the Pan-American Exposition* (Buffalo, NY: Charles Ahrhart, 1901), 5.

87. The hemisphere nations attending were Argentina, Bolivia, Brazil, Canada, Chile, Colombia, Costa Rica, Cuba, the Dominican Republic, Ecuador, Guatemala, Haiti, Honduras, Jamaica, Mexico, Nicaragua, Peru, Puerto Rico, El Salvador, Uruguay, and Venezuela.

88. Robert W. Rydell, *All the World's a Fair: Visions of Empire at American International Expositions, 1876-1916* (Chicago: University of Chicago Press, 1984),

152; President McKinley was assassinated after this speech on September 6, 1901.

89. Elihu Root, *Speeches Incident to the Visit of Secretary Root to South America* (Washington, DC: Government Printing Office, 1906), 12.

90. Albert Shaw, ed., *President Wilson's State Papers and Addresses* (New York: George H. Doran, 1918) 32-36; Gordon E. Harvey, "'Without Conscious Hypocrisy': Woodrow Wilson's Mobile Address of 1913," *Gulf Coast Historical Review* 10 (1995): 25-46; for a general study of President Wilson's Latin American policy, see: Mark T. Gilderhus, *Pan-American Visions: Woodrow Wilson in the Western Hemisphere, 1913-1921* (Tucson: University of Arizona Press, 1986).

91. *Congressional Record*, 64th Cong., 2nd sess., (December 7, 1915), vol. 53: 95, 96.

92. Haring, *South America*, 14.

93. *The Foreign Student in America* (New York: Association Press, 1925).

94. Frances FitzGerald, *America Revisited: History Schoolbooks in the Twentieth Century* (New York: Vintage, 1980), 49, 94.

2

Bolton Develops the Americas Concept, 1890-1919

By the early twentieth century, the Americas concept had still not entered college curricula; it remained an obscure undercurrent of American historiography. Between the end of the Spanish-American War and World War I, the United States was rapidly emerging as a world leader and greater emphasis was being placed on the Western Hemisphere. The Americas concept needed a historian who could further define it and bring it to the attention of other historians.

Thus, the stage was set for the coming of Herbert E. Bolton and the development of his ideas. For Bolton, this intellectual development was a continuum that began in the closing decade of the nineteenth century and continued throughout most of his life. Working toward the concept of the history of the Americas and building on the work of his predecessors, he established a number of important subfields within American historiography, such as the Spanish Borderlands and comparative colonial history. However, Bolton's most significant work was the history of the Americas.

At first glance, Bolton's rural Midwestern upbringing gives little indication of the direction he would take and the subsequent impact that direction would have on history. Bolton was born on July 20, 1870, in Wilton, Wisconsin, and was raised in the rural countryside where Spanish America and the role of Spain in American history were little known or appreciated.[1] As a matter of fact, in correspondence written during the Spanish-American War, Bolton identified himself as a "'still unreconstructed' Black Legend man, the traditional American who found little, if any, good to say of the Spaniards, past and present, in their relations with the Americas."[2]

Despite the attitude Bolton carried toward Spain as a graduate student, growing up in Wisconsin did provide him with valuable experience. In the late nineteenth century, local Winnebago Indians were still a part of the landscape and the French experience on the fur trade frontier was still part of local memory.

Bolton's formal higher education began in 1890 when he enrolled in a two-year teaching certificate program at the Milwaukee State Normal School (today University of Wisconsin-Milwaukee). He received his state certification in June 1891. He was hired that fall as the principal at Fairchild, Wisconsin, where he remained through 1892. During this time, Bolton began to contemplate and prepare for returning to college, studying German and developing a reading program of which he would later write:

I read a good many fine books, and some of them stand out even today with startling vividness. Amongst these I remember for example Abbott's *Biography of Hannibal* and Prescott's *Conquest of Mexico*. From the time that I read the latter book to the time when more than a decade later I journeyed to the land of the Aztecs I carried with me a clear picture of the Valley of Mexico, and its romantic charms. They were particularly the product of my imagination shaped by Prescott's wizard word picture, but they were not by any means erroneous.[3]

As his reading progressed, Bolton contemplated whether he should study mathematics and history or possibly civics and history, which might be better preparation for a career in law. In the fall of 1893, he enrolled at the University of Wisconsin-Madison as a junior in the pre-law program.

Although most of his courses involved various aspects of law, Bolton did come into contact with the European historian Charles Homer Haskins, who taught English constitutional law. While studying under Haskins, Bolton developed a fascination with history, and his course load reflected that fascination.

In the fall of 1894 Bolton enrolled in two American history courses. One of these was taught by Frederick Jackson Turner, who was in the process of establishing himself as the premier historian of the American frontier. In summer of 1893 Turner had presented his epic-making ideas in his talk "The Significance of the Frontier in American History," in which he stated that the frontier experience was a major influence in the development of the United States and the American character.

Turner was a major influence on Bolton's career. First, Turner served as one of the final influencing factors in Bolton's selection of history for a career. Second, he played an important role in the general development of Bolton's frontier approach to history. In a letter written in 1928, Bolton speaks of Turner's influence:

Nevertheless, Turner's influence upon my teaching and writing has been very direct and very real, although it may not be evident to others. My interest has been a study of the process of European expansion in the western hemisphere. This has been in no small part a study of the development of European civilization on a succession of frontiers. Professor Turner's field of research was lain very largely in the advance of the Anglo-American frontier. My special researches have lain more particularly in the advance of the Spanish frontier and the meeting of the international frontiers. He has been especially interested in the institutional effects of frontier influences. I have had a similar interest in the institutional forms resulting from frontier experience in Spanish America. One evidence of this may be found in my essay "The Mission as a Frontier Institution in the Spanish American Colonies." But more especially have I been interested in the international aspect of frontier history. My special researches have lain pretty largely in the Borderland area between Spanish North America and English North America, but in my teaching I have attempted to synthesize the story of frontier expansion and its international results throughout the whole hemisphere. It is this effort which has eventuated in my freshman, sophomore course on the History of the Americas.[4]

Bolton promoted this expanded Turnerian frontier approach among his students as well. He expressed his pleasure in a letter to Arthur S. Aiton of the University of Michigan upon the publication of the latter's work on the first Mexican viceroy, Mendoza:

It is a most excellent contribution, and will form one of the stones in the great edifice which will some time be built commemorating the march of European civilization from the Caribbean to California. This work of yours, and the companion studies that are being made by others, are bound to influence immensely the historiography of the western hemisphere.[5]

As historian Gerald D. Nash later observed, "Bolton reflected multicultural and multinational perspectives in his writings.... In a certain sense, [Bolton] was extending the Turner Thesis from a nationalistic to an international dimension."[6]

While Bolton was pursuing his academic career, he also found time to write letters to Gertrude Janes of Tunnel City. This relationship eventually led to a wedding in August 1895. Between 1897 and 1913 the Boltons had seven children, and their financial well-being was on Bolton's mind as he pursued his academic endeavors.[7]

After graduating with a Bachelor of Letters degree, Bolton pursued a master's degree *in absentia* through the University of Wisconsin-Madison during the 1895-1896 academic year. He was an accomplished student, passing all of the exams that Turner sent to him. In the fall of 1896, he returned to Wisconsin, and although he was majoring in history, he had not decided on an area of emphasis. Although there was the possibility of working under Haskins in European history and Bolton was considering staying at Wisconsin to pursue his doctorate, his plans changed when he was not awarded one of a limited number of fellowships.

Professor Turner came to his aid, and eventually Bolton received a six hundred dollar fellowship from the University of Pennsylvania. John Bach McMaster immediately accepted Bolton as one of his graduate students and agreed to direct his dissertation. Bolton also studied under the established European historian Edward Potts Cheyney. Herman Vandenburg Ames and Dana Carleton Munro rounded out the array of historians under whom Bolton studied at Pennsylvania.[8] John F. Bannon wrote about

Bolton's development under these historians:

McMaster had deepened Bolton's Turner-given awareness of social factors in history. Haskins, Cheyney, and Munro had kept him, mindful that American history, to be sound and truly understandable, must have many Old World roots; in their own several ways they trained him to be an expert American colonist. Few men of Bolton's generation, or any other for that matter, were as fortunate as he had been in being exposed to such a galaxy of "greats."[9]

Bolton quickly moved toward the development of a dissertation and had selected a topic by mid-October 1897. His topic was the status of the African American as slave, and the first title was "The Status of the Negro in 1860." Bolton refined his topic and eventually defended a dissertation titled "The Free Negro in the South Before the Civil War." Although Bolton thought that it was a "good orthodox subject," in reality it was a radical departure from dissertation topics that graduate students were developing at the time. It might also be seen as a precursor to his study of the Americas with its leveling effect of the mingling of races on equal historical terms throughout the hemisphere.

Bolton noted the direction of American history at this time, writing, "I was trained in the good old fashioned way. My instruction in American history was good orthodox American history—it all happened between the 49th parallel and the Rio Grande."[10] While Bolton was strongly influenced by his mentors, his creativity allowed him to reach beyond the scope of his education.

In 1898 the Boltons returned to Wisconsin for the summer. Bolton dreamed of traveling to Europe, experiencing the Old World and possibly learning a foreign language to help develop a better understanding of a culture for his research. Because he was interested in the Renaissance, Italian was his first choice. Ironically, Spanish was his last choice![11]

Upon receiving his Ph.D. in 1899, Bolton returned to Wisconsin, where he obtained an instructorship at Milwaukee State Normal School.[12] Although he would have preferred to teach history, as a new faculty member Bolton taught civics and economics and was promised some history classes the following year. Unfortunately for Bolton, the Normal had not reached a level of specialization and, as a result, he taught mathematics, economics, ancient history, and a variety of courses as they were needed.[13] In the summer of 1900, he taught summer school in Appleton, Wisconsin, to augment his salary, but American history still was not part of his teaching schedule. Bolton was not satisfied with his teaching schedule because he was teaching "everything" but American history. The prospect of a growing family and few offers for a permanent position added to his dissatisfaction.

Despite the fact that he was not teaching American history, Bolton did find time to reflect upon ideas of American history. His professors had prepared him well. In 1901, while teaching at Milwaukee State Normal

School, he developed a study titled, "The Place of American History in the High-School Course" and presented his findings at the Interscholastic History Conference at Madison. He wrote:

Apperceptively considered, a knowledge of American history must be insufficient unless based on some knowledge of the world's history. American history did not begin with John Smith nor with Christopher Columbus. This the student must not only know in the sense of having read or heard it so stated, but he must realize it by having come in touch with the history of other nations that contributed to the making of America. He must see the fundamental institutions of America in their relation to the history of mankind.

After including an appropriately lengthy quotation from John Fiske's *American Political Ideas*, Bolton concluded, "In short, American development is the crowning work of a great part of human development."[14] For Bolton, American history must be seen from a broader perspective, a concept that he would soon be developing in the college classroom.

As if to solve his dilemma, on September 10, 1901, Bolton received a letter from the chairman of the University of Texas History Department. Professor George P. Garrison asked Bolton whether he would be interested in teaching courses in medieval and modern European history. Garrison was faced with a problem that needed immediate attention; the current professor, Lester Bugbee, was ill with consumption and was unable to teach his courses. Classes would begin in a few weeks, and the salary was $1,500. Bolton considered his options, discussed the matter with his family, and corresponded with Garrison. In 1929, Bolton reminisced, "I don't know where it came from, but a flash came to me at the time that I corresponded with Professor Garrison. I knew just enough about Spanish American history to know that Texas was once Spanish so I asked Professor Garrison if I might play with Southwestern history."[15] Garrison agreed to the request but established strict limitations. Since Southwestern history was Garrison's field, he would not permit Bolton to teach in the field, but he would allow Bolton to work with the archives. Bolton considered over his options and decided that Texas would be a good opportunity. On September 25 he wrote to his brother, Frederick, "The die is cast. They offered the Texas place to me and I accepted."

Bolton's first teaching assignment included two sections of medieval history and one section of modern European history. Garrison's promise of "odds and ends" consisted of Bolton's helping to edit the *Quarterly* of the Texas State Historical Association, "a very high grade magazine which I have known since it started." Six days after his arrival at the University of Texas, Bolton wrote to Frederick, "Garrison...is building up a center for Southwestern history for which Texas has unsurpassed opportunities." He continued, "Though I am down for European Hist[ory], I think he will encourage my working in his field—Southwestern History—which I shall prefer to European. I shall get up Spanish at once, which they say is easy."

A few days later he wrote, "I must learn Spanish at once for Southwestern history which everybody here must 'work' I am glad to say."[16]

The possibility of teaching American history and using some of Turner's insights and ideas along with his own would have to wait. In late 1901, the opportunity Bolton had been waiting for presented itself. Garrison was plotting out the 1902-1903 history schedule and offered Bolton the course "European Expansion: Commercial and Colonial Activities, Sixteenth and Seventeenth Centuries," which he accepted. In a letter to Frederick dated January 5, 1902, Bolton observed, "I think I shall in time be able to block out a field of *my own* here."[17] He expanded on the role and importance of his experience in Texas to the formation of his career in a letter dated January 24:

I believe that Texas is preferable for History to any place outside the [Old] Northwest or the far west…. Texas has the key to Spanish American history. I am grubbing Spanish, so that I may be able to turn the lock. My new course is a triumph for me, for it is Garrison's permission to tramp on his ground.[18]

When he was made a fellow of the Texas State Historical Association, Bolton thought that "it is in the line I wish to be known in and as the list of fellows appears in the cover of each *Quarterly* it will give me some advertisement."[19]

Bolton was developing a knowledge of the Spanish language. On March 13, 1902, he noted, "I am studying Spanish on the side. I want to handle it well by Fall. It is easy, but not so easy as French, I think. I hope to learn to speak it too, as Mexico is so near."[20] By the end of June, when he could read ten pages of ordinary Spanish in an hour, Bolton observed, "I would like to fully conquer Spanish now that I am at it. It is the key to Southwestern history, on which I must work as long as I am here."[21] On July 8, he continued in the same vein:

I am making hard efforts to get the Spanish language now, and want to get into the heart and core of southwestern history by getting familiar with Spanish civilization and the mine of sources that lie in Mexico. To go to Mexico is the best way to do that…. I want to lay my lines here deep enough, and my plans broad enough, so that if, in the future, chance should leave an open field, I will be master of the situation. To do it one must know the Spanish archives and the Spanish language.[22]

Garrison had told him of the wealth of Spanish documents in Mexico City, Saltillo, and elsewhere, and in the summer of 1902, armed only with a rudimentary knowledge of Spanish, Bolton ventured for the first of many times into Mexico. In August and September 1902, he researched in the Archivo General de la Nación in Mexico City and also found time to retrace the route of Cortés. Upon his return, Bolton noted that he had a profitable summer, and the documents he collected "will keep me in powder for shooting off historical fireworks most of the year."[23]

Bolton's trips to Mexico had another influence on his career. During these trips Bolton began "looking at the map from the bottom up, and in California, looking at it from the Pacific Ocean." He commented further on the influence of these trips:

I moved beyond the borders [of traditional United States history] into the Southwest, Mexico, and the Pacific Coast and began to realize that two-thirds of the history of North America before the end of the 18th century belongs not to United States history in a restricted sense, but to the story of European expansion in the continent of North America. No framework less comprehensive will unify all the varied threads of influence during that period.[24]

By this early date, Bolton was formulating basic ideas that would lead to the Americas concept. With the start of fall classes, Bolton was prepared for his usual course load but now had the additional responsibility of "European Expansion: Commercial and Colonial Activities, Sixteenth and Seventeenth Centuries." The course description provides insight into the nature of the course and its influence on the development of Bolton's history of the Americas:

[The course is] a study of the social, economic, religious, and political forces that led to the commercial and colonial activities of the European nations during the sixteenth and seventeenth centuries; the methods employed by the important nations; the field occupied by each; and the effects of these expansion activities upon the parent states.[25]

However, as would happen with History 8 in 1919, Bolton was faced with a lack of textbooks for the course and limited library facilities. In response to this problem, he began formatting his lectures into a text for the course, and by the end of the year he had completed the first chapter.[26]

The development of this course shows Bolton's movement toward a comprehensive approach to colonial history. This process continued in the fall semester of 1903, when he began to emphasize Spanish colonization. The course bulletin for the following year lists Bolton's selected texts: John Fiske, *The Discovery of America*; Bernard Moses, *The Establishment of Spanish Rule in America*; Justin Winsor, *Narrative and Critical History of America*; Frank W. Blackmar, *Spanish Institutions in the Southwest*; and Hubert H. Bancroft's works.[27] The use of these illustrates the critical link between these historians and their concepts and the development of Bolton's approach toward a broader view of United States history. Bolton would soon follow Moses's ideas.

[Moses's monograph] aims, moreover, to suggest that American history is not all told in the history of the United States, and, by making accessible in a concise form a general account of the Spanish colonies in their earlier decades, to offer an introduction to the neglected half of American history.[28]

Moses compares and contrasts the English and Spanish colonial experiences in the New World in the concluding chapter of his work, demonstrating the connection between his concern for the presentation of the broader approach to United States history and Bolton's future treatment of the history of the Americas.[29]

By the fall of 1905, Bolton had retitled his course "Spanish Colonization," replaced Fiske's text with Edward Bourne's recently published *Spain in America*, and again emphasized the use of "sources and of other older authorities, of which a fair supply is available."[30] It is presumed that Bolton was going to use either the local Bexar Spanish archives, the transcriptions that he had retrieved from Mexico, or a combination of both sources.

As the years passed, Bolton fine-tuned the subject matter and direction of the "Spanish Colonization" course. In 1906-1907 he emphasized the development of Spanish colonial institutions in America, and in 1908-1909 his added course prerequisite of a reading knowledge of either French or Spanish indicated his expansion of the colonial experience to include the French.[31]

Bolton had "found" at least one of his fields — the Spanish Southwest — and he would continue to make annual trips to Mexico, where he worked long hours transcribing and becoming familiar with the national and provincial archives. He returned to Austin with suitcases bulging with transcriptions and soon got to work developing articles for the *Quarterly* of the Texas State Historical Association, such as "Some Materials for Southwestern History in the Archivo General de Mexico" (October 1902) and "Tienda de Cuervo's Ynspección of Laredo" (January 1903). In 1903 he was also translating materials for the multi-volume Blair-Robertson series of documents on the Philippines.[32] Throughout his life Bolton stressed the importance of utilizing original documents, which his publications and seminars evidenced. He would go on to publish *Guide to Materials for the History of the United States in the Principal Archives of Mexico* in 1913.[33]

Bolton set his mark for the future while at the University of Texas. He had been creative with new courses and productive in his research, publications, and in his attendance and presentation of papers at the American Historical Association's meetings.[34] For him, Hispanic American history was his field of study. But then he was faced with reality. In 1907, Bolton later recalled, Dr. Garrison called him into his office to tell him that professorships were being developed and distributed. Garrison would retain the English and American history courses, and he offered Bolton a professorship in either medieval or modern European history. Bolton later related:

"Neither," I replied. "I prefer to specialize in Southwestern and Spanish American history." His reply was, "Man, you're crazy. There will never be a professorship in that subject. There are none anywhere. I'm sorry, but I fear I shall have to call someone over your head." "All right," I replied. Two years [1909] later I began my professorship in my chosen field. Texas is now one of the leading centers for Hispanic studies.[35]

It was fortunate that Garrison jealously guarded the field of American and Southwestern history, because this forced Bolton to seek a foothold in United States history and begin the development of ideas that would eventually lead to Bolton's Americas thesis. In 1923, Bolton recalled his formative days at the University of Texas in a diary he kept while attending the annual meeting of the American Historical Association:

[Here in Texas] I always feel at home. Here I found myself and a field. Had I kept on with my old line of work, I doubt I should have ever emerged from the ranks of followers of beaten paths. I probably should have been a respectable teacher of second-hand stuff—for a time—and then from the very *ennui* of it I should have quit, because I could not have stood that kind of an existence long. I at least discovered Free Negroes and first of all wrote them up. But here in Texas there was a wide expanse, scarcely charted, scarcely trail broken. I felt the tingle of its romance at the first touch. I had found my love. She had been waiting for me. Turned my back on Free Negroes without a pang. Five hundred pages of them, more or less, have been resting quietly somewhere amid my junk, I know not where. And I have wooed my new mistress ever since, ardently and faithfully. And she has always given back response without stint.

Bolton continued his description of his experience:

The most formative chapter of my life is comprised in those eight years when I was learning my Spanish, roaming over Texas, thrilling with the experience of following old trails and identifying lost sites, and then running every summer to old Mexico to find my documents. Only a few will ever know that most of the gatherers in those archives are followers on trails blazed out for them. And why should they? This has been true of most people, even writers and scholars, throughout all generations of human existence. But it is the trail breakers who have the fun, and the thrills that come with discovery, and those scarcely less joyful, yes even more ecstatic thrills that come with danger. What McKenzie [*sic*] or David Livingstone would change place with a millionaire grocer? He never lived! Or who would roll safely and tamely along on a boulevard in the level valley when he could be dangerously courting mountain trails[?][36]

Other institutions actively sought Bolton's expertise, and soon Stanford University had contacted him. The correspondence between E. D. Adams of Stanford University and Bolton, beginning in September 1908, provides insights into the man and his work. Bolton saw himself as an American historian who preferred teaching undergraduate courses in the history of the West, the Spanish Southwest, and the social and economic history of the United States, and graduate courses in the Spanish Southwest and the Anglo-American West. This young historian impressed Adams as having carved out for himself "the most logical field for special development by our Pacific Coast universities, and that it seems to offer the greatest opportunities for new and original work.[37] As their correspondence continued concerning the new position at Stanford, Adams provided clarification regarding the course:

By American history here I do not mean to limit the field to United States history at all, but rather to emphasize Spanish American history. In short I should hope that you would continue the work you have begun so excellently and really develop this field.[38]

Bolton accepted the position at Stanford University, and in the fall of 1909 he began teaching a graduate seminar in Southwestern history, another, unspecified seminar, and an undergraduate course on Spain in America. He viewed himself as the first man teaching American history with specializations in Southwestern and Spanish American history.

However, late in the summer of 1910, Bolton began thinking of returning to the University of Texas. Stanford did not impress him as a major academic institution, and it lacked a research library. Garrison, who had been an obstacle to him, had died, and thus the chairmanship of the department was open. In a letter to Bolton, President Sidney Mezes expressed his hope that Bolton would join them in Texas.[39]

In the midst of his discussions with Texas, a crucial development took place. Henry Morse Stephens, chair of the History Department at the University of California-Berkeley, learned of Bolton's dissatisfaction with Stanford and his possible move to Texas. Bolton's work impressed Stephens, and he felt that Bolton would be an asset in developing a new field of study compatible with the location and direction of the University of California's History Department. Stephens further observed, "If we cannot have [Frederick Jackson] Turner," who had gone to Harvard, "let us have Turner's most promising pupil."[40]

After several weeks of indecision, on September 21, 1910, Bolton accepted Stephens's invitation to join the Berkeley faculty. He was attracted by the research possibilities at the Bancroft Library and the fact that he considered a position at Berkeley the most influential west of the Mississippi.[41] Bolton wrote of his move to Berkeley in a letter to Frederick Jackson Turner:

I hope that we shall be able to build a strong department in Western and Spanish American history, for both of these areas in the center of the stage. My own personal interest lies on the border between the two and I expect plenty of help on the two flanks.[42]

The development of the Bolton tradition and Latin American history at the University of California can be directly traced to Henry Morse Stephens (1857-1919). Born in Edinburgh, Scotland, and trained at Oxford University, Stephens came to the United States to teach at Cornell University in 1894. University of California President Benjamin Ide Wheeler, who had been a former colleague of Stephens at Cornell, invited Stephens to Berkeley, and by 1902 Stephens had become Sather Professor of History.

As a European historian, Stephens emphasized English history but also had written on Portuguese topics and created the journal *India*. He had a multi-faceted background and was a brilliant and well-liked professor. His concern for students using original and accurate sources led to his vocal push for the University of California's acquisition of the Bancroft Library.[43]

Bolton lived up to Stephens's expectations. After they received their Ph.D.s, Berkeley added two of Bolton's graduate students, Charles E. Chapman (Ph.D. 1915) and Herbert I. Priestley (Ph.D. 1916), to the faculty. Chapman, a former baseball player and a prolific writer, specialized in Hispanic American and California history, while Priestley complemented Bolton by his concentration on Mexican history. Bolton stressed the role of the Spanish in the American West and the Borderlands, European rivalry in North America and eventually the history of the Americas. This academic threesome turned the University of California into one of the premier national centers for the study of Latin American history, as Stephens reported in 1918. Furthermore, Stephens convinced the Native Sons of the Golden West to donate three thousand dollars annually for fellowships to assist graduate students with their foreign research.[44]

During 1911-1920, while Bolton's concepts were being developed and refined, other developments were occurring on a non-academic level. American interest in Latin America had continued to exist into the twentieth century. Government and business planners had a strong interest in the Caribbean and Mexico because of their proximity to the United States. As the Panama Canal moved toward completion in the early years of the twentieth century, American military strategists developed a defensive attitude toward the Caribbean region. During the Mexican Revolution (1911-1920) the American Government renewed its interest in and concern for Mexico, the immediate neighbor of the United States. Over 900,000 refugees poured into the United States as a result of the revolution, and most of the news coming out of Mexico was not encouraging. Marines landed in Veracruz, and General John J. Pershing led a punitive raid into the northern part of the country. At the same time American interest in all aspects of Mexican life was growing.

Americans had long been interested in a "New West" south of the Tropic of Capricorn, otherwise known as the Southern Cone, including Argentina, Chile, Uruguay, Paraguay, and southern Brazil. Between 1850 and 1930, there was hope that this area, especially the pampas, could be developed much as the American West had been developed. Great hope rested on the building of a transcontinental railroad between Buenos Aires, Argentina, and Santiago, Chile, and the settlement and integration of the mineral lands, forests, and grasslands of the region. Although by 1930 this idea had died, it promoted interest all the way to the remotest corners of southern South America.[45]

Economic interest in southern South America caused a number of agencies to fill the gaps in scientific information about the area. Early in the twentieth century, the Pan-American Union collected and published new data on the region. By the 1920s, Union materials were in classrooms, and Rand McNally had been commissioned to produce maps of Latin America. The goal of the Pan-American Union to foster travel between North and South America was realized by the mid-1920s, when there were six thousand Latin American students in the United States and a variety of media publications promoted tourist and business travel.[46]

Both the American Geographical Society, founded in 1851, and the National Geographic Society, formed in 1888, were influential in promoting Latin America during these years. Through scientific expeditions to the Andes, where Hiram Bingham rediscovered Machu Picchu in 1911, and the production of maps and articles in the *Geographical Review* and the *National Geographic*, Latin America was kept before the public.[47]

During World War I, as markets, scholarly contacts, and other activities with Europe were terminated or weakened, Americans fervently looked to the Western Hemisphere to recapture their commercial fortunes. This interest is evident in a number of areas. For example, in 1910 there were approximately five thousand students enrolled in Spanish-language classes in the United States on the secondary school level; by 1915 the figure had risen to 35,000; and in 1922 there were over 260,000 students enrolled. This development corresponded to similar expansions at the college and university level. In December 1917 this growing linguistic interest found representation in the founding of the American Association of Teachers of Spanish, with an initial membership of over four hundred. In 1916, the University of Missouri had inaugurated the first American-taught course in Spanish-American literature.[48] With the creation of the *Hispanic American Historical Review* in February 1918, the embryonic field of Latin American history gained acceptance in America.[49]

Various universities and libraries throughout the United States expanded their scholarly collections during this period. Since 1898, the Library of Congress had been developing its holdings in Latin American subjects. The University of California purchased the Bancroft Library, and in 1921 the University of Texas purchased the private library of Mexican historian Genaro García for its Latin American collection.[50] Similar developments were taking place throughout the nation.

Between 1909 and 1919, historians and educators across the United States downplayed ancient and medieval history and stressed the modern era instead.[51] They developed fields in the history of the Far West, Latin America, and Canada, and paid increasing attention to the areas of social, agricultural, and military history to name a few.[52] A number of these educators adopted positions that would eventually culminate with Bolton's approach to the history of the United States and the Americas. Lew Allen Chase, professor at Northern State Teachers' College, in

Marquette, Michigan (now Northern Michigan University), first developed his ideas about the importance of the fluid nature of the United States-Canadian boundary while visiting Edmonton in the summer of 1913.[53] Later he wrote of the transnational nature of the fur trade that existed despite the international boundary along the northern frontier.[54] Now that enthusiasm for Latin American history had been raised, W. N. Stearns stressed the role of studying Canadian history as well, stating that it would be a crime not to train youth in Canadian history because Americans share the continent and a common destiny.[55] In 1916, Isaac J. Cox, Bolton's friend and a professor of history at the University of Cincinnati, stressed the European background of American history in his classes; two years later, Bolton's colleague at Berkeley, Professor Chapman, placed an emphasis on Hispanic history.[56]

In 1913, at Berkeley, Professor Stephens emphasized the history of the American West, which he noted must include the northward movement of the Spanish from Mexico, the southward movement of the French from Canada, and the southward movement of the Russians from Alaska.[57] Others, like the Englishman Charles Prestwood Lucas, wrote about the importance of the West Indian islands. "Europe, Africa, Asia," he noted, "have all colonized the West Indian islands. America has not." He said that students in the United States should have their consciousness raised because at one time the West Indies "overshadowed the old North American colonies."[58] Professor William I. Hull of Swarthmore College felt that an "inter-nationality" approach to history should be taken by secondary teachers:

[To] teach our people that beyond the Rockies and the Pacific, beyond the Atlantic, the Rio Grande and the Andes, there are not only people, with aspirations like unto our own, but that their past and present are inextricably interwoven with ours and that their future, for weal or woe, we must assuredly share with them.[59]

At the 1916 annual meeting of the Pacific Coast Branch of the American Historical Association, held in San Diego, historians presented this more diverse approach to the teaching of history, and a number of professors responded to it. Professor Waldemar C. Westergaard of Pomona College presented a paper titled "The United States in the Caribbean," focusing on the idea that "an air of provincial insularity...surrounded colonial history," and then used Caribbean history to show how this antiquated approach was no longer necessary. When Westergaard completed his presentations, a number of professors commented on its concept.

Professor Stephens, who followed Westergaard, stressed the importance of a knowledge of Caribbean history and pointed out that the history of America included the endeavors of France and Spain and other nations that settled the mainland and the islands. He further noted that American history was actually a phase of European history, and that Spanish civilization in America was important long before Jamestown. Stephens concluded by stating that historians and teachers must get rid of the conception of American history as an autonomous unit.

Bolton spoke to the same effect. "He pointed out that while the main stress has hitherto been laid upon a 50 years' struggle between France and England, the struggle with Spain began practically from the settlement of Jamestown, and the Americans were rivals of the Spanish in their movement all the way across the continent to California." Other professors took a similar position, stressing the valuable historical perspectives students could gain if the Caribbean Islands were studied.[60] Bolton had taken a similar position in a University of Texas course a dozen years earlier.

N. Andrew N. Cleven, who was teaching at San Diego High School and Junior College, was deeply committed to the promotion of Latin American history. In 1917, he was concerned that "the almost pathetic provincialism of the average American is very generally reflected in the boys and girls of our secondary schools." Cleven proposed that teachers enrich and enlarge the scope of their history courses because the "colossal tragedy of World War I" had focused thought on the very fundamentals of human society. The post-World War I era was a period of reconstructing the secondary school curriculum. For Cleven this meant that there should be four divisions dealing with the histories of British America, the Pacific nations, the United States, and Latin America. The essentials of ancient, modern, English, and Oriental history should also be taught in order to provide the necessary background for a comprehensive view of the contemporary Americas and Pacific Rim nations. If this system was not possible, Cleven proposed that there be a separate study of Latin America. An internationalist in outlook, Cleven concluded, "There should result a larger conception of international-mindedness, a type of mind which the exigencies of the times make imperative."[61]

Other articles promoting the study of Latin American history followed Cleven's. In October 1917, Professor Westergaard highlighted American interest in the West Indies, and in November, Laura F. Ullrick, a history teacher at New Trier Township High School in Kenilworth, Illinois, pointed out that the school had been offering a course in Latin American history for several years.[62]

Other historians, like Carl Wittke of Ohio State University, noted that while interest in Latin America had led to the development of courses in the area, courses in Canadian history did not appear in college and university bulletins. He emphasized the French role in colonial history and provided evidence of why Canadian history should be studied in the United States—yet another historian who challenged the concept of "American history" or the history of the United States. A. H. Buffington of Williams College focused his comments in an article titled "British and French Imperialism in North America."[63] Bolton was developing his concepts in an academic environment where the best approach to history was considered a broad, international one.

On another front, Isaac J. Cox, of the University of Cincinnati and later of Northwestern University, was an early believer in the Americas approach to history. In a 1919 special section of the *Hispanic American Historical Review* titled, "The Teaching of the History of Hispanic America," Professor Cox presented his views, concluding that although between 1914 and 1919 there had been a flurry of activity in the teaching of Hispanic American history, it was still too soon to bring it to the high school classroom. He took a more conservative approach that focused on using a broader Americas concept when bringing these ideas to the general public:

For the present, the utmost we may hope to do in our higher institutions is to train teachers and men of affairs who will interpret our history from a wider point of view — one that includes Hispanic factors among those of European origin affecting our development — and who will treat our inter-American relationships with more definite and sympathetic knowledge of fundamental economic and racial questions. Under such expert guidance, we may hope to shift the emphasis in our ordinary textbooks, introducing new topics and changing the interpretation of others, and thus present the history of the Americas in truer perspective, recognizing that it has an Iberian as well as a British background, and that the former can no longer be ignored after a cursory review of early Spanish exploration.[64]

In his History 20: "The History of Hispanic America," Cox introduced materials which presented a comparative colonial approach. He discussed the Spaniards in North America; under a section titled "Early International Conflicts in America," he brought in colonial rivalry along with the French, English, and Dutch; and finally he took an Americas approach with "International Relations in the Americas" in the late eighteenth century.[65]

Even in Bolton's vicinity, a broader approach to traditional history had entered the secondary schools. By 1915 the Berkeley public school system was taking this approach with "History of the Pacific," a course offered to high school freshmen that dealt with the role of Spain in California and the Northwest, the meeting of the Hispanic and Anglo-Saxon civilizations, and commercial and cultural relations with Latin America stimulated by the 1914 opening of the Panama Canal.[66]

While Bolton was developing his ideas on the West Coast, similar ideas were being discussed on the East Coast. At a special session at Columbia University following the Second Pan-American Scientific Conference in early 1916, a number of participants expressed views similar to Bolton's. Dr. Ernesto Quesada, member of the faculty at the University of Buenos Aires and the University of La Plata, and president of the Argentine delegation, stressed the idea that Pan-Americanism was based on history and geography, which were intimately interwoven. He further noted that the oceanic separation was an important factor in determining the difference between the Americas and the rest of the world. Seth Low, president of the New York State Chamber of Commerce, pointed out that the European tradition was brought to the Americas, and after independence a new civilization emerged that was bound neither by old traditions nor by the spirit of empire. The vice president of the Chilean delegation and professor of public finance at the University of Chile, Dr. Julio Philippi, stressed the idea that at the basis of Pan-Americanism was an understanding of people, their languages, literatures, and histories, and the search for common solutions to similar problems among Anglo-Saxon and Latin minds. Finally, Dr. Luis Anderson, president of the National Society of International Law in Costa Rica, observed, "we must look to the university centers, to the intellectuals, the patriots, and the statesmen of the three Americas, to maintain on its pedestal the superb and majestic tower of Pan-Americanism."[67] Others pointed out that Americans should be educated in order to understand the peoples and cultures of the Western Hemisphere.[68]

The combination of past and present influences impacted Bolton as he was developing, discussing, and testing his various ideas, forming a continuum for his comprehensive approach to the history of the Americas. He was also influenced by the "school of history" that had blossomed at Berkeley between 1911 and 1921.[69]

Bolton received encouragement from William R. Shepherd of Columbia University, who had published an article that focused on the role of the non-English nations in the colonization of North America. In a letter to Bolton, Shepherd stated that he was taking a broader approach in his courses because he felt that the role of the French and Spanish in United States history had been sadly neglected in the past. In addition, conservative, traditional United States historians dealt with the Americas approach with a great deal of hostility. Shepherd summed up this tradition:

We must struggle constantly against the traditional notion that all that is worthwhile in the history of the United States — incidentally, also a monopoly of virtue and of the essential forces which have put this country into the foreground of the progressive nations of the world — has been and still is concentrated in the area east of the Connecticut River, and certainly between the Piscataqua and the Allegheny.[70]

The emergence of Bolton's concept of the Americas is as important as the concept itself. As we have seen, Bolton brought Turner's concept of the frontier and his expansion of this concept outside of the United States to the University of Texas. While he was in Texas, his research trips to Mexico, where he encountered a wealth of documentation that drastically changed his historical outlook, influenced his beginning interest in Spanish colonial history. When his department head, Garrison, would not allow him to focus on Spanish Texas and the Southwest, Bolton used the internationalization of the Caribbean Basin during the colonial era as a class theme. Then Bolton broadened his view to include the international rivalries in the Caribbean basin, Spanish colonial history in the Southwest, and eventually the Borderlands or the southern region of the United States from Florida to California. This was the situation as of 1911 when Bolton moved to Berkeley and continued his comprehensive approach to the history of the Western Hemisphere.

Prior to 1911, there is no evidence that Bolton publicly discussed or published his ideas on the role of Spain in the United States. That year Bolton chaired a session devoted to the study of the Southwest at the annual meeting of the American Historical Association. He also presented his ideas about the importance of the Southwest in national and international history. Before his colleagues he noted the benefits of such a focus:

[It offered] the richest opportunities afforded by our country for the study of archaeology and ethnology; that as the theater for two centuries of a contest between Spain and barbarian America, it was the place where the Spanish colonial institutions were subjected to their severest test and where they can be most profitably studied; that the continuous international struggle of which it was for the same period a constant scene, struggle of which it was for the study of the colonial and diplomatic history of America; that it played a leading part in the slavery question, the westward movement, and the development of imperialism; and that its recent growth offers ethnic, economic, architectural, social, and intellectual forces and features peculiar to itself.[71]

He also stressed that extended work needed to be done on narrative history of the region along with the publication of the documents that had recently been uncovered. Only after this preliminary work could an accurate history of the Southwest be written. Once this history was developed, it could be integrated into the larger national history of the United States.

Bolton's interest in the development and publication of documentary resources continued to be enthusiastically promoted. On December 18, 1911, shortly after his arrival at Berkeley, Bolton sent a detailed report to Benjamin Ide Wheeler, president of the University of California, outlining the need for the publication of a comprehensive body of documents relating to the Spanish in the United States. Bolton opened with the assertion that "One of the greatest needs in the field of American History is the publication of a comprehensive body of historical materials relating to Spanish activities within the present limits of the United States." Further, he wrote, "A more fundamental explanation of the neglect of the Spanish period and of the West generally in American history is the fact that down to recent times the history of the United States has been written almost solely from the standpoint of the East and of the English colonies." Bolton also noted that Frederick Jackson Turner had recently highlighted the West, but "he and his school have contributed very little to the history of the Southwest and the Far West." He concluded that the History Department at Berkeley was taking the lead to remedy this situation in American his-toriography.[72]

At a 1913 meeting of the Pacific Coast Branch of the American Histori-cal Association, which had convened jointly with the Southern California Social Science Association, Bolton promoted the importance of using origi-nal documents in the study of history. He stressed the importance of ac-quainting American youth with historical materials and urged that the nature of these materials must be understood. Historical evidence, Bolton believed, was an important element in the discipline of history. However, he concluded with an expression of traditional sentiments:

The interest in the good of one's own community or nation is one of the best results of teaching of history. The patriotism and enthusiasm of the South in mat-ters affecting the State probably come from courses in local history.[73]

Bolton held this concern for a solid foundation upon which to build historical studies as a keystone concept throughout his life. In 1946, he summed up how he and his students should approach the study of his-tory:

While the ultimate objective of historical investigation may be regarded as a search for the synthetic and the general, a person who has never put the fabric of history under a microscope and watched the genesis of society in process will not arrive at sound generalizations with regard to its origin and significance. Facts must go before theories. No generalization can reveal more than the merest suggestion of the full richness of the pattern and substance of the fabric which become apparent when examined in detail.[74]

Bolton followed the guideline of a good historian by first developing a program to gather historical documents and then proceeding to the gen-eral synthesis. (Figure 2.1)[75]

Figure 2.1
Ideological Model Used by Historians

While establishing the importance of Spain in North America, Bolton began to broaden his ideas to include a comparative colonial history of the United States. In a June 1912 letter to his brother, Frederick, he ex-plained that in his general course in Western history, "I have established a point of view which will cause a rewriting of text books, much as Turner's work did." The Spanish Borderlands, as yet unnamed, were coming into being. He continued in the letter, "I approach American history from a continental and European standpoint, instead of from the standpoint of England alone."[76]

The European role in the development of the world, specifically of the Pacific Rim, further enhanced Bolton's ideas. The Panama-Pacific International Exposition was held in San Francisco a year after the 1914 opening of the Panama Canal. As part of the celebration, the American Historical Association authorized the Panama-Pacific Historical Congress to convene. A group of international scholars presented papers focusing on the history of the Pacific Rim as a unit, uniting Europe, Asia, and America and a part of world history.[77] Bolton, who gave a paper at one of the sessions, was possibly influenced by these historians and their broader approach to history, which strengthened Bolton's convictions.

This unorthodox, wider approach would soon lead to Bolton's work written with his former student Thomas M. Marshall, *The Colonization of North America*. Bolton saw this work as the story of European expansion in North America:

To grasp the unity of early North American history, one must conceive of several foci, from which streams of influence went forth, and must follow those streams and their interminglings. The Spanish stream started in the West Indies, spread to Central America, Mexico, the northern provinces, the Philippines; the French stream started from two foci (Canada and the West Indies); two streams went out and met in the West (Louisiana, the Illinois, the Saskatchewan). The Russian stream proceeded southward; the English stream was a unit until 1783; then it split into the American westward movement and the expansion of British Canada. The frontiers of the different nations clashed. The Franco-Spanish and the Anglo-French border conflicts ended in 1765 (not counting the Anglo-French contest in the West Indies in the later 18th century), but the Anglo-Spanish contest, beginning in the 16th century, continued till the 20th (in the Caribbean); the two English streams met and clashed all along the Canadian border from 1783 to 1846, especially in the Oregon-British Columbia country. Thus have the nations hammered out their boundaries.[78]

This concept, a comparative colonial United States history, was the final step in Bolton's development of the history of the Americas.

Bolton's move into comparative colonial history ran into some criticism because it presented traditional history in a broader context. When Bolton and Marshall completed *The Colonization of North America* in 1916, the editor at Macmillan sent it to a reviewer for reaction. The fact that the work included so much of the little-known, non-English story of colonial North America shocked one unidentified reviewer. He noted that "one third of the whole is devoted to the period before 1606, that is to say, before there were any permanent English settlements in America." The reviewer was rather disturbed that "nearly twice as much space is given to this early period of exploration as to the whole of the revolutionary movement from 1763 to 1783." He concluded that this focus was "impractical" for a college textbook "or as the first part of a history of the United States."[79] The manager of the College Department of Macmillan, R. R. Smith, further expounded this criticism and noted that this review "represent[s] pretty accurately the attitude regarding a college text on American history of men in the states east of the Rocky Mts., with the possible exception of a few of those in the south-western states."[80]

After a long, convoluted history, Macmillan published *Colonization* in 1920. Frederic Paxson quickly critiqued the new comparative approach. He felt that Bolton had created a new subject rather than built on traditional colonial history and agreed that the unorthodox distribution of space shocked some traditional historians. Finally, he was sorry to see colonial history changed, but the book would be instrumental in creating a new comparative approach.[81]

If Bolton had moved toward comparative United States colonial history, by 1916, through this publication, he was a short step away from the implementation of his history of the Americas concept. However, once again it is important to review the external developments that paralleled and complemented Bolton's thought processes.

In late 1917, the Semi-Centennial Committee of the Founding of the University of California appointed a March celebration of the Committee on International Relations. As a member of this committee, Bolton was responsible for developing a program dealing with historical questions relating to contemporary issues in the Pacific Basin. He persuaded Stanford professor Payson Jackson Treat to be the main speaker at the celebration.[82] Bolton was simultaneously developing other global concepts. In February 1917, Carl R. Fish sent Bolton a paper on the frontier that sparked Bolton's "The Frontier, a Word Problem." Bolton expressed this idea and hoped to pursue the topic, but he never did.[83] Prior to Bolton's development, the concept of the history of the Americas seemed to exist in fragments that certainly had a great impact on his thinking.

With the United States' entry into World War I, Bolton believed that a phase in hemispheric history had come to a close. The future would lie with the nations of the Americas, and he would have to present his concept.

Other developments also may have influenced or strengthened Bolton's larger outlook. The University of California Publications in American Archaeology and Ethnography first appeared in 1903-1904, but it was not until 1916 and afterward that its papers began to take an Americas approach—looking at Mexico and Peru, for instance. In 1918 Bolton was involved with the Center for Hispanic-American Culture. The Spanish government charged the Center with organizing a congress to be held in Seville during the Hispanic-American Exposition that would take place at the end of the war. The primary purpose of this congress was to study the principles whereby the governments of Hispanic America and Spain would unify their laws dealing with culture, science, trade, and commerce. It was hoped that these laws would become a common base for Spain and the American republics. All Spanish-speaking hemispheric nations, institutions, societies, and groups were encouraged to take an active role in this congress.[84]

Not only was Bolton interested in Hispanic concerns, but early in 1918, he and other faculty members were on the Committee on International Relations.[85] They met at the Faculty Club in March to discuss a proposed international conference. In Hawaii or Japan, representatives from Pacific Rim nations would meet in 1919 to consider international cooperation in the fields of commerce and trade, diplomacy, education, labor, and science.[86]

On the eve of the Versailles Peace Conference, Bolton, William M. Sloane, and John J. Van Nostrand issued a statement stressing the importance of history for understanding the causes of the war and how they might be avoided in the future.[87]

Besides this interest in world affairs, Bolton was further developing and refining his concept, but now in the field of cartography. In correspondence dating from 1917 with L. P. Denoyer of the Chicago map firm Denoyer-Gepper, Bolton promoted a series of maps that took an Americas approach.[88]

By the end of the second decade of the twentieth century, Bolton's historiographical thought process had reached the apex of its development. It had its genesis with local colonial Texas and its full-grown development as the Americas approach. Bolton summed up his approach in late 1920: "So you see my thesis is not local history, but American history in the largest sense. The Spanish Borderlands are only a bit of the whole." He further revealed, "Of course the entire thesis is too vast for one person to master except in outline, but I believe I have had a vision which is destined to reconstruct our teaching. We shall have general courses in American history, and special courses in national history (United States, Canada, Mexico, etc.)."[89]

Over the years, Bolton continued to refine his idea of the history of the Americas. In 1950 he recollected, "Through research in borderland areas it dawned upon me that what we in this country, used to call American history was really United States history — the story of only one of the twenty American nations." As he moved toward the Americas concept, Bolton realized that he was breaking with tradition and "my great and admired teachers," who included Frederick Jackson Turner, John McMaster, and others.[90] The die had been cast. In the coming decades, a new era in American historiography would unfold.

NOTES

1. The standard biography of Bolton is John Francis Bannon, *Herbert Eugene Bolton: The Historian and the Man* (Tucson: University of Arizona Press, 1978). A good portion of this chapter has been based on chapters 1-2.

2. Ibid., 24. In a letter to his brother, Frederick, on the eve of the Spanish American War, Bolton wrote of Spain: "Most of her possessions have been lost by revolutions all through incompetency. This seems to be her last stand in which she is rising unheard of methods to maintain her hold [over Cuba]." Herbert E. Bolton to Frederick Bolton, 04/08/1898, Bolton Papers, Out, Bancroft Library, University of California, Berkeley. The Bolton Papers are cataloged according to an "in" and "out" system. Hereafter: Bolton Papers, In or Out.

3. Bolton to Mr. Tubbs, 05/14/1920, Bolton Papers, Out.

4. Bolton to M. E. Curti, 09/07/1928, Bolton Papers, Out.

5. Bolton to Arthur Scott Aiton, 05/05/1927, Bolton Papers, Out.

6. Gerald D. Nash, *Creating the West: Historical Interpretations, 1890-1990* (Albuquerque: University of New Mexico Press, 1991) 18.

7. The Bolton family consisted of Frances (1897), Helen (1899), Laura (1901), Eugenie (1904), Gertrude (1907), Jane (1910), and Herbert, Jr. (1913).

8. During his stay at Pennsylvania, Bolton's course work included a bibliography sources course from Dana Munro; "England and the Continent, 1400-1700" from Edward Cheyney; "American Constitutional Law" from Herman Ames; and an economics course from Simon W. Patten.

9. Bannon, *Herbert Eugene Bolton*, 26.

10. "Rambles in Mexico by Herbert E. Bolton," 03/07/1929, Bolton Papers, the Mary L. Ross Papers, sec. 4, Professional Papers 4-8, file 3, (Hereafter: Bolton-Ross Papers.) Georgia Department of Archives and History, Atlanta.

11. Bannon, *Herbert Eugene Bolton*, 25.

12. The University of Wisconsin-Milwaukee administration has commemorated one of the university's noted graduates and instructors by naming a building after Bolton.

13. Frederick Bolton, "Random Memories of an Admiring Brother," *Arizona and the West* 4 (1961): 72-83.

14. Herbert E. Bolton, "The Place of American History in the High-School Course," *School Review: The Journal of Secondary Education* 9 (1901): 516-525.

15. Bolton, "Rambles in Mexico."

16. Bolton to Frederick Bolton, 10/16/1901, 10/26/1901, Bolton Papers, Out.

17. Bolton to Frederick Bolton, 01/05/1902, Bolton Papers, Out.

18. Bolton to Frederick Bolton, 01/24/1902, Bolton Papers, Out.

19. Bolton to Frederick Bolton, 02/01/1902, Bolton Papers, Out.

20. Bolton to Frederick Bolton, 03/13/1902, Bolton Papers, Out.

21. Bolton to Frederick Bolton, 06/29/1902, Bolton Papers, Out.

22. Bolton to Frederick Bolton, 07/08/1902, Bolton Papers, Out.

23. Bolton to Frederick Bolton, 09/10/1902, Bolton Papers, Out.

24. Bolton to Guy S. Ford, 04/30/1921, Bolton Papers, Out.

25. *Bulletin of the University of Texas* no. 12. (April 1, 1902): 85.

26. Bolton to Frederick Bolton, 10/06/1902, 10/13/1902, Bolton Papers, Out.

27. *Bulletin of the University of Texas* no. 31 (June 1, 1904): 81.

28. Bernard Moses, *The Establishment of Spanish Rule in America: An Introduction*

to the History and Politics of Spanish America (New York: Putnam's, 1898), iii.

29. Ibid., 293-312.

30. *Bulletin of the University of Texas* no. 54 (June 1, 1905): 108.

31. *Bulletin of the University of Texas* no. 73 (April 1, 1906): 100; no. 103 (February 15, 1908): 93.

32. Herbert E. Bolton, trans., "Affairs in the Philippines Islands, by Fray Domingo de Salazar" [1583], and "Two Letters to Felipe II" (Gerónimo de Guzmán and Jhoan de Vascones, 1585), in Emma Helen Blair and James Alexander Robertson, eds., *The Philippine Islands, 1493-1803*, 55 vols. (Cleveland: Arthur Clark, 1903-1909), 5:210-255, 6:76-80.

33. Herbert E. Bolton, *Guide to Materials for the History of the United States in the Principal Archives of Mexico* (1913 repr. New York: Kraus, 1965).

34. By 1909 Bolton had published one co-authored book and some fifteen articles.

35. Herbert E. Bolton, "Hispanic American History in the United States: Retrospective and Prospective," Bolton Papers, pt. III, carton 11, Bancroft Library.

36. Bolton, "On Wisdom's Trail, a Westerner in the East: Notes on a Trip to the American Historical Association Held at New Haven, Connecticut, December 1922," Bolton Papers, books I-IV, folder 26, Bolton-Ross Papers, 42-43.

37. E. D. Adams to Bolton, 10/03/1908, Bolton Papers, In.

38. Adams to Bolton, 11/02/1908, Bolton Papers, In.

39. Bolton to Sidney Mezes, 07/30/1910; Bolton Papers, Out. Mezes to Bolton, 08/06/1910, Bolton Papers, In.

40. Henry Morse Stephens to Bolton, 08/12/1910, Bolton Papers, In.

41. Bolton to Frederick Bolton, 01/30/1911, Bolton Papers, Out.

42. Bolton to Frederick Jackson Turner, 12/27/1910, Bolton Papers, Out.

43. "Henry Morse Stephens, 1857-1919," Correspondence and Papers, ca. 1890-1919, C-B 926, Key, Bancroft Library, 1.

44. "Hispanic and Hispanic American Studies at the University of California," 1918[?], Bolton Papers, Out.

45. J. Valerie Fifer, *United States Perceptions of Latin America, 1850-1930: A "New West" South of Capricorn?* (Manchester: Manchester University Press, 1991), provides the best single study on this interest and concern by United States citizens. For a more specific study, see Joseph Tulchin, *The Aftermath of War: World War I and U.S. Policy Toward Latin America* (New York: New York University Press, 1971).

46. Fifer, *Perceptions*, 153-158.

47. Ibid., 158-162.

48. Henry G. Doyle, "Spanish Studies in the United States," *Bulletin of the Pan-American Union* 60 (March 1926): 223-234; "The First Annual Meeting," *Hispania* 1 (1918): 15; J. R. Spell, "Spanish Teaching in the United States," *Hispania* 10 (May 1927): 141-159.

49. Charles E. Chapman, "The Founding of the Review," *Hispanic American Historical Review* 1 (1918): 8-23; J. Franklin Jameson, "A New Historical Journal," *Hispanic American Historical Review* 1 (1918): 2-7.

50. Carlos E. Castañeda and Jack Autry Dabbs, *Guide to the Latin American Manuscripts in the University of Texas Library* (Cambridge, MA: Harvard University Press, 1939), vii; Library of Congress, *Hispanic Foundation*, Departmental and Divisional Manual no. 12 (Washington, DC: Library of Congress, 1950), 3-4; *New York Herald*

Tribune, 10/05/1930, sec. 2, p. 5.

51. An interesting study on this subject is Edith M. Clark, "The History Curriculum Since 1850," *History Teacher's Magazine* 11 (February 1920): 58-68.

52. "A Decade of History Teaching [1909-1919]," *History Teacher's Magazine* 10 (December 1919): 497.

53. L. A. Chase, "The Last American Frontier," *History Teacher's Magazine* 6 (February 1915): 37-46.

54. Chase, "How the Furs Came Down from the North Country," *History Teacher's Magazine* 7 (February 1916): 44-46.

55. W. N. Stearns, "Canadian History Next?" *History Teacher's Magazine* 6 (November 1915): 294.

56. Isaac J. Cox, "The European Background for the History Course in American History," *History Teacher's Magazine* 7 (1916): 163-169; Charles E. Chapman, "A Producing Class in Hispanic-American History," *History Teacher's Magazine* 9 (1918): 84-86.

57. H. Morse Stephens, "Courses in History in the Junior Colleges," *History Teacher's Magazine* 4 (1913): 154.

58. Charles Prestwood Lucas, "The ABC of West Indian History," *History Teacher's Magazine* 6 (1913): 184, 187.

59. William I. Hull, "International Interpretation of United States History," *History Teacher's Magazine* 5 (1914): 135.

60. William A. Morris, "Report of the Proceedings of the 13th Annual Meeting of the Pacific Coast Branch of the American Historical Association," in *Annual Report of the American Historical Association for the Year 1916*, 2 vols. (Washington, DC: Government Printing Office, 1919), 1:124-125.

61. N. Andrew N. Cleven, "Latin American History in Our Secondary Schools," *History Teacher's Magazine* 8 (1917): 219-220.

62. Waldeman Westergaard, "American Interest in the West Indies," *The History Teacher's Magazine* 8 (1917): 249-253; Laura F. Ullrick, "Latin American History in the High School: An Experiment," *History Teacher's Magazine* 8 (1917): 296.

63. Carl Wittke, "Canada—Our Neglected Neighbor," *History Teacher's Magazine* 10 (1919): 485-488; A. H. Buffington, "British and French Imperialism in North America," *History Teacher's Magazine* 10 (1919): 489-496.

64. Isaac J. Cox, "Courses in Hispanic American History," *Hispanic American Historical Review* 2 (1919): 399.

65. Cox, "Syllabi of Courses: The History of Hispanic America," *Hispanic American Historical Review* 2 (1919): 425-427.

66. William John Cooper, "Berkeley Public Schools—Courses in History," *History Teachers' Magazine* 6 (1915): 328-330.

67. *The University as a Factor in American Relations*, International Conciliation, Pan-American Division, Bulletin 9 (New York: American Association for International Conciliation, Pan-American Division, 1916), 10, 33, 23-24, 28.

68. Peter H. Goldsmith, *The Next Steps in Interamerican Relations*. International Conciliation, Pan-American Division, Bulletin no. 14 (New York: American Association of International Conciliation, Pan-American Division, 1917), 8-9, 11.

69. Bolton to unknown, 02/23/1921, Bolton Papers, Out.

70. William R. Shepherd to Bolton, 12/15/1911, Bolton Papers, In.

71. "The Meeting of the AHA at Buffalo and Ithaca [December 27-30, 1911]," in

Annual Report of the AHA for the Year 1911, 2 vols. (Washington, DC: Government Printing Office, 1913), 1:28.

72. Report, Bolton to Benjamin Ide Wheeler, 12/18/1911, Bolton Papers Out; copy in John F. Bannon, ed., *Bolton and the Spanish Borderlands* (Norman: University of Oklahoma Press, 1964), 23-31.

73. William A. Morris, "Proceedings of the Tenth Annual Meeting of the Pacific Coast Branch of the American Historical Association," in *Annual Report of the AHA for the Year 1913*, 2 vols. (Washington, DC: Government Printing Office, 1913), 1:73.

74. Outline for a seminar given in Mexico City in the summer of 1946, preserved in the Bolton Papers, Bancroft Library, University of California at Berkeley; see Bannon, *Bolton and the Spanish Borderlands*, 68-69.

75. Bannon, *Herbert Eugene Bolton*, 275-282.

76. Bolton to Frederick Bolton, 06/02/1912, Bolton Papers, Out.

77. For a presentation of these ideas and concepts, see H. Morse Stephens and Herbert E. Bolton, eds., *The Pacific Ocean in History* (New York: Macmillan, 1917).

78. Bolton to Mr. Glasgow, 11/06/1920, Bolton Papers, Out.

79. R. R. Smith to Bolton, 03/21/1917, Bolton Papers, In.

80. Ibid.

81. Frederic Paxson to Bolton, 12/16/1920, Bolton Papers, In.

82. Bolton to Payson Jackson Treat, 02/19/1918, Bolton Papers, Out.

83. Bolton to Carl Russell Fish, 02/23/1918, Bolton Papers, Out.

84. "Congress for Hispanic American Culture," 1918, Bolton Papers, Out.

85. Committee members included Herbert E. Bolton, H. H. Guy, W. MacDonald, J. C. Merriam, C. H. Rieber, W. E. Ritter, P. J. Treat, O. G. Villard, and F. F. Westbrook (president of the University of California).

86. "Committee on International Relations," Faculty Club, University of California Campus, 03/21/1918; "Meeting for Consideration of Recurrent Conferences on International Problems of the Pacific," Wheeler Hall #312, 03/22/1918, Bolton Papers, Out.

87. "History," 1918?, Bolton Papers, Out.

88. Bolton to L. P. Denoyer, 12/20/1918, Bolton Papers, Out.

89. Bolton to Mr. Glasgow, 11/06/1920, Bolton Papers, Out.

90. Herbert E. Bolton, "The Confessions of a Wayward Professor," *The Americas* 6 (1950): 361.

3

The Americas Concept
Emerges, 1919-1929

One of the curious aspects of the historiography of the history of the Americas is the fact that the Americas concept became more closely associated with teaching than with research. Bolton directed his efforts toward teaching the concept in his famous History 8 class. Given the fact that between 1919 and 1928 he published ten of his most important works, which focused primarily on the Spanish Borderlands, there was little time to complete a projected textbook or an interpretative work on the Americas. Much like his mentor Frederick Jackson Turner, who did not publish much more than his historic "Significance" speech of 1893, Bolton published little on the Americas concept. All that is left is his correspondence, a number of articles, the "Epic" speech, and History 8. It was Bolton's classroom teaching that actually brought the concept to thousands of students, and thus it is important to understand the History 8 course as a vehicle for expounding the history of the Americas.

April 16, 1919, proved to be a fateful day for Bolton and the history of the Americas. Phoebe Apperson Hearst, philanthropist and friend of the University of California, had died a few days before, and many of the university faculty attended her funeral. As the well-loved chairman of the History Department, Henry Morse Stephens, was returning from the funeral, he fell dead of a heart attack. The man who had brought the Bancroft Library to Berkeley, along with Native Sons' Fellowships, Herbert E. Bolton, and a Hispanic-oriented faculty, was gone. For Bolton it was "an incalculable and irreparable loss" with as yet unknown ramifications.[1]

Bolton's career changed quickly. First, Berkeley's president appointed Bolton acting chair and then chair of the History Department. In this position he would have to lead the department without Stephens, teach his classes for the rest of the semester, and develop new classes for the anticipated increase in veterans' enrollment following the end of World War I. Bolton covered Stephens's popular Western Civilization course, which attracted as many as seven hundred students; however, in the months that followed, the history faculty reorganized the lower-division program.

As department chair, Bolton was now in a position to take positive action on his dream of creating and teaching a course on the history of the Americas. Since 1911 he had been "advocating a course in the history of the Western Hemisphere, which in a way should parallel the general course in the history of western Europe." As Professor Lawrence Kinnaird (Ph.D. 1928) noted in 1942, "Professor Bolton dared to suggest that a knowledge of the New World might be of more practical value to Americans." In order to achieve this, a history of the peoples who came to the Americas should be presented rather than the history of individual political units.[2]

At this time the curricula of most colleges and universities required students to take a general survey of European history. Traditionalists then and now stress the importance of a thorough knowledge of European history. American history, which followed in importance, was organized along nationalistic lines.[3]

There is evidence of a conflict between Bolton and Stephens over the teaching of an Americas-type course. Bolton alluded to this problem when he wrote that the course was one "which I never expected to give, but which fell to me through the death of Professor Stephens and the great increase in our freshman enrollment."[4] In 1966 J. Fred Rippy (Ph.D. 1920) described Stephens as "an incurable optimist in respect to the ultimate destiny of the world under Anglo-Saxon leadership."[5] Had Stephens blocked the introduction of this course because it dealt with Latin and Anglo history as equals, or was there another reason? Was it perhaps the voice of a traditionalist seeking to maintain the status quo over Bolton's new perspective? These questions may never be answered.

Exactly two weeks after the death of Stephens, Bolton wrote, "New possibilities have opened here for the development of my personal work and I have to decide soon which path I wish to follow."[6] On May 26, within forty days of Stephens's death, Bolton had organized the course, titled it "History of the Americas," and placed it among the fall semester offerings.

Over the years, Bolton provided numerous insights into the value of the history of the Americas. His first analysis of the educational value of the history of the Americas is found in his response to the Committee on History and Education for Citizenship in the Schools, based in Washington, DC, in which Bolton outlined the importance of the history of the Americas for schoolchildren.[7] He wanted the Committee to use the term "American history," so that the nations of Latin America and Canada could be included. He reasoned that in order for students to become "fully equipped American citizen[s] of the post-war period," they must "have some definite knowledge of world affairs as well of strictly national affairs." He continued, "For no field is this knowledge so eminently desirable and at the same time so painfully lacking as for that of the Hispanic American countries to the south of us. In only a lesser degree is this true of our neighbor on the north."

Bolton believed that American participation in World War I completed a cycle of American history. In the sixteenth and seventeenth centuries, the Europeans "transmitted a culture, a congeries of institutional traditions, and a potent civilization." Then for three centuries, the Americans further developed that civilization, so that when World War I was in process, they could "enter the conflict and give the incisive victory to the cause of humanity." Furthermore, Bolton believed that knowledge of the Western Hemisphere was necessary for economic and political reasons, such as "promoting better relations with Hispanic America, to the unity of interests of the nations of this hemisphere, and to our own growing need of foreign markets where we may compete to advantage against the great mercantile powers in the world."

Bolton's enthusiastic statements placed him in a dilemma. On one hand he outlined how this new history could be taught, but in the next statement he noted that there was no room for it in elementary and secondary curricula. However, he pushed forward with the concept and wrote that certain "unities and parallels" allowed it to be taught by "an ever-growing body of men." He ended with the admonition that historians from the Far West, because of international contacts and foresight, knew what was best for national education and "believe in battering down those traditions of American history which have...unduly restricted its scope." His statements are those of an enthusiast for the concept and do not take into consideration the reality of introducing such a radical concept into educational systems throughout the nation. Bolton's enthusiasm for the concept later caused him to promote the idea because it was the right thing to do, but he never really developed a philosophical approach to explaining it.

Having created the concept for the course, Bolton "brashly announced a lower division lecture course in the history of all the Americas in one synthesis" in the fall of 1919.[8] This new endeavor, which Bolton called "Universal American History, that is the History of the Americas from North Pole to the South Pole from Columbus to Now," was filled with new challenges.[9] Known as History 8, it was conceived as a two-semester course. History 8A covered the colonial era, and the following semester History 8B dealt with the national era.[10] The history faculty was convinced of the importance of this comparative approach. Over the years, the required status of the course within the department varied; in 1933 it was an elective although other departments did recommend the course.[11]

Response to the course was overwhelming. Much to Bolton's surprise and dismay, 722 students were awaiting his lecture in Wheeler Auditorium on the first day of fall classes in 1919. At the start of the second semester in January 1920, there were 1,258 students in the class — standing room only. When Bolton urged students to drop the class because of a lack of seats, they said that they were content to stand and remained in the course. This was the highest enrollment ever allowed. Subsequent restrictions kept the numbers to around one thousand.[12] For the next twenty-five years, Bolton lectured to between six hundred and eight hundred students twice a week, assisted by half a dozen teaching assistants who "helped me to organize that Seven Ring Circus." Students and faculty considered the course to be the largest purely elective course at Berkeley.[13]

Bolton later reflected that he had made "very little preparation for the course" prior to its presentation, "and gave it in a rather hand-to-mouth fashion." As a result, he "spent day and night reading, made a day-by-day syllabus of one mimeographed page, drew maps on manila paper, and later published the syllabus and maps in a three-hundred-page book."[14] Two of his students, Arthur S. Aiton (Ph.D. 1923) and Ralph Kuykendall (M.A. 1918), assisted Bolton and developed the first crude bibliographies. Aiton noted, "You were always a lap ahead of the wolf that year and we were two laps behind."[15] It was common for Bolton to spend a week preparing a lecture, and at times he stayed up beyond midnight fine-tuning these lectures. Furthermore, he created three new sets of maps and hired nine graduate assistants.[16]

One of Bolton's former teaching assistants, J. Manuel Espinosa (Ph.D. 1934), described the mechanics of Bolton's teaching of History 8. The classes were large lecture sections held in Wheeler Auditorium, where Bolton began lecturing promptly at 11 A.M. two days a week. Notes were kept on the podium while he walked across the stage with the pointer. He covered the published syllabus in-depth in the lectures and used original examples to get the students to focus on the concepts. Behind him was a 12-by-30 foot map that he pointed to with a six-foot pointer. At times he would lean on the pointer in a resting mode.

The graduate assistants were required to attend the lectures and take attendance. Each discussion section had twenty-five students. In the discussions the assistants expanded on points of interpretation and reading materials from the syllabus. Through this experience most of Bolton's graduate assistants, like Espinosa, were trained to be the instructors who would keep the course going into the late 1960s.[17]

The course themes followed aspects of Frederick Jackson Turner's concept that the frontier experience modified the newly arrived European culture in the Americas, creating a true American character. Bolton began the course with "a general sketch of the European background of America," and once he got the Americas occupied, he moved into "the transmission of European civilization (Spanish, Portuguese, Swedish, Dutch, French,

English and Russian)." The first half of the course featured colonial expansion, then international rivalries, and ended with the fateful year 1776. The second half of the course began with the completion of the independence movements and then turned to the creation and development of the American republics and the evolution of Brazil and Canada. Once the nations were established, Bolton shifted his emphasis to the relations and interrelations between the nations of the Americas and the rest of the world, and ended with a look at the contemporary states of the Americas and their role in the world.[18]

The comparative approach unraveled in the latter half of the course because Bolton relied on individual national histories rather than taking a broad thematic approach to the national period. This approach was similar to the traditional Latin America history that continues to be taught and presented in textbooks as a series of separate national experiences. Later, Bolton confided to Woodrow Borah that the national period was harder to fit into his concept of unity. However, Bolton was confident that in the future a historian would work a way out of this dilemma.[19]

The average student in the course experienced a certain excitement created by Bolton's "infectious enthusiasm," the backdrop of large maps, and the new approach of comparative history. In the 1990s, a number of former students left their impressions of the experience of History 8.[20] Engel Sluiter (Ph.D. 1937), a former graduate assistant (1932-1935), observed the course's effect on students:

The course was an eye-opener for students: it gave them new and exciting perspectives; it put the national history they knew as "American" history in a larger hemispheric framework; it introduced them to different peoples, cultures, and institutions; and it gave them a chance to become more tolerant of races and cultures different from their own.[21]

Ursula Lamb (M.A. 1937) entered the University of California as a German immigrant in the 1930s. She recalled Bolton's approach:

Bolton would make a strong and at times a combative case for what he called, "Las Americas." He pointed out that civilization approached the United States from the Southwest northward and he constantly stressed this point. He could not be happier than when he stressed this point. He would say, "Mexico City had a great cathedral when Boston was a fishing village." As a European, I thought he was overemphasizing the idea [of the history of the Americas] because it was so obvious. His stressing of the unity idea was overdone until I realized that my fellow American students had no idea of this European-type unity in hemispheric history.[22]

Donald E. Worcester (Ph.D. 1940) commented on Bolton's hemispheric focus:

His purpose was simply to show freshman that there was much more to what went on in the hemisphere than the coming and spread of the English. He resented the insularity and anti-Spanish biases of U.S. historians, and his aim was to counteract it [*sic*]. He took the approach he enjoyed and which suited his purpose—narrating events.[23]

Besides Bolton's comparative approach to the history of the hemisphere, there were other reasons for the success of History 8. In 1963, John W. Caughey (Ph.D. 1928) wrote about Bolton's teaching style:

The paradox was that he did not seem to be a good lecturer. He was neither dramatic nor spectacular. He did not try to entertain, nor was he truly eloquent. Instead, he offered a down-to-earth exposition, a straightforward narrative, together with his observations on the meaning. Clearly he was talking out of solid knowledge. More important, he showed his keenness for the grand development that was his subject and his zest for the study. He achieved a contagion of interest in the pursuit and recapture of a fleeting past.[24]

Professor Thomas Bailey noted that Bolton was "a highly effective lecturer"—his voice carried well in Wheeler Auditorium. The other part of his appeal was the published syllabus that students could purchase, thus giving them time and the opportunity to "scribble down more meaningful notes." Bolton's "infectious enthusiasm" and use of memorable, well-placed anecdotes to emphasize a point also contributed to his success as a lecturer.[25] Bolton brought the same narrative style he used in his publications to the classroom, a practice that made history come alive and was popular with students.

Throughout his life Bolton saw the value of private institutions and organizations, rather than federal government programs, promoting cultural relations programs. Thus, for Bolton, the university was the best environment for this comparative history of the Americas. Here nationalistic provincialism could be challenged, hopefully contained, and his new approach could take hold.[26]

Bolton sought to destroy the provincialism of the Americas not only through his courses and writings but also through fostering visiting professorships.[27] He oversaw the arrival of Professor Raúl Ramírez, the first exchange professor from Chile (University of Santiago), at the University of California. He arrived in May 1920 and stayed for the year, teaching courses in the traditional and intellectual history of South America. Such visits forwarded Bolton's vision because through this personal contact, students could "develop an intelligent and sympathetic knowledge of our Hispanic-American neighbors."[28]

It is interesting to speculate about what Bolton learned from his encounter with Ramírez, who had been educated in a system that stressed Diego Barros Arana's history of the Americas. The two professors probably exchanged views of the history of the Americas.

Bolton promoted the concept of the history of the Americas in lectures and talks whenever the opportunity arose. In April 1920, he was in communication with the director of the University of California Extension Service, L. J. Richardson. At the invitation of Professor Klingsberg, Bolton proposed going to Los Angeles to deliver two lectures: "New Viewpoints in American History" and "Opportunities for Historical Research."[29]

At the same time, Bolton received an invitation from President Abbott L. Lowell of Harvard University to present a series of lectures on United States-Latin American relations at the Lowell Institute. Bolton declined to speak on the proposed topic, but on December 13, 1920, he presented the first of eight lectures under the title "The Expansion of the Spanish Empire in America." In New England, the bastion of traditional colonial history, Bolton was presenting a non-traditional view of hemispheric history.[30]

The annual meetings of the American Historical Association provided both a private and a public forum where Bolton could present his ideas. In December 1922, he boarded a train in Oakland and began his eastward journey to attend the annual meeting of the American Historical Association at New Haven. In a journal he kept of the trip, he recorded his meeting with historians and his analysis of their reactions to his ideas.[31] On December 27, at a session at the Taft Hotel attended by thirty-four people, Bolton was the principal speaker; his topic was "Two Types of Courses in American History." In his speech he acknowledged that courses in the history of the Western Hemisphere were needed, but there was also a need for courses in national history or histories. To facilitate his ideas, Bolton submitted a brief outline of his course. In his diary Bolton noted, "My position seemed to be approved quite generally." His colleagues Victor Andrés Belaúnde, John M. Merriman, and Charles H. Haskins discussed Bolton's concept, but no one took issue with him. However, Bolton noted that in a "peppery" fashion, Merriman said that what Bolton was saying could be found in Edward Bourne's work, published earlier in the century.[32]

The following day Bolton attended a luncheon conference whose topic was "The General College Course in American History"; N. W. Stephenson of Yale presided, and other participants included Ralph Gabriel of Yale, Dixon R. Fox of Columbia, Arthur Schlesinger, Sr. of the University of Iowa, and Beverly Bond of the University of Cincinnati. Although Bolton sat between Claude Van Tyne and Frederick J. Turner, the men only exchanged pleasantries and did not seem to discuss the presentations. Later, Bolton left a critical assessment of his impressions of the men and their ideas:

The discussion rather amused me. The notion of a "general course" in American history as expressed by the speakers struck me as almost pitiful, when there is so large and rich a field for a broad course (most of which still lies beyond the ken of the profession). They merely urge a little more detail here, or a little more drill without changing the scope of the course one whit.[33]

Bolton had a discussion with Schlesinger concerning his broad approach to United States colonial history. Schlesinger volunteered the opinion that the East generally regarded *The Colonization of North America* "as the most significant contribution of recent times." His only complaint about the book was that the Preface was not more pretentious! Bolton replied, "I studied restraint in writing the Preface, in order not to seem too far from the old [traditional conservative] idea." In a new edition, Bolton said, he would revise the Preface to "safely tell what the book is about."[34]

Ever the advocate of the history of the Americas, at New Haven, Bolton stayed up past midnight explaining the course to Professor Ralph H. Gabriel, who was teaching a freshman course at Yale based on the "Chronicles of America" series. Gabriel remarked "that it seemed strange, though evident, that the most 'remote' institution is giving the interpretation of American history."[35]

University of Michigan professor Arthur Aiton (Ph.D. 1923) asked Bolton to present a lecture or series of lectures dealing with the Americas topic at his university. A staunch believer in the Americas approach, Aiton noted that it "will be excellent missionary work to deliver them [the lectures] here."[36]

Although lectures and conference presentations helped to spread the new Americas approach, a monograph, whether a textbook or an interpretative work, would have been more beneficial and have wider-ranging effects. From the beginning, Bolton contemplated writing a text for his course. Because no text existed, he had to rely on an extensive syllabus filled with readings that were placed on reserve. Although this could be used in his specific circumstances—he could have the university purchase sixty copies of a book to be placed on reserve—it was not possible for teachers at less generous institutions who were planning to teach the course.

Bolton's first publication on the subject was a modest endeavor. In the first few years after word spread of the success of History 8, Bolton received "so many inquiries…that it has not been possible to answer all individual inquirers"; as a result, in 1924 he published a brief outline of the course in *Historical Outlook*, thereby bringing the concept to teachers throughout the United States.[37] If individuals found this new comparative approach difficult to teach because of a lack of knowledge of Latin American or Canadian history, Bolton advocated that they start with what they knew and gradually ease into the rest while they developed their knowledge base.

During the 1920s, Bolton's writing schedule was full.[38] However, despite his busy schedule, in 1919 he contemplated writing a two-volume textbook on the history of the Americas. Such a work would illustrate the importance of his ideas and allow them to enter mainstream American history.[39] At the December 1919 meeting of the American Historical Association (AHA) in Cleveland, Bolton, still reeling from the success of the first semester of History 8, met with William W. Appleton of D. Appleton & Company. Bolton discussed two possible titles for his study: "The Expansion of Spanish Dominion in North America" or "The Development of the Americas in the Western Hemisphere." His enthusiasm and the potential of profitable sales interested Appleton, and there ensued correspondence between the two on the matter for a year. At the 1922 AHA meeting, Bolton showed Appleton his unfinished manuscript, "Outline of the History of the Western Hemisphere." Discussions and meetings continued for several years, and Appleton urged Bolton to complete his manuscript as soon as possible.[40]

However, for some unexplained reason Bolton opened discussions with representatives from Macmillan. Once again there were visits to Berkeley, contracts were presented to Bolton, and pleas were made for a completion date. By the closing years of the decade, Bolton continued to promise a finished manuscript, now titled "History of the Western Hemisphere," but Macmillan would be disappointed despite the fact that Bolton restarted discussions on the book in 1930.[41] Apparently dissatisfied with his discussions with Macmillan, in December 1926 Bolton opened correspondence with yet another publisher, Harper & Brothers, which also did not lead to publication.[42]

Despite all of these discussions and negotiations with frustrated publishers, the idea of a full-blown text became lost in Bolton's busy publication schedule. However, negotiations with Ginn & Company agents would finally bear fruit. In late 1924, Bolton proposed both a text and a syllabus. Since Ginn & Company saw the idea of a text as vague and illusive, it realistically agreed to publish the syllabus for the growing college market. The syllabus was on firmer ground because it already existed, having first appeared in mimeograph form in 1919-1920. For years following, the University of California Press had printed it but had not published it. On November 17, Bolton signed a contract with Ginn & Company in which he would receive 15 percent royalties from its sales.[43] It took Bolton several years to make the necessary corrections and revisions. Finally, on October 15, 1928 Ginn & Company published the syllabus, *History of the Americas: A Syllabus with Maps*. Except for the "Epic of Greater America" address presented in 1932, this would be the closest that Bolton would ever get to the development of a monographic study on the history of the Americas. Although the syllabus provides some insights, it is not an interpretative work that could set the stage for a full study and analysis of the concept.

Bolton saw the syllabus as a pioneer work and noted, "Pioneer trails generally are neither smooth nor straight, but those who come after me will remedy these defects. The Syllabus makes no pretence of finality." In letters to colleagues, he reiterated the fact that the syllabus was far from complete, being only a survey of Western Hemisphere history in the form of sixty lectures. The main concepts were presented in introductory para-graphs and detailed outlines, and an extensive bibliography served as a guide for further study. The work contained some ninety detailed maps, which Bolton believed were in great demand and which many praised for their detail.[44]

Publication of the syllabus quelled the desire of both Bolton and his publisher to realize a two-volume masterpiece on the Americas. Early in February 1929, Bolton discussed his ideas for a two-volume work on the history of the Western Hemisphere in a letter to Frederick Jackson Turner, an idea that had been "rattling around in my brain for some time." He was looking not at a textbook but at a broader interpretative work that would be of interest to the general public. The parameters of his work were beginning to come into focus.[45]

In July 1929, Bolton received a letter from an English Catholic, Edward Eyre, who was concerned with the anti-Catholic history taught to Catho-lic children in English schools. He proposed that Bolton write a work of 60,000 to 100,000 words that took a comparative approach to New World history for the Westminster Catholic Federation.[46] Eyre's suggestion in-trigued Bolton. He responded that he was writing a two-volume work tentatively titled "The Historical Development of the Western Hemi-sphere"; it was being developed both for the general reader and as a text-book with a more cultural focus than that found in the syllabus. He con-cluded with an ambitious plan to take his two-volume work and revise it into a one-volume work for Eyre's purposes, but his plan was never real-ized.[47]

Although this was the nationalist 1920s, there were other historians who, like Bolton, were concerned with promoting inter-American friend-ship and understanding within academic circles. Harvard professor Clarence H. Haring fostered the idea of gaining a better understanding of the peoples of the Americas.[48] In Chicago, the Norman Wait Harris Me-morial Foundation at the University of Chicago sought to promote better understanding between Americans and their neighbors, and in 1924 held what became an annual institute.

Although a monograph on the history of the Americas that could be analyzed and discussed did not exist, historians were becoming familiar with Bolton's approach. Writing soon after he heard about History 8, a long-time advocate of Bolton's approach, William R. Shepherd of Colum-bia University, responded positively to the concept and hoped that the course would be introduced into all of the major United States universi-ties. His only caveat was that it might be difficult to find a professor "whose profound scholarship, gift of presentation and broad historicity of out-look would compare in some measure with your own [Bolton's]."[49] This warning manifested itself during the decline of the course in the 1960s.

In 1921, Professor O. G. Libby noted the importance of Bolton's broad approach to the colonial history of the United States. The approach was "distinctly a product of our twentieth-century experience and international alliances." For Libby it was "the very antithesis of that American insularity" which European critics projected onto American manners and morals. It was Libby's hope that a broader study of the Western Hemisphere could be created which would help to supplement the works in European history. He concluded that the United States growth as a world power made it imperative "that we abandon the self-centered type of history writing and attempt something on a somewhat more generous and catholic basis." Finally, he hoped that in the future a large number of influential scholars and general readers would see "that its methods are fully justified by results and that a new field of scholarship has definitely been opened for future work."[50]

Bolton's broader approach impressed the colonial historian Charles M. Andrews. In the Bolton and Marshall book, *The Colonization of North America*, Andrews was able to read about Spanish administration and quickly see the contrast between it and English administration. He concluded that Bolton's work set a standard, and now English colonial historians would have to catch up in their field.[51]

The publication of the syllabus pleased Isaac J. Cox, one of the early promoters of the Americas concept. Cox thought the syllabus would have "a marked effect on the teaching in the field." He saw it as "a piece of missionary work and as one of immediate value to those of us who are already giving courses in the field."[52]

As early as 1917, Bolton's mentor and friend, Frederick Jackson Turner, had words of both encouragement and caution for Bolton. He was impressed with Bolton's work in the Spanish Borderlands and its bearings on a broader approach to American history. He saw Bolton's Borderlands orientation as a new field of study that "admirably fits in with my own studies of the American advance, and makes it possible to understand the meaning of that advance."[53]

Best known for his frontier thesis, Turner had looked favorably upon the comparative historical method as far back as 1904. He felt that the use of comparative methodology would be an important contribution to the study of the history of the United States. He further observed that "we should undoubtedly find most fruitful results" in comparative frontier studies of the United States, Russia, Germany, and English colonization in Canada, Australia, and South Africa.[54] Thus, in terms of the history of the Americas, the fact that this approach would "have a real and important influence upon the study of American history" satisfied Turner.[55]

Realizing the nature of American historians and historiography, Turner cautioned Bolton about his new approach to American history because of the conservative nature of United States historians.[56] He encouraged Bolton to develop a book on the subject so that traditional "eastern and northern scholars" would appreciate the "rich field you are working and what its bearings are on general American history, in the larger sense." However, Turner concluded with an additional cautionary note:

Some of us are converted already, even if we are not adepts, but you must water your rum, and offer it in a small glass to the man who is brought up on the Parkman light wines — Or words to that effect! — You get the idea.[57]

Taking a more realistic position, Frederic L. Paxson had his doubts about how this broader approach would be accepted by United States historians. Bolton and Marshall's, *The Colonization of North America*, which contained "marked excellences that will gain a wide adoption" impressed him; however, he thought that if given a choice between a broad colonial approach and the narrower English story, most historians would opt for the latter. Paxson also believed that the history of the Americas should be widely studied but, given the traditional nature of United States historians, "I expect the heavy traffic will be in the history of the United States." Paxson saw Bolton as the master of a new field and wanted to continue their discussions of the broader approach. The syllabus caught Paxson's interest and attention, but he continued to be "less than certain" about the Americas approach although he had to admit "You make a most persuasive presentation of it in this little volume."[58]

Bolton's students spread his historical ideas from the University of California to colleges and universities throughout the nation. He attracted hundreds of students in the field of American history in its broader sense, and his graduate seminars became famous throughout America. By the time of his retirement in the early 1940s, Bolton had trained some five hundred students who received master's degrees and were teaching in high schools and junior colleges throughout the United States. Furthermore, under his guidance, approximately one hundred students secured doctorates in history. Many of these went on to obtain influential teaching positions at major colleges and universities throughout the nation. They took with them the fundamental Bolton concept of teaching the history of the Americas.[59]

In the Midwest, the idea of a broader approach to United States history had taken hold even before Bolton developed his course. William L. Schurz, who began teaching at the University of Michigan in 1915, was soon offering a course on Spain in North America and the Pacific area. When Arthur S. Aiton, a recent Bolton student, joined the University of Michigan faculty in 1922, he strengthened this tradition. Between the 1920s and 1950, Professor Aiton presented the non-English approach to United States history to hundreds of students.[60]

Within a decade after Bolton introduced the idea, the history of the Americas had spread across the United States and Canada; thirty-four colleges, universities, and junior colleges were teaching the course and using the syllabus.[61] Some professors were uncomfortable teaching the new approach and used the syllabus in their United States survey courses or for their United States-Canada courses. In 1921 at Hamilton College in Clinton, New York, Professor Milledge L. Bonham inaugurated a two-semester course on the colonization of North America that devoted 20 percent of its time to Canada. At the University of Montana, Professor Paul C. Phillips presented a similar course to some forty students annually. Sold on the idea of a broader approach to United States history, in 1923 Professor Ralph Gabriel began to teach a single semester course on the history of North America at Yale that spent 50 percent of its time on Canada.

Professor Isaac Cox began to offer a course similar to Bolton's in 1921. Lewis Hanke, who would later become an ardent promoter of the "Bolton theory," studied under Cox, becoming familiar with this new approach and one of its ardent disciples. Within a year the University of Nevada and the University of Southern California had introduced Bolton's approach to hemispheric history.[62]

Early in 1929, a representative of Ginn & Company proudly announced that the syllabus headed the firm's list of books sold in the Pacific Coast territory.[63] The largest number of institutions teaching the course were located in the West, with some nineteen (55.8%) reporting. Given Bolton's influence on California graduates, 52.6 percent of the reporting institutions were concentrated in California. In the East, eight (23.5%) schools were teaching the course, three (8.8%) in the Midwest, and only one (2.9%) in the South. In Canada, three (8.8%) institutions taught the course.[64] Despite the fact that this was a revolutionary approach to history in the United States and Canada, historians and students liked the comparative approach.

Some institutions had made the history of the Americas their introductory course and a prerequisite for advanced work in United States history. At Berkeley it was an elective for history majors, and students in other majors were encouraged to take it. The only problem some historians saw was the fact that the broad nature of the course and the limited time of two semesters made certain topics like the history of Canada or Canadian-American relations difficult to deal with in two or three weeks. In general, the primary contribution to students was the presentation of a point of view that Edith E. Ware referred to as "the contribution of the remarkable experiment."[65]

Junior colleges, especially those in the American West, borrowed the title and imitated the content of "History 8A-8B—History of the Americas." Edith Ware commented on the importance of teaching the course in the junior colleges as a mechanism to help reach a wider audience, thereby having a greater impact. She concluded that it "is a wholesome departure from the narrow nationalism which has too often limited the historical horizon of immature students to the region south of the Lake of the Woods and north of the Rio Grande."[66]

As an example of the popularity of the course, the president of Sacramento Junior College, J. B. Lillard, wrote to Bolton early in 1931, seeking graduates who could teach the Americas course. The course was popular, the demand was great, and his institution needed teachers to meet the demand. This problem was growing throughout the nation and Canada.[67]

At other institutions the content remained the same, but the title changed. At Elmira College it was titled "The History of the Western Hemisphere"; at Bucknell University, "Our Neighbors, Canada and Mexico"; at the University of Pennsylvania, "Latin-American and Canadian History"; and at Occidental College, "The Pacific Ocean History." Out of sixteen titles that were submitted to Edith Ware's *The Study of International Relations in the United States*, these were the four best. In some cases these courses were directly stimulated by Bolton's work, whereas other courses were created in order to keep Latin American history from becoming isolated from continental relationships.[68]

By 1930, nineteen professors teaching at colleges and universities throughout the United States and Canada lent their support to this pioneering work.[69] Edward E. Curtis at Wellesley College noted that the "course has attained a nation-wide fame and is the envy of all teachers in the same field." Others stressed that it was an excellent concept that someday would "become the standard for all our preparatory history work." Others shared this idea, feeling that in the past, history was studied "in isolated and detached fragments and not as a unified subject." Finally, many suggested that the course "will destroy much of the unfounded prejudice and provincialism so characteristic of our teaching and will lay a foundation for a more just appraisement of the contribution made by the different European countries to our history."

Even in Canada, the Americas concept was taking hold against strong traditions. Early in the twentieth century, traditionalists dominated Canadian historiography, stressing either Canada's imperial relations or constitutional questions.[70] Furthermore, the public and most Canadian scholars were so engrossed with their own affairs and the influence of the United States that interest in Latin America or any concept of Canadian involvement in Latin American affairs was virtually ignored.[71] Interest in lands south of the United States was so limited that prior to the 1960s, Canada was not a full participant in the Pan-American Union.[72]

By the 1920s a growing interest in the United States role in the development of North America initiated a change in the direction of Canadian historical thinking. Canadian constitutional historians were infused with a commitment to internationalism that found the model for a supranational state in French-English cooperation and the Canadian imperial relationship. Younger historians who were exponents of North American history also shared the idea that Canadian history was an international history. How could you teach the French colonial story without including the colonial history of the mid-continent United States and the trade and commerce in the Caribbean?[73]

Canadian-born and United States-educated Reginald G. Trotter (1888-1951) was one of the leaders of the movement to promote cooperation between Canada and the United States, and more generally among the nations of the world.[74] After receiving his doctorate from Harvard in 1921, Trotter obtained a position at Stanford University, which he held until his 1924 appointment as Douglas Professor of Canadian and Colonial History at Queen's University in Kingston, Ontario. His Canadian upbringing, American education, and years at Stanford that coincided with Bolton's Americas approach at Berkeley all had an effect on Trotter.[75]

Interestingly, in 1922, two years prior to Trotter's arrival at Queen's University, "History 3: Colonial History" took a comparative approach, looking at the Spanish, French, and English experiences in the New World.[76] Thus, with his background and the comparative approach already taken in colonial history at Queen's, Trotter found a place for a broader approach to Canadian history that coincided with Bolton's concept of the study of the Americas.

In terms of Canadian historiography, it was Trotter who promoted the internationalist view of the link between Canada, the United States, and Britain. This is evidenced in his *Canadian Federation* (1924), in which, Carl Berger observed, "Trotter elevated the achievements of responsible government and Confederation to a higher plane when he noted that Canada had been the principal exponent of national autonomy preserved within an internationalist commonwealth." From this position, Berger continued, "It was a short step to seeing Canadian relations with the United States as pointing toward a more co-operative and peaceful international order and away from the truculent and suspicious nationalism."[77]

Trotter's expansive view of Canadian history allowed him to make some use of Bolton's concept of the Americas. In a letter to Bolton in 1938, Trotter explained his own approach in dealing with a broader view. Since he was unable to focus on Spanish American history due to history department requirements, he used the vehicle of Canadian history. Up to the American Revolution, Trotter presented a broad Americas-style approach in dealing with North American history—or, as he put it, "The general colour of the early part of the course is greatly affected by the influence of your [Bolton's] own emphasis on the importance of seeing the history of any American country against the wider American background."[78]

Furthermore, a review of his teaching materials and syllabi show Trotter's familiarity with and acceptance of the Bolton approach. In his class notes for the history of Canada, Trotter included Bolton's lecture outline pertaining to Canadian topics along with Bolton and Marshall's *The Colonization of North America*.[79] In his *Canadian History: A Syllabus and*

Guide to Reading, Trotter noted, "The task of placing Canadian history in its continental setting is helped by such works as...." He proceeded to list Bolton and others as useful sources.[80] In his large Canadian history course of the 1930s, Trotter drew from both Bolton's *History of the Americas* and Bolton and Marshall's *The Colonization of North America* or John Brebner's *The Explorers of North America.*[81]

Early in 1927, when Trotter was preparing his article on the study of Canadian history in United States universities, he sent questionnaires to colleagues throughout the nation. He specifically asked Bolton for information on the history of the Americas course.[82] Bolton responded by listing the Canada-related courses at the University of California, and although he did not discuss the Americas course, he added that his "History of the West" (History 181) was in reality "a history of colonial North America...down to the middle of the nineteenth century," in which he devoted "a very considerable space to Canada," presenting lectures on French Canada, Anglo-French rivalry, the British conquest of Canada, establishment of British rule, the British fur trade in the Northwest, and the contest for the Pacific Northwest and the North Pacific in the later eighteenth and early nineteenth centuries. Characteristically, Bolton highlighted the fact that he subordinated "national history to the larger aspects of the historical development of the continent."[83]

In 1927 Trotter made some grand statements about the role of Bolton's concept. The Americas course allowed students to "gain about as much familiarity with the outline of Canadian history as with the history of the United States or Latin America." The subordination of "national history to the larger aspects of the historical development of the continent" also impressed him.[84] Trotter concluded by noting that the publication of Bolton and Marshall's *The Colonization of North America* "facilitated elsewhere the broadening of scope in courses on early American history, and stimulated the growth of a similar attitude toward the latter period as well."[85]

George W. Brown was also a strong proponent of the Americas idea. In 1924, he was the first North American-trained Ph.D. (University of Chicago) to be appointed to the faculty of the University of Toronto. Brown took a positive position toward Herbert Priestley's 1929 book, *The Coming of the White Man*, and stressed the importance of the Bolton concept when he wrote: "The many comparisons between the various European colonies are a valuable feature of the book, especially as historians have been far too much disposed to study the colonies of some one nation rather than colonial America as a whole."[86]

John B. Brebner was another Canadian historian who promoted a broader view of the history of the Americas. Born in Toronto, he was educated at the University of Toronto and then at St. John's College, Oxford. He taught at Toronto between 1921 and 1925, and then joined the faculty at Columbia University. In his first work, *New England's Outpost: Acadia before the Conquest of Canada*, Brebner studied a border region where the French and English collided. This study laid the groundwork for a follow-up history of Nova Scotia, *The Neutral Yankees of Nova Scotia: A Marginal Colony During the Revolutionary Years*. His *The Explorers of North America* covers the entire region and its participants, and his seminal *North Atlantic Triangle* presents the interplay of the United States, Canada, and Great Britain.[87] Later Brebner would respond to Bolton's "Epic" speech before the American Historical Association, calling it a "remarkable synthesis" and pointing out that he had been promoting the Americas concept for a number of years as well.[88]

Prior to World War I, students at the University of British Columbia studied United States colonial history in connection with Canadian history, which presented a broader than usual approach. Subsequently, Walter N. Sage and F. H. Soward continued teaching this larger historical approach and stressed United States history as well.

In 1928 Professor Sage took a comparative frontier approach in his presentation of the history of Canada and the United States. In a July 13 letter to Bolton, he explained: "I'm putting on a new course on Western Canadian History, modeled to a large extent on your History 8, but on a more restricted field." Sage noted that some seventy-five students were enrolled in the course, which was the first of its kind offered in British Columbia or anywhere else in Canada.[89] He pointed out that until that time, Canadian historians had paid little attention to the Canadian westward movement and to its parallel with the movement in the United States. In his article on the subject, Sage presents a tight comparative history.[90]

A long-time friend of Bolton, Professor Sage maintained correspondence with him and offered suggestions for improving the Americas course. Early in 1929 Sage shared a syllabus of his British Columbia history course with Bolton that he hoped Bolton would find useful, particularly the bibliography. A few months later he sent Bolton more information on Canada and the Americas course and a copy of his article on the Canadian frontier.[91]

McGill University in Montreal instituted the study of European colonization and expansion in 1918. Four years later the faculty inaugurated a course on the history of Canada and the United States.[92] Professor Edward R. Adair joined the history faculty in 1925.[93] He quickly incorporated his interest in the Americas into a new course, and as a result, during the 1926-1927 academic year, "British and European History" was offered for the last time. Adair, who at that time was teaching "History of Canada and the United States" introduced "General History of North and South America" in the fall of 1927.[94] Although Trotter would point out that this was the most Bolton-like course offered at the time in Canadian colleges and universities, he expressed cautious optimism: although Canadians had begun to focus on hemispheric history, they were still attached to European history because of their membership in the British

Commonwealth.[95]

In Latin America the hemispheric approach to history had been in vogue since the mid-nineteenth century in Chile. Schoolchildren had been using Diego Barros Arana's *Compendio elemental de historia de América*, the first Americas textbook revised for popular use by students, since its first publication in Santiago, Chile, in 1865. Until 1932, editions were published in Santiago and Buenos Aires for use in the local schools.[96]

Since the 1850s, Frei Camilo de Monserrate, the director of the National Library, had been discussing the idea of actually teaching a history of the Americas in Brazil.[97] Unfortunately, Brazilian educators took little heed of the Benedictine priest's suggestions for a broader approach to hemispheric history. By 1886 non-American events were taught at length, but only United States independence and the Mexican Revolution were discussed in detail. At this time, the director of the National Library, Benjamin Franklin de Ramiz Galvão, tried to promote his predecessor's Americas approach to history, but again to little avail. However, the idea began to make some progress among Brazilian historians like Manuel de Oliveira Lima (1867-1928), who presented a lecture in the United States titled "Historical Evolution of Latin America Compared with That of English America" at Stanford University in 1914. Soon after, the concepts were published under the title *The Evolution of Brazil Compared with That of Spanish and Anglo-Saxon America*.[98] It would be over a decade before the history of the Americas entered the Brazilian curriculum in the 1930s.

Besides the academic setting, conferences and other organizations promoted the idea of the history of the Americas. In September 1922, the International Congress of the History of America was held in Rio de Janeiro to commemorate the centennial of Brazilian independence. A former Boltonian, William L. Schurz, represented the University of California. During a special session entitled "The Americas," Percy A. Martin, Mary W. Williams, N. Andrew N. Cleven, and Charles L. Chandler presented papers that took a comparative approach.[99]

The Pan-American Union further promoted an inter-American conception of history and geography. At the Sixth International Conference of American States, which met at Havana in 1928, the delegates adopted a resolution that created the Pan-American Institute of Geography and History. It was headquartered in Mexico City, and the Mexican government provided a permanent building for its use. The Institute's purpose was the collection and dissemination of information on geographical and historical questions of interest to the American republics.

The work of the Institute would eventually move toward the study and development of an Americas approach. At its 1935 meeting, United States Secretary of State Cordell Hull welcomed the delegates and added that the study of hemisphere geography and history are "well calculated to stir and unite the interest of our twenty-one nations." Taking the Boltonian

approach, he continued, "From colonies we have become free and independent nations, established in lands unhampered by the bonds of the
past. Can anything conceivably draw us closer together intellectually and
culturally, than dispassionate and earnest study of our various environ-
ments and of our histories as independent states but neighboring
peoples...?"[100]

The Americas approach and the interest in Latin American history were
evidently having a positive impact in the United States. If the Spanish
people and their history had been presented in a negative light in the nineteenth century, textbook writers of the early twentieth century gradually
changed their position. Some, like Reuben Post Halleck, began to make
concessions. In *History of Our Country*, Halleck commented on Spanish
contributions to history:

The Spanish lacked "moral and ethical character," but they had made certain contributions to the New World; they had, after all, discovered it, and they had brought
it Christianity, mission architecture, and domestic animals.[101]

Did Bolton and his students bring about this changing attitude? Bolton
was part of the changing position toward the Spaniards and, by the 1930s,
had helped to define a more balanced approach that gradually displaced
hispanophobia.

Although historians still dealt hesitantly with a full Americas approach,
a broader approach to American history was gradually making inroads
into mainstream United States historiography. Yale University Press's
publication of the "Chronicles of America" series had as its goal presenting a balanced history of the United States and its neighbors. As a result,
the series grew, and the press included Bolton's *The Spanish Borderlands*
along with volumes on New France and William R. Shepherd's *The Hispanic Nations of the New World* (1919). Once the series was complete, Ralph
H. Gabriel and Arthur B. Darling produced *The Yale Course of Home Study
Based on the Chronicles of America*, which they published in 1924. In the
Preface the authors stated, "This outline has been prepared for the use of
the person who wishes to become familiar with the story of his country;"
however, the outline did allow students to obtain an in-depth view of
American history very much in line with Bolton's broad Americas con-
cept.[102]

Bolton, who was working at full capacity and was unable to complete
his Americas text manuscript, now contemplated a major book series with
an Americas theme. He had a conversation with a representative of Ginn
& Company, in which he discussed a series of short volumes similar to
those in the "Chronicles of America" series. They could be written in a
similar style for the general reader and for use as supplementary readings
for high school and college students. With these, Bolton was trying to
solve the dilemma of inadequate supplemental reading facing instructors

of the history of the Americas. In a letter to G. H. Moore of Ginn & Company he wrote, "As a matter of fact, I think the time is close at hand when large textbooks will be replaced by very brief textbooks, supplemented by 'interesting' little books dealing with special topics." However, Bolton saw that his concept differed from that of the "Chronicles" in two respects. First, the volumes of the "Chronicles" were too broad in their scope, and thus much like textbooks. "Each episode," he wrote, "should be rather special and written with interesting detail." Second, he wanted his proposed series to cover the entire Western Hemisphere with topical volumes taken as they come rather than developed around a general scheme. He even included a list of contributors for the series, a number of whom had demonstrated their ability when they had been his students.[103] Unfortunately, Bolton never developed the series, and there is little further mention of it.

If Bolton was unable to produce a work on the history of the Americas, others would have to meet the demand for a broader interpretation. A colleague on the Berkeley faculty, Herbert I. Priestley, filled the void. In 1929, as a part of the thirteen-volume "History of American Life" series edited by Arthur M. Schlesinger and Dixon R. Fox, Priestley completed a social history, poorly titled *The Coming of the White Man, 1492-1848.* The approach was Boltonian in nature, dealing with the history of the Spanish, French, Swedish, and Dutch societies in North America. "Such pictures have a special interest," commented Priestley, "as by similarity or contrast they bring out the colors of that fuller view of the Anglo-American settlements grouping into the community of the United States...."[104]

Book reviews reveal how historians reacted to this Bolton-styled, broader approach to American history. In his review of the book, O. M. Dickerson wrote that it should have been titled *The Non-English Colonization of America.* Although Dickerson did stress the importance of this comparative approach, which was approved by "every student of American history," he complained that possibly the entire story of Latin American colonization should have been included.[105]

Isaac J. Cox, a pro-Bolton man, used a book review to express his views on this broader approach to American history. The comparison that appeared in Priestley's book pleased Cox because it created a certain unity, and allowed a better understanding of land-holding, trade policy, church organization, social expression and other colonial institutions.[106] He understood that limited space prevented the inclusion of Central America and the West Indies, and he concluded his review by noting that the adjective "American" had been stretched far beyond the limits of the United States — "a concession that was not possible a decade ago."[107]

In a book review for the *Hispanic American Historical Review,* Professor Arthur P. Whitaker wrote that he was impressed with the book's "pioneer character" and "the use of the comparative method." He also expressed the role of this new form of history: "Here was a subject that not only lacked obvious unity but also required the writer to prove to many a doubting Thomas that such a study has a place in the history of life in the United States."[108]

While Bolton and his colleagues throughout the Americas were developing, implementing, and promoting the Americas concept behind the "ivy-covered walls" of academe, United States foreign policy toward Latin America was taking on a broader, pro-Latin America approach. President Woodrow Wilson's idealism "evolved into a kind of moral meddling, resulting in a series of interventions in the internal affairs of several Caribbean powers."[109] The Mexican Revolution caused friction between the two republics. Then in 1921, with the coming of President Warren Harding and his pro-Latin American Secretary of State, Charles Evans Hughes, change was in the air. President Harding appointed Herbert Hoover Secretary of Commerce, and although Hoover could not change government foreign policy with Latin America, he could influence trade and commercial policy. During the Coolidge administration the government reverted to an interventionist position.

The election of President Hoover in November 1928 brought a new cooperative approach to United States-Latin American affairs. He regarded the improvement of United States-Latin American relations as of vital interest to the hemisphere.[110] Thus it was not surprising that one of his first acts as President-elect was to go to Latin America on a six-week visit in November-December 1928.[111]

Typical of the speeches that Hoover made on this trip is a portion of one that sounds similar to concepts Bolton used in his history of the Americas:

There is abundant reason why friendship and understanding between us should be so deeply rooted in the hearts of the people of both of our nations. We have on both sides a history of common labor, of building in the New World a new form of government founded upon a new conception of human rights; the supreme experience of rebellion from the political and social systems of the Old World; the subjugation of the wilderness; of development of economic life through the application of the great discoveries of science; the effort to lift the moral and cultural levels of our countries.[112]

Journalists who accompanied Hoover concluded that the trip "was one of the most important contributions ever made by an American statesman to good-will on the American continents, and to the smooth functioning of diplomatic and economic relations."[113] Frank H. Simonds took on a Boltonian tone when he promoted the Americas concept: "What Mr. Hoover did clearly accomplish was to put South America on the map for our part of North America." He elaborated that during the trip, Latin America, "which has never enjoyed a tithe of the prominence bestowed upon it in the past weeks," filled the media and the conversations of United

States citizens.[114] As a result, President-elect Hoover taught the American public, who had been "disastrously ignorant" of Latin America, the importance of understanding Latin America, its people, and its culture. However, Simonds was realistic and stressed that it would be a long and ongoing process.

In the area of foreign policy, President Hoover brought about a reversal in United States policy vis-à-vis Latin America. The words of his inaugural address on March 4, 1929, in which he devoted a paragraph specifically to inter-American relations set the tone for this change in United States foreign policy. No longer would the United States dominate Latin American affairs; rather, it would work with them as a "good neighbor."[115]

In order to facilitate travel and mail service to Latin America, President Hoover promoted the establishment of Pan-American Airways, which began service in 1930. Furthermore, in order to achieve immediate results, he stressed better organization of intellectual exchanges between students and professors. At the first Pan-American Day exercises, on April 14, 1931, President Hoover promoted the concept of educational cooperation in understanding Latin America:

> It is of the greatest importance that the people of the United States become better acquainted with the history, the traditions, the culture and the ideals of the other republics of America. To an increasing extent, courses in the languages, literature and history of the nations of Latin America are being offered in the educational institutions of the United States. A similar realization of the importance of becoming better acquainted with the history and development of the United States exists in the countries of Latin America. Increasing numbers of students from the countries to the south are being enrolled in the colleges and universities of the United States. I cannot emphasize too strongly this important aspect of inter-American relations. These cultural currents not only contribute to better international understanding, but also emphasize the essential unity of interest of the American republics.[116]

Thus by the 1930s, there was a unique blending of a historiographical development with American foreign and commercial policy. Interest in Latin America and inter-American ties were being fostered by President Hoover. Public and private individuals promoted the idea while Bolton and his colleagues promoted similar ideas in academe.[117] Despite the fact that Bolton was challenging the traditional nationalistic approach to history, many historians saw the value of the Americas concept in historiography and praised this new comparative approach to history. In a curious twist-of-fate, this idea was promoted primarily by word-of-mouth, as Bolton never wrote an analytical study on the subject.

NOTES

1. Herbert E. Bolton, "Report of the Department of History for the Year 1918-1919," Bolton Papers, Out.

2. Lawrence Kinnaird, "Herbert Eugene Bolton: Historian of the Americas," *Andean Quarterly* (Santiago, Chile) Christmas iss. (1942): 3.

3. Ibid.

4. Bolton to Arthur Schlesinger, Sr., 11/26/1919, Bolton Papers, Out.

5. J. Fred Rippy, *Bygones I Cannot Help Recalling: The Memoirs of a Mobile Scholar* (Austin, TX: Steck-Vaughn, 1966), 97.

6. Bolton to Andrew C. McLaughlin, 04/30/1919, Bolton Papers, Out.

7. Bolton to the Committee on History and Education for Citizenship in the Schools, Washington, DC, 05/26/1919, Bolton Papers, Out. Much of the material that follows comes from this selection.

8. "A New Course in American History at the University of California," 1919, Bolton Papers, Out.

9. Bolton to Roscoe R. Hill, 08/06/1919, Bolton Papers, Out.

10. In the University's catalog for 1920-1921, "History of the Americas" is described thus: "A general survey of the history of North America, South America, and Central America, from the discovery to the present time." The course was designed for freshman but was open to sophomores as well. A fee of $1.50 was charged for the famed syllabus.

11. Bolton to Edith E. Ware, 04/04/1933, Bolton Papers, Out. History 8 remained in a prominent position until the late 1940s when Professor John D. Hicks introduced History 17A and 17B, the United States survey up to and from the Civil War.

12. Bolton to John C. Merriam (Dean of Faculties), 01/26/1920; Bolton to Edith E. Ware, 04/04/1933, Bolton Papers, Out.

13. Kinnaird, "Herbert Eugene Bolton," 3.

14. A copy of an early or even an original syllabus is in the Columbus Memorial Library, Organization of American States, Washington, DC; a copy is in the Magnaghi Papers, Central Upper Peninsula and University Archives, Northern Michigan University, Marquette (hereafter: Magnaghi Papers). A review of it shows how the course slowly emerged. There were only twenty-four lectures listed and an unidentified lecture topic at the end with readings on British North America. Lectures on Spanish and English colonial life and culture, and the international rivalry of the eighteenth century are missing. Bolton to Mr. Platt, 05/17/1921, Bolton Papers, Out.

15. Arthur S. Aiton to Bolton, 07/05/1929, Bolton Papers, In.

16. Bolton to Miss Steel, 02/03/1920; Bolton to William Carey Jones (Administrative Board), 08/22/1919, Bolton Papers, Out.

17. Interview with J. Manuel Espinosa, Washington, DC, 11/05/1992, Magnaghi Papers 4.

18. Bolton to Arthur Schlesinger, Sr., 11/26/1919, Bolton Papers, Out.

19. Woodrow Borah to Magnaghi, 07/21/1992, Magnaghi Papers, In.

20. Irene Paden, "Dr. Bolton as I Knew Him," 10/18/1959, C-D 5035.5, Bancroft Library. During the 1930s a number of Bolton's former students wrote to Frank Lockwood, who was compiling information on their mentor, and expressed their insightful views of Bolton and his teaching methods. See letters from Arthur Aiton

(03/01/1932); William C. Binkley (02/26/1932 and 11/17/1932); Charles E. Chapman (02/29/1932); William H. Ellison (02/17/1932); Charles W. Hackett (02/ 1932); George P. Hammond (02/29/1932); Andrew L. Neff (02/25/1932); Charles T. Neu (03/10/1932); J. Fred Rippy (03/27/1932); Mary Ross (03/24/1932); Francis Stanger (02/29/1932); Wilhelmina A. Stockwell (05/01/1932); Alfred B. Thomas (02/29/1932); Rufus K. Wyllys (02/17/1932), Frank C. Lockwood Papers, Correspondence, Bancroft Library.

21. Engel Sluiter to Magnaghi, 07/30/1992, Magnaghi Papers, In.

22. Interview with Ursula Lamb, 10/03/1992, Magnaghi Papers, In.

23. Donald E. Worcester to Magnaghi, 01/01/1992, Magnaghi Papers, In.

24. Wilbur R. Jacobs, John W. Caughey, and Joe B. Frantz, *Turner, Bolton, and Webb: Three Historians of the American Frontier* (Seattle: University of Washington Press, 1963), 47.

25. Thomas A. Bailey, *The American Pageant Revisited: Recollections of a Stanford Historian* (Stanford, CA: Hoover Institution Press, 1982), 80. Some half-century earlier, Professor Bailey noted the value of the syllabus and the importance of Bolton's enthusiasm: Thomas A. Bailey to Bolton, 04/22/1930 and 02/18/1933, Bolton Papers, In.

26. Ben M. Cherrington to Bolton, 06/15/1939, U.S. Department of State, Division of Cultural Relations, Bolton Papers, In.

27. Speech by Bolton to the Department of History for Ramírez, 11/1920, Bolton Papers, Out.

28. Bolton to President David P. Barrows, 12/01/1920, Bolton Papers, Out.

29. Bolton to L. J. Richardson (Director, UC Extension), 04/05/1920, Bolton Papers, Out.

30. Bolton to David Barrows, 04/30/1920; Bolton to Abbott L. Lowell, 05/05/ 1920; and program from the Lowell Institute, Bolton Papers, Out.

31. Herbert E. Bolton. "On Wisdom's Trail: A Westerner in the East: Notes on a Trip to the American Historical Association Held at New Haven, Connecticut," December 1922, Bolton Papers, books I-IV, folder 26, Bolton-Ross Papers.

32. Ibid., 5-6.

33. Ibid., 8.

34. Ibid., 9.

35. Ibid., 9-10.

36. Arthur S. Aiton to Bolton, 05/03/1923, Bolton Papers, In.

37. Herbert E. Bolton, "An Introductory Course in American History," *Historical Outlook* 15.1 (1924): 17-20.

38. During this time Bolton would publish seven articles and ten books. Some, like Francisco Palóu's *Historical Memoirs*, ran to four volumes. For more detail, see John F. Bannon. *Herbert Eugene Bolton: The Historian and the Man, 1870-1953* (Tucson: University of Arizona Press, 1978), 279-280.

39. Bolton to Thomas M. Marshall, 02/06/1919; Bolton to William Boyd, 02/ 10/1919, Bolton Papers, Out.

40. William W. Appleton to Bolton, 01/07/1920, 07/15/1920, 10/19/1921, 03/ 12/1923, 12/06/1923, Bolton Papers, In.

41. R. R. Smith to Bolton, 07/10/1925, 12/22/1926, 04/25/1928, 02/14/1929; T. C. Morehouse to Bolton, 04/14/1930, 11/29/1930, 01/24/1931, Bolton Papers, In; Bolton to Guy Stanton Ford, 04/10/1931, Bolton Papers, Out.

42. Frank S. MacGregor to Bolton, 12/16/1926, Bolton Papers, In.

43. C. H. Thurber to Bolton, 10/11/1924; "Articles of Agreement," 11/17/1924, 11/18/1924, Bolton Papers, In.

44. Herbert E. Bolton, *History of the Americas: A Syllabus with Maps* (Boston: Ginn, 1928), iv-v.

45. Bolton to Turner, 02/07/1929, Bolton Papers, Out.

46. Edward Eyre to Bolton, 07/19/1929, 09/16/1929, Bolton Papers, In.

47. Bolton to Edward Eyre, 08/02/1929, Bolton Papers, Out.

48. Clarence H. Haring, *South America Looks at the United States* (New York: Macmillan, 1928), 63.

49. William R. Shepherd to Bolton, 06/16/1920, Bolton Papers, In.

50. O. G. Libby, review of *The Colonization of North America*, by Herbert E. Bolton and Thomas M. Marshall, *Mississippi Valley Historical Review* 7 (1921): 397-399.

51. Charles M. Andrews to Bolton, 12/21/1921, Bolton Papers, In.

52. Isaac J. Cox to Bolton, 12/11/1928, 4/10/1929, Bolton Papers, In.

53. Frederick Jackson Turner to Bolton, 8/12/1925, 8/31/1925, Bolton Papers, In.

54. Frederick Jackson Turner, "Problems in American History," in *Congress of Arts and Science, Universal Exposition, St. Louis, 1904*, ed. Howard J. Rogers, 2 vols. (Boston: Houghton Mifflin, 1906), 2:192.

55. Frederick Jackson Turner to Bolton, 02/04/1929, Bolton Papers, In.

56. Wilber J. Jacobs, *The Historical World of Frederick Jackson Turner*, with selections from his correspondence (New Haven: Yale University Press, 1968), 215-216; Turner to Bolton, 01/30/1916(?), Bolton Papers, In.

57. Jacobs, *The Historical World* 215-216.

58. Frederic L. Paxson to Bolton, 04/30/1921, 02/07/1929, Bolton Papers, In.

59. Kinnaird, "Herbert Eugene Bolton," 3.

60. University of Michigan catalogs that tell this story are found at the Bentley Library, University of Michigan, Ann Arbor.

61. The following institutions were either teaching the course or using the syllabus: Bakersfield Junior College (CA); Brigham Young University (UT); William J. Snow; Columbia University (NY); Fresno State College (CA); George Washington University (DC); Goucher College (MD); Mercer College (GA); McGill University (QU); Edward Adair; Northwestern University (IL); I. J. Cox; Occidental College (CA); Porterville Junior College (CA); Rice University (TX); Royal Military College of Canada (ON); Rutgers University (NJ); Sacramento Junior College (CA); St. Louis University (MO); Rev. Kenny; St. Mary-of-the-Wasatch (UT); Lucy M. Hazard; San Diego State Teachers College (CA); San Mateo Junior College (CA); Seattle College (WA); Skidmore College (NY); University of Buffalo (NY); University of California, Berkeley; University of California, Los Angeles; University of Hawaii; Thomas Bailey; University of Idaho; University of Minnesota; University of Nevada; University of Southern California; Syracuse University (NY); University of Texas, Austin; University of Western Ontario; University of Wichita (KS); and Wellesley College (MA).

62. Edith E. Ware, ed., *The Study of International Relations in the United States, Survey for 1934* (New York: Columbia University Press, 1935), 282-283; Reginald G. Trotter, "Canadian History in the Universities of the United States," *Canadian Historical Review* 8 (1927): 194-195.

63. Selden C. Smith to Bolton, 01/11/1929, Bolton Papers, In. Between 1928 and 1934 (excluding 1930 and 1933, which are missing) the financial reports show Ginn made $12,777.73 and Bolton realized royalties of $1,916.67. This was a handsome fee in the midst of the Great Depression.

Ginn & Company, the publishers of *History of the Americas: A Syllabus with Maps*, promoted the new approach for financial reasons. When the book first came out, besides meeting Bolton's requests to have the book sent to United States historians, the company sent copies throughout Canada. The lack of interest in American history in England caused the firm not to promote the book there. In the 1930s there is evidence that the revised edition was sent to Latin American scholars. By 1943, Frederick Rice reported to Bolton that there continued to be a great demand for the syllabus and for the textbook if it were ever completed.

64. This information was gathered from Bolton's correspondence and business records between 1928 and 1929. In particular, see Selden C. Smith to Bolton, 09/19/1928, 1/11/1929; Frederick A. Rice to Bolton, 11/20/1928, 01/1929?, 05/13/1929, Bolton Papers, In. I consider this a conservative figure because a number of colleagues expressed interest in the course but did not indicate whether or not they were teaching it.

65. Ware, *The Study*, 282.

66. Ibid., 283.

67. J. B. Lillard to Bolton, 01/16/1931, Bolton Papers, In.

68. Ware, *The Study*, 283.

69. These professors were E. A. Adair (McGill University); Arthur S. Aiton (University of Michigan); Robert G. Albion (Princeton University); Walker Brown (Board of Education of Louisiana); N. Andrew N. Cleven (University of Pittsburgh); I. J. Cox (Northwestern University); Edward E. Curtis (Wellesley College); Walter L. Fleming (Vanderbilt University); J. Montgomery Gambrill (Columbia University); Chester Lloyd Jones (University of Wisconsin); Elden V. Jones (Kansas State Agricultural College); Charles E. Martin (University of Washington); P. A. Martin (Stanford University); Julius W. Pratt (University of Buffalo); J. Fred Rippy (Duke University); William J. Snow (Brigham Young University); George Tays (University of California, Berkeley); Reginald G. Trotter (Queen's University, Kingston, Ontario); Arthur P. Whitaker (Western Reserve University).

70. Carl Berger, *The Writing of Canadian History*, 2nd ed. (Toronto: University of Toronto Press, 1986), 137-159.

71. See J.C.M. Ogelsby, *Gringos from the Far North: Essays in the History of Canadian-Latin American Relations, 1866-1968* (Toronto: Macmillan, 1976).

72. F. H. Soward and A. M. Macaulay, *Canada and the Pan-American System* (Toronto: Ryerson, 1948), 21.

73. Berger, *Writing*, 182.

74. Trotter received the following degrees: B.A. from Yale in 1911; M.A. from Yale in 1915; Ph.D. from Harvard in 1921.

75. R. G. Trotter Papers, Guide; Mario Creet, "R. G. Trotter — Additions, Collection 1063 — Boxes 22-27, April 1988," Reginald Trotter Papers, Queen's University Archives, Kingston, Ontario.

76. *Calendar of the Faculty of Arts, Queen's University, Kingston, Ontario* (Kingston: Jackson Press, 1922), 103. At the time the texts being used for the courses included Edward Bourne, *Spain in America* (1904); Carl Becker, *Beginnings of the American*

People (1915); Charles P. Lucas, *New France* (1923); and W. L. Grant, *History of Canada* (1919).

77. Berger, *Writing*, 147.

78. Trotter to Bolton, 06/16/1938, Bolton Papers, In.

79. Folder 81, Canadian History...; Folder 82, Canadian History: Syllabus; Folder 86, Canadian History: Syllabus; Box 3, ser. B, Manuscripts, R. G. Trotter Papers, Queen's University Archives, Kingston, Ontario.

80. R. G. Trotter, *Canadian History: A Syllabus and Guide to Reading* (Toronto: Macmillan, 1934), 148.

81. Trotter to Mr. Johnson (of Macmillan Company of Canada), 03/06/1935, Folder 8, Trotter Papers; *Calendar of the Faculty of Arts, 1933-1934. Queen's University* (Kingston, ON: Jackson Press, 1933), 219.

82. Trotter to Bolton, 05/03/1927, Bolton Papers, In.

83. Bolton to Trotter, 05/10/1927, Bolton Papers, Out.

84. Trotter to Bolton, 05/03/1927, Bolton Papers, In. Trotter sent a form questionnaire to professors throughout the United States, asking about the role of Canadian history in the United States universities. On Bolton's he attached a special note about the Americas and how he needed specific information from Bolton.

85. Trotter, *Canadian History*, 194.

86. George W. Brown, review of *The Coming of the White Man, 1492-1848*, by Herbert I. Priestley, *Canadian Historical Review* 12 (1931): 69.

87. John B. Brebner, *New England's Outpost: Acadia Before the Conquest of Canada* (New York: Columbia University Press, 1927); *The Neutral Yankees of Nova Scotia: A Marginal Colony During the Revolutionary Years* (New York: Columbia University Press, 1937); *The Explorers of North America* (New York: Macmillan, 1937); *North Atlantic Triangle: The Interplay of Canada, the United States, and Great Britain* (New Haven: Yale University Press, 1945); "Personal—Recent Deaths," *American Historical Review* 63 (1958): 859.

88. John B. Brebner to Bolton, 04/04/1933, Bolton Papers, In.

89. Walter N. Sage to Bolton, 07/13/1928, Bolton Papers, In.

90. Sage, "Some Aspects of the Frontier in Canadian History," *Canadian Historical Association Report* 6 (1928), 62-72.

91. Sage to Bolton, 01/29/1929, 03/02/1929, Bolton Papers, In.

92. Reginald G. Trotter, "Canadian Interest in the History of the United States," *Queen's Quarterly* 36 (1929): 98.

93. Adair was associate professor (1925-1944), chairman of the department (1941-1946), member of the academic senate (1943-1946), and professor of history (1945-1953). See "Staff Card Index," McGill University Archives, Montreal.

94. *McGill Calendar, 1926-1927* (Montreal: McGill University, 1926), 170; *McGill Calendar, 1930-1931* (Montreal: McGill University, 1930), located in McGill University Archives, Montreal.

95. R. G. Trotter to Edith E. Ware, 04/26/1933, Trotter Papers, Correspondence, 1933, Folder 6, Queen's University Archives, Kingston, Ontario.

96. The *Compendio elemental*...was published at Santiago in 1865, 1894, and 1908, and at Buenos Aires in 1887, 1891, 1904, 1910, 1913, 1916, and 1932.

97. This section on Brazil is taken from Hélio Vianna, "Ensino e conceito de história da América," in his *Estudos de história colonial* (São Paulo: Companhia Editora Nacional, 1948), 15-32.

98. Manuel de Oliveira Lima, *The Evolution of Brazil Compared with That of Spanish and Anglo-Saxon America* (Stanford, CA: Stanford University Press, 1914).

99. The papers presented at the conference were published in a special volume of the *Revista instituto histórico e geográfico Brasileiro* 1-2 (1922), entitled *Anais do Congreso Internacional de história da América realisado pelo Instituto Histórico e Geográfico*. The comparative papers included Percy A. Martin (Stanford University), "Minas Gerais and California: A Comparison of Certain Phases of the Historical and Sociological Evolution," 250-270; Mary W. Williams (Goucher College), "The Treatment of Negro Slaves in the Brazilian Empire: A Comparison with the U.S.A.," 273-292; N. Andrew N. Cleven, "James Watson Weble, U.S. Minister to Brazil, 1861-1869," 295-394; Charles L. Chandler, "Commercial Relations Between the United States and Brazil," 397-414.

100. *Second General Assembly of the Pan-American Institute of Geography and History, Washington, October 14-19, 1935* (Washington, DC: Pan-American Union, 1935), 2.

101. Frances FitzGerald, *America Revisited: History Schoolbooks in the Twentieth Century* (New York: Vintage, 1980), 95.

102. Ralph H. Gabriel and Arthur B. Darling, *The Yale Course of Home Study Based on the Chronicles of America* (New Haven: Yale University Press, 1924), v.

103. Bolton to G. H. Moore, 02/10/1929, Bolton Papers, Out.

104. Herbert I. Priestley, *The Coming of the White Man, 1492-1848* (New York: Macmillan, 1929), xviii.

105. O. M. Dickerson, review of *The Coming of the White Man, 1492-1848*, by Herbert I. Priestley, *Mississippi Valley Historical Review* 16 (1930): 565.

106. Isaac J. Cox, review of *The Coming of the White Man, 1492-1848*, by Herbert I. Priestley, *American Historical Review* 35 (1930): 374.

107. Ibid., 375.

108. Arthur P. Whitaker, review of *The Coming of the White Man, 1492-1848*, by Herbert I. Priestley, *Hispanic American Historical Review* 10 (1930): 63.

109. For a thorough survey of this era, see Mark T. Gilderhus, *Pan-American Visions: Woodrow Wilson in the Western Hemisphere, 1913-1921* (Tucson: University of Arizona Press, 1986).

110. Herbert Hoover, *The Memoirs of Herbert Hoover: The Cabinet and the Presidency, 1920-1933* (New York: Macmillan, 1952), 211.

111. During the trip President-elect Hoover and his party visited Honduras, El Salvador, Nicaragua, Costa Rica, Ecuador, Peru, Chile, Argentina, Uruguay, and Brazil and spoke with presidents and other officials of common problems. Hoover also met with the president of Bolivia and planned to visit Cuba and Mexico in the future.

112. Hoover, *Memoirs*, 211.

113. Mark Sullivan, "With Hoover in Latin America," *Review of Reviews* 79 (February 1929): 53-54.

114. Frank H. Simonds, "Hoover, South Americanus," *Review of Reviews* 79 (February 1929): 67.

115. Alexander DeConde, *Herbert Hoover's Latin-American Policy* (Stanford, CA: Stanford University Press, 1951), 45.

116. "Address on Celebration of Pan-American Day," Presidential Press release, April 14, 1931.

117. There is no evidence indicating that Bolton had any direct influence on President Hoover or his staff. The developments paralleled each other.

Bolton (R) and his roommate, Will Naylor at the University of Wisconsin (ca. 1893). At this time he was studying under Frederick Jackson Turner. Source: Bancroft Library, #7.

Herbert E. Bolton in May 1920 at the time he inaugurated History 8A–B, History of the Americas at the University of California. Source: Bancroft Library, #15.

Bolton seated in front of one of his famous maps used in his Americas classes (1930s). Source: Bancroft Library, #50.

Bolton at the Los Angeles Colosseum. In later years he continued to promote Hemispheric unity in public forums, especially during World War II. Source: Bancroft Library, #43.

Cartoon of Bolton made by "Lario" at the Hotel Ritz while on tour in June 1942. Source: Bancroft Library, #61.

4

The Epic of Greater America, 1930-1953

The last phase of the unfolding of the Bolton concept lasted nearly a quarter of a century, from 1930 through Bolton's death in 1953. These were the golden years of the history of the Americas, when, through a number of important developments, historians' interest in the concept reached its pinnacle. It opened with Bolton's "Epic of Greater America" address at the annual meeting of the American Historical Association (AHA) in Toronto. The presentation acted as a catalyst for historians throughout the Americas to analyze and critique the man and his concept. Bolton sought this reaction immediately after the "Epic" address; it was the "echo" he had hoped for. This presentation and resulting analysis represented an important step in the process of getting the Americas concept incorporated into American historiography.

The expansion of college courses treating the Americas continued, and the concept reached the elementary and secondary school systems as well. To meet the demand for a textbook, which Bolton had not yet produced, a number of historians, both Boltonians and others, began writing textbooks on the Americas, thereby realizing Bolton's dream.

Beyond the halls of academe, the United States Department of State promoted the Good Neighbor policy as the official policy toward Latin America. Many Boltonians helped implement this policy as members of the State Department staff. As World War II approached, the Good Neighbor policy evolved into one of hemispheric solidarity. Action among inter-American organizations flourished as Bolton's academic interests merged with external forces. The Pan-American Union, through agencies like the Pan-American Institute of Geography and History and others, promoted an inter-American approach not only to history and geography, but to archaeology, anthropology, and cultural exchanges as well. This was an exciting period for hemispheric history and related studies. As Bolton reached his sixth decade, the Americas approach was maturing and Bolton was at the pinnacle of his career.

In late December 1932, Bolton traveled to Toronto to attend the annual meeting of the American Historical Association, where he would be appointed its president. In Toronto, a number of honors were bestowed upon him for his work on the Americas concept. In a ceremony conferring an honorary degree on Bolton at the University of Toronto, Chester Martin read a lengthy citation extolling Bolton's accomplishments. After noting Bolton's work on the Spanish in America, Martin emphasized that Bolton was "carrying his studies into a still higher realm. He is seeking to make a synthesis of these various influences which have contributed to the making of this continent."[1] A formal presentation of the first of two festschrifts, *New Spain and the Anglo-American West*, edited by some of Bolton's former students, followed this convocation. In the Preface the editors noted Bolton's role as the creator of the Americas concept:

It is true that his interest in the History of the West has continued; but new ideas, facts, and interpretations appear in his studies of New Spain and in his broader view of the history of both North and South America. He was one of the first to discard the narrowly national method of historical presentation and to recognize the fundamental unity of New World development. American history with him is not merely the story of the thirteen English colonies and the United States but a more correctly proportioned narrative of the Western Hemisphere in all its international aspects. He is the creator of the *History of the Americas* as it is now taught in scores of colleges and universities.[2]

The editors concluded with the statement that these studies "may help to form a basis for the ultimate synthesis of these important branches of American history."[3] This tribute from his students deeply moved Bolton, and his biographer, John Francis Bannon, felt that it "meant more to him than the Toronto degree, the AHA presidency, and most other things which had happened to him."[4]

When a new president of the AHA takes office, it is customary for him to present an address that characterizes his work. During the summer of 1932, Bolton was selecting an appropriate topic for his presidential address. At first he planned on "The Other Jesuits in North America." His idea was to talk about the Jesuits of Mexico, whom Francis Parkman had completely ignored in his mistitled work *The Jesuits of North America*. During this time, Bolton sketched out the first part of the planned address. As late as October 7, when he applied for funding from the University of California, he listed as his topic "The Jesuits of New Spain."

At some point Bolton changed the topic of his address. In the introduction to his speech, he noted that the expanded membership and outlook of the AHA, along with the fact that the Association was meeting in Toronto, made it appropriate for him to present "some of the larger aspects of Western Hemisphere history."[5] Bolton used "the past for purposes of the present,"[6] and his presentation, "The Epic of Greater America," was a condensation of his work for the past thirteen years, now divided into eight distinct sections.[7] First, Bolton pointed out "a need of a broader treatment of American history, to supplement the purely nationalistic presentation to which we are accustomed." For him, "much of what has been written of each national history is but a thread out of a larger strand." He went on to point out:

It is time for a change. The increasing importance of inter-American relations makes imperative a better understanding by each of the history and culture of all. A synthetic view is important not alone for its present day political and commercial implications; it is quite as desirable from the standpoint of correct historiography.[8]

Next Bolton moved into the historical development of his presentation, focusing on discovery, exploration, and colonization. Here he took a Turnerian approach, stating that "Europeans settled on the land, adjusted themselves to the American environment, devised systems for utilizing natural resources, and transplanted European culture." Within the colonial systems that were transported to the New World, Bolton highlighted the fact that "Likenesses in the colonial systems were more striking than differences." These common points included mercantilism, "government...adapted to the American frontier...," the vestige of feudalism, African slavery in the tropical areas, and European policies toward Native Americans. On the latter point he noted that although "Indian tribes were everywhere used as buffers against European rivals," there was a point of contrast: "In one respect the Indian policies of the Latin countries differed essentially from those of the Saxons. The Latins considered the Indian worth civilizing and his soul worth saving."[9]

The third section of Bolton's address returned to the Turnerian theme: "Everywhere contact with frontier environment and native peoples tended to modify the Europeans and their institutions. This was quite as true in the Latin as in the Saxon colonies." Finally, he stressed that "Colonial expansion involved international rivalry." A lengthy discussion of international rivalry throughout the Americas followed this introductory statement, which was probably more than his listeners desired at the time.[10]

Having set the foundation for the colonial era, Bolton moved into the revolutionary era in the Americas. He noted that the American Revolution "was by no means a local matter." In the United States, the "shadow of Europe" that "lay deep over the West" menaced independence and the growth of the new republic. For Bolton, Canada's development to nationhood was the product of the French colony and the coming of the Loyalists from the United States, which led to "the great Dominion of Canada." He also noted that Brazilians gained their independence without bloodshed. However, he had the most to say about the Hispanic American struggles, which "were an imposing military drama." He noted the similarities and differences of United States and Hispanic struggles. External influences, causes, and the use of outside aid were common to both; however, the greater landmass, distances, natural obstacles, and the existence of numerous separate movements made the Hispanic story different. Bolton ended the section by promoting the commonality of the post-revolutionary era, for which he has been criticized by historians. Typical of a United States historian of the time, he discussed the role of the Monroe Doctrine in an uncritical tone.[11]

Section V was reserved for a detailed discussion of the westward movement in United States and Canadian history, once again with Turnerian overtones:

This division of the western seaboard of North America was highly significant. It cut off from Spanish America the remaining borderland areas which had been only partly Hispanized and placed the boundary near the frontier of effective Spanish colonization. It gave both Canada and the United States frontage on the Pacific. It enabled them both to assimilate added millions of Europeans. Built on the national domain, in both countries the West became a powerful nationalizing force. The process of growth kept both nations young with continued frontier experience; it prolonged opportunity for social experimentation, and perpetuated early American and Canadian characteristics.[12]

The next two sections were reserved for a discussion that "the territorial bases for the national system had been laid." Bolton continued, "In this whole process of national growth and unification in the nineteenth century the outstanding factors were boundless natural resources, foreign immigration, foreign capital, and expanding markets" that were hemispheric in extent. Here he stressed material progress throughout the Americas.[13] While passing over the United States' development of "solidarity and power," Bolton discussed Canada, Argentina, Brazil, and Chile in some detail. However, he also noted that for Latin America "prosperity was one-sided," and this had led to the Mexican Revolution. He ended by stressing that "Progress towards nationality in the Western Hemisphere has been attended by international adjustments."[14]

Bolton closed his address by stating that the presentation was an "imperfect way...to indicate some of the larger historical unities and interrelations of the Americas." The fact that work in the field had progressed well in recent years and more light was being shed on formerly little-known aspects of this history was encouraging to him. For Bolton the "new synthesis" was merely a beginning for other historians to conduct research on new Americas-related topics.[15]

Analysis of the address shows that Bolton presented a lengthy narrative[16] that many viewed as an encapsulation of History 8. The presentation was a chronological narrative, as he said of his course, "from pole to pole and from Columbus to the present." Bolton readily admitted, as did those who were in contact with him, that he was not an intellectual historian, and thus he did not provide an in-depth analysis of the concept in terms of its role in and value to comparative history.[17] However, Belgian and French historians, Henri Pirenne and Marc Bloch, were in the early stages of developing this type of history. It is possible that if the Americas concept had been presented in Bloch's analytical approach, the results might have been different. But this was not to be the case. Bolton had laid aside plans for a monograph on the subject that could have provided him with the opportunity to more completely develop the analytical framework for the Americas concept. He had provided the framework for future historians to further develop a "new synthesis."

Bolton minimally treated or ignored many facets of the Americas story. His comments concerning culture, literature, and philosophy in the Americas were not well developed. For instance, he did not deal with the spirituality of the Saxon and Latin peoples and the impact of religion on their ideas, values, and aspirations. He also glossed over difficult problems such as the impact of the Mexican-American War, and he brought into question the role of hemispheric solidarity during World War I. Bolton stated, "I have endeavored to indicate some of the larger historical unities and interrelations of the Americas." However, he did not discuss the differences and the reasons for them.

Bolton was committed to the concept and had been teaching it for over a dozen years, so he was puzzled by the lack of reaction from his colleagues. He lamented, "I have heard very few echoes from my speech and the silence is ominous."[18] He must have forgotten that since 1919, many prominent and influential historians had been aware of the history of the Americas and had responded to his new concept through correspondence, personal discussions at conferences, and book reviews.

As was true of all presidential addresses, the *American Historical Review* reprinted the talk, now titled "The Epic of Greater America," in April 1933. The *American Historical Review* summarized the talk as an appropriate theme for a meeting in Canada, a "masterly synthesis of the development of the Western Hemisphere," and it hoped that the talk would broaden "our perspectives in considering the history of the Americas, South as well as North." Thus Bolton's ideas were not only heard by most of the 423 AHA members who had attended the December meeting, but also were available to many more scholars. In reality "echoes" from historians began in 1933 and continued for some eight years.

A Bolton friend and Europeanist, William E. Lingelbach of the University of Pennsylvania, was an immediate convert to Bolton's concept: "All in all, your address was one of the most stimulating I have listened to and I am glad you adhered strictly to your own field [Americas]." He went on to note, "the classical frontier — or shall I say the Turner frontier — came in for a decided beating. Our New England friends certainly were none too happy and I am surprised that they did not come to the defense of the older position after Paxson's paper on Thursday morning."[19]

Walter Sage of the University of British Columbia and Reginald Trotter in conservative Toronto sent Bolton notes of appreciation and recognition. In a March 1933 letter, Sage concluded:

From what I have heard your address was much appreciated and it was a real pleasure to know that you had been able to preach your gospel of the history of the Americas in the rather conservative attitude of Old Toronto. We here in British Columbia regard the Toronto view of Canadian history just as you do the New England tradition in the history of the United States. So to me, at any rate, it is a real pleasure to know that you spoke as you did in Toronto.[20]

Professor Trotter, of the University of Toronto, sent Bolton a congratulatory note right after the "Epic" speech was given. He wrote, "It was certainly a sweeping presentation of a great interpretation or rather reinterpretation which it has been one of your achievements to make." He concluded that Bolton's presence in Canada would be "a just and unprecedented stimulus to the cause of history in this country."[21]

John B. Brebner of Columbia University addressed similar congratulations to Bolton within a few weeks. He was glad that Bolton could "bring the impact of your remarkable synthesis to bear directly on those who attended and also on the many readers of the *Review*. Further, he noted that in recent years he had been promoting the idea among his English friends and had "presented a slight counterpoint of your recent paper to the Canadian Historical Association."[22]

An American colonial historian, Curtis P. Nettels of the University of Wisconsin, read a reprint of Bolton's presentation with "the greatest interest, and appreciated its importance for American history." Nettels, who was "brought up on the thirteen colonies interpretation of American history," appreciated the Spanish influence in the New World and the role of the Caribbean as a center for the development of many British policies. For Nettels, Bolton's reprint "greatly broadens the horizon of American history."[23]

In 1934 J. Manuel Espinosa, who had studied under Bolton, wrote to Bolton praising his speech. Bolton's address inspired Espinosa to write a short article on Bolton and the concept.[24] He believed that the speech had a great influence in stimulating an interest in the study of Hispanic America in Catholic schools.[25]

Mexican historians also reacted to Bolton's address. Bolton sent a copy of the article to Vito Alessio Robles, who was delighted with it, and said, "It is a serious and sensible work..." that pulled together Bolton's ideas of the history of the Americas. Robles was so enthusiastic about the work that he strongly urged Bolton to have it translated into Spanish and made available to everyone "in all the nations of the Western Continent."[26] In a brief review of the translated version of "The Epic," another Mexican historian, Silvio Zavala, wrote that Bolton's experience as "[an] intelligent cultivator of American history gives his conclusions obvious authority and results in agreeable reading."[27]

Professor Alessio Robles's eldest daughter, Carmen, presented the idea of promoting the history of the Americas to the Second Mexican Historical Congress at Mérida, Yucatán, in November 1937. In her presentation she noted that in the past Mexicans had given preference to European affairs and concerns, and as a result they knew little or nothing of the republics of Central and South America. Furthermore, even though Mexican history had been bound to that of the United States, most historians had fragmentary knowledge of their neighbor to the north. Since American life was becoming increasingly independent from Europe, and because great powers had arisen in North and South America, Carmen Alessio Robles thought it was time to develop mutual knowledge and understanding in an attempt to realize Bolívar's dream "for effecting the union of all the peoples in the continent." To realize this, Alessio Robles suggested that the Congress send an invitation to the Mexican Department of Education, Mexican colleges and universities, and state governments to develop a preliminary Americas course in the national curriculum to be taken prior to a Mexican history course.[28]

Unfortunately, a group of "pseudo-Communists" broke up the meeting before action could be taken on this proposal. Fortunately, the faculty of the National Autonomous University of Mexico introduced two courses on the history of the Americas in 1936, and Professor Alessio Robles was placed in charge of them.[29]

Alessio Robles pursued the idea of having the "Epic" speech translated and published. Discussions with the director of the Pan-American Institute of Geography and History, Pedro C. Sánchez, led to the publication of the translated edition as part of the Institute's ongoing series titled "Publication."[30]

Critiques of the Bolton concept of the history of the Americas emanated from a number of sources in the late 1930s. Arthur P. Whitaker, in a review of the recent reprint of the "Epic" speech in *Wider Horizons of American History*, took the opportunity to react to the concept.[31] He questioned Bolton's assertion of the "essential unity of the Western Hemisphere" and "fundamental Western Hemisphere solidarity" since independence. Whitaker felt that it might be a fine future ideal but certainly did not reflect the past. He was also critical of the fact that Bolton's emphasis in the field of Latin American history was Mexico and the Spanish Borderlands rather than Spanish South America or Brazil. He noted that "it is also illustrated by his statement that 'till the end of the eighteenth century...Mexico City was the metropolis of the entire Western Hemisphere' — a statement that would not be accepted at Bahía or Rio de Janeiro or Lima any more than at Boston or Philadelphia or Quebec." However,

Whitaker concluded with high praise for Bolton:

His frequently demonstrated talent for grasping the larger significance of local history has set a high standard for scholars engaged in that kind of work. The courage with which he has forsaken the ivory tower of monographic writing for the battlefield of synthesis is an example which many will admire and a few may even emulate.[32]

From the pen of Edmundo O'Gorman, a member of the staff of the Archivo General de la Nación, came critical comments. The University of Havana approached him to write a response to Bolton for the 1939 issue of *Universidad de la Habana*.[33] In his article, titled "Hegel y el moderno panamericanismo," O'Gorman took the position that in reality there was little that was unifying in the Americas tradition. For him, many of the unities and interrelations Bolton discussed could be found in any society. He feared that the study of local themes might become too narrow in scope and thus detrimental to a hemispheric approach. Further, he took Bolton to task for not including the human element and for ignoring culture, religion, and intellectual life. O'Gorman also attacked Bolton for his emphasis on the idea of progress or, as he put it, "material prosperity."

A few months after this publication, O'Gorman, who did not know Bolton, sent him a copy. In the cover letter O'Gorman noted Bolton's "important discourse" and wanted to let Bolton know of his work; he also asked Bolton to respond to his article.[34] There is no indication that Bolton responded directly to O'Gorman at that time; however, he indirectly reacted to O'Gorman's position in a letter to William C. Binkley in 1941:

I have read Mr. O'Gorman's dissertation with great interest. There is no doubt of the truth of much of what he says of the differences between Latin America and Anglo America. In some circumstances "parallel phases" and "interrelations" may be better expressions than "common history." I am glad to note that he believes "that the time has come to go beyond the nationalistic view of history in America," and that he recognizes "the pedagogical necessity of conceiving the facts of the Western Hemisphere within a total structure." That has been the basic thought in all my endeavors in developing my History of the Americas. Moreover, I think that you will do well to keep the emphasis of the discussion [during a session of the AHA] on that aspect of the matter rather than on a quibble over terms. Contrasts between Anglo and Hispanic America should find a place in a Western Hemisphere view, but overemphasis of them should not result in losing sight of the whole picture. I quite agree with Mr. O'Gorman that there is danger that "history which generalizes is history which falsifies." That is why I have spent most of my life in minute research. I have wished to know intimately the substance of history. Nevertheless, I approve his attempts to present a generalized history, which constitutes the essence of his paper. If you put your emphasis on the broader aspects of the Western Hemisphere, somewhat as I outlined them in the opening paragraphs of my Toronto address and insist on keeping the discussion there, it will not degenerate into a quibble over terms and phrases.[35]

When the State Department asked Bolton to prepare a speech for one of its sponsored meetings, he was probably mulling over O'Gorman's comments. In November 1939 Bolton presented a talk titled "Cultural Coöperation with Latin America" to an inter-American conference of educators and professionals in Washington, DC. He stressed the cultural unity of the Americas and answered some of O'Gorman's criticisms. This piece was subsequently published in a number of journals and became a corollary to the "Epic" speech.[36]

In response to this work, Peter M. Dunne, S.J. (Ph.D. 1934), of the University of San Francisco wrote to Bolton: "The former ["Cultural Coöperation with Latin America"] is surely a classic synthesis and nobody else could have written it. No wonder that it carries the day and that it is being spread all over the Americas. The good it will do is going to be very great."[37]

A historical controversy developed around Bolton's Americas concept, and Lewis Hanke, the director of the Hispanic Foundation at the Library of Congress, was interested in bringing the concept to a scholarly forum.[38] Hanke proposed to Professor Nettels of the University of Wisconsin, program chair of the 1941 American Historical Association meeting, a special symposium to discuss the question "Do the Americas have a common history?" In January 1941, Nettels invited Bolton to participate in a round table discussion on the subject because "It is our belief that the growing interest in the field of Latin American history and its relation to the history of the United States and Canada warrants a general session on this question."[39] It is important to remember that while these plans were being formulated, Europe was seeing some of the darkest days of World War II; it was being overrun by the Nazis, and the last hope of stopping this aggression seemed to be in the hands of Europe's offspring, the Americas.

Plans went forward for the session, and invitations were extended to George W. Brown, professor at the University of Toronto and editor of the *Canadian Historical Review*, Edmundo O'Gorman of the Mexican archives, and Dr. William E. Binkley, who consented to serve as chair of the symposium. The session was tentatively scheduled for December 29, 1941, and because of its importance, there were no conflicting sessions on the program.[40]

Although Bolton eventually withdrew from the session for personal reasons, his correspondence provides insights into aspects of the subject.[41] At this time Bolton finally responded to O'Gorman's criticisms. Concerning the question of commonality, Bolton believed that the question being posed — Do the Americas have a common history? — "might be regarded as a call for argument rather than for enlightenment, and offer a temptation to excel in debate rather than in historical scholarship." He thought that a title such as "Common Factors and Interrelations in the History of the Americas" would be more constructive and would avoid any unnecessary debate.[42]

On December 15, William C. Binkley expressed his regret that Bolton had found it necessary to withdraw from the program. He went on to say, "I feel that no one could be as effective as you in presenting the comprehensive point of view."

At the afternoon session on December 29, generically titled "History of the Americas," the round table discussion "Do the Americas Have a Common History?" opened.[43] Neither Bolton nor Hanke participated. Clarence H. Haring chaired, and the rest of the program remained as planned, except that Germán Arciniegas replaced Hanke. William Binkley of Vanderbilt University presented the United States position.[44] He stated that if historians and educators were going to deny the possibility of a synthetic history of the Americas, they must demonstrate that the American nations lack common experiences susceptible to synthetic treatment and contemporary bonds of interest. He concluded that these factors were not present. The Canadian position, represented by Brown, showed the two opposing tendencies in Canadian development: (1) the tendency toward complete Canadian autonomy and (2) cooperation with Britain. Given the fact that World War II was raging, Brown "pointed out that in relation to the problem of world order the Americas have had a common history—a history which challenges them to a common responsibility." Arciniegas, who presented the Colombian position, asserted that the forces of the New World made Americans of Europeans as they struggled to dominate the environment. American history could be discussed as a result of this struggle.

The lone dissenter was O'Gorman. For him, American colonization was similar to all of the colonies. The difference was "the fact that colonial Latin America was a projection of medieval Spain and Portugal, while the colonization of British America represents the antagonistic spirit of modern Britain." He denied that the struggles for autonomy in the two Americas were similar, and concluded by advocating the recognition of the inherited distinctiveness of the two regions as the key to an understanding of Pan-American history.[45]

Over twenty-five years later, Silvio Zavala, the latter-day dean of the history of the Americas, addressed the question of unity and diversity. He wrote in an introductory statement to his monumental work, *El mundo americano en la época colonial*:

Before continuing this train of thought and adding our own profession of faith to preceding ones, it should be noted that the main arguments in this debate have been extensively set forth by excellent minds on both sides. The hypothesis herein proposed is that we should speak with greater propriety if, instead of accepting a flat verdict in favor of the unity or the diversity existing among the histories of the American countries, we should be willing to recognize that the history of the New World embraces both unities and diversities. Further, such unities and diversities are varied in origin, follow different directions, and change over periods of time.

Zavala's introduction then proceeds to expand his point.[46]

Charles C. Griffin wrote in his introduction to *The National Period in the History of the New World*, concerning the question of unity and diversity:

The task of ordering the disparate material presented in the various preliminary regional outlines proved difficult.... In addition to differences in the course of United States history from that of Latin America, there were important differences within the latter area. There were many similarities and parallels in the different countries and regions, but no single overall pattern, even for Spanish America alone. This makes it clear that American history combines unities and diversities and that any plan for a general history must take both into account.[47]

Thus, the circular debate over whether unity or diversity directed the history of the Americas was laid to rest. The authors of these landmark studies proceeded with a broader interpretation and explanation of the concept that would incorporate similarities and differences of the various regions and nation-states within an increasingly synthetic Americas concept.

The Good Neighbor policy of the United States and the development of hemispheric solidarity during World War II encouraged further discussion and redefinition of the Americas concept. In Argentina on August 7, 1940, Victoria Ocampo, editor of *Sur*, a literary journal, organized a round table discussion titled "Is America a Continent?," which *Sur* published soon afterward. This open-ended discussion brought forth a variety of concepts and opinions, and showed how the discussion of the concept of Americas' unity had spread among intellectuals.[48] In the following years the Pan-American Union published a series of discussions in the series "Points of View," discussing various aspect of life in the Americas, and illustrating the interest and concern that intellectuals had for this position.

In separate developments, there were others who added to the debate. Enrique de Gandía, Secretary of the National Academy of History in Buenos Aires, presented his views on the controversy. He disagreed with O'Gorman and took the position that the interchange of ideas in the Americas had been more of a unifying factor than most people realized. Furthermore, Western Europe had influenced the Americas, and each nation had developed its own national culture. He could not agree with Bolton's idea "that American cultural development had always followed material prosperity" and concluded, "our American history [was] born of different peoples and nourished by different cultures but...was guided, at times, in a parallel way by the same ideal, by an identical aim: that of independence, liberty, and democracy."[49]

The pro-indigenist Aprista movement influenced the Peruvian intellectual Luis-Alberto Sánchez, and he took a different position on the common bond in the Americas. In 1941 he stated that the use of tradition existed throughout the Americas, but its presentation differed between North and South America. Thus, it was important to try to understand the underlying foundation of the many parts of Latin American society in order to properly understand its people and traditions.[50] In a further development of this traditionalist position, Sánchez wrote of the Aprista concept of an "Indo-America" rather than merely a "Hispanic-America," in an attempt to more clearly define exactly what developments comprised Latin America.[51]

In 1943, the Mexican diplomat Luis Quintanilla used the totalitarian threat of World War II as backdrop in his book *A Latin American Speaks*. He opened by asserting that "The America of today must be viewed as a unit" and then critically discussed the role of unity in the Americas. In the process he took issue with O'Gorman's Hegalian view that America has no history.[52]

Of the many scholars who commented on the Americas approach, Philip C. Brooks (Ph.D. 1933) made one of the best analyses in a 1949 presentation. He noted that Bolton's written statements on the concept can be found in the *Syllabus* for his history of the Americas course and in his presidential address, "The Epic of Greater America," presented in 1932. Both of these key works were "essentially narratives, rather than expositions of broad factors of history." Brooks believed that "this elementary narrative characteristic" was "an important reason why professional historians have not come to know and appreciate better the fundamental principle behind the *History of the Americas*."

The most convincing part of the narrative, the part in which hemispheric common factors are best brought out, is that covering the colonial period. This is a natural result of Dr. Bolton's own training, career, and interests....[53]

Brooks regarded two of Bolton's works as significant to the development of his historiography: *The Colonization of North America* and *The Spanish Borderlands*. Unfortunately, both of these works focused on the interweaving of European expansion rather than stressing the thesis of the Americas concept. As a result, in 1937 Michael Krause, in his *History of American History*, mistakenly emphasized Bolton's role as a frontier and sectional historian. Brooks felt that Bolton "would not eschew the label 'frontier historian,' that is too restricted, and the word 'sectional' is the antithesis of his broad view." Finally, Bolton's concern with colorful narrative of the heroes in history "has tended away from the philosophy of American history and emphasis on the common factors behind developments in various areas."

In his critique of Bolton's approach, Brooks came to the conclusion that there were three ways to approach the history of the Americas. The first was to view it as a series of national histories, and the second was to view national histories as they impinged on the history of the United States." The third approach was to imagine oneself on a platform in space and look at the Western Hemisphere as a whole," which "is the ideal of the Bolton school." Of these approaches, Brooks thought that the first was used for expediency when teaching college students, especially in regard to the nineteenth century. The second approach was widely utilized by diplomatic historians and others. With mature scholars as an audience, Brooks recommended that the Bolton thesis be developed in terms of broad historical factors, rather than a mere narrative outline.[54]

For Brooks this was the way to look at the hemispheric concept. The factors must be unique to the Americas and distinguishable from the rest of the world. First there was the geographical location of the Americas. Vast oceans separate the continent from the rest of the world, yet physically they are linked together as neighbors. The distance dictated the types of people who came, and the linkage was apparent in commerce and war. The role of the native peoples was another common bond for the hemisphere. The encounter with and the legacy of the native peoples had a profound influence on Americans. The role of African-Americans in terms of slavery, racial policy, manumission, and continuing interaction was another important feature. The encounter of the three peoples — black, red, and white — created a common and unique experience in the hemisphere. The common European heritage that dominated the continent was another all-inclusive feature of the story. The economic resources of the Americas was another common aspect of the continent from the colonial era to the present day. A comparative analysis of the development of mercantilism and free trade would be an important feature of the Americas history. Bolton also did not stress industrialization in his presentation. The wars of independence proved that "the Americas had grown up, in thought as well as in government." Brooks thought that Bolton had presented this idea satisfactorily, but his concept of ideological development was the weakest element. There was also literary development, the arts, the common interest in democracy, and the promotion of the rights of the individual. And finally there was the strong bond of Christianity throughout the Americas.

If Bolton initially believed there was little interest in the history of the Americas idea, the responses from historians and the demands for publication of the address and possibly a monograph on the subject were significant enough to allay this belief. By the mid-1930s William Lingelbach was the general editor of the "Historical Essay Series" for Appleton-Century. In late 1935 Bolton wrote to Lingelbach to see if he would be interested in including some of Bolton's presentations in a volume. Lingelbach expressed immediate interest in the idea of a volume on "Greater America" and concluded, "I know of nothing more opportune than a volume that would draw attention to another aspect of the same general movement" of historical ideas or concepts.[55] As usual, Bolton was slow in sending a final copy of the essays to Lingelbach.[56] After much prodding, in September 1938 Lingelbach received the essays and wrote to Bolton, "[I] have always felt they should be republished in a form available for larger circulation which we can now give them." At the time the proposed title, "Greater America" was retained, but by its publication in 1939, it was titled *Wider Horizons of American History.*[57]

This work brought together a number of Bolton's concepts from diverse publications. The topics included the Americas concept, the defensive nature of the Spanish Borderlands, the role of the mission as a frontier institution in Spanish America, and the role of the Jesuits in New Spain. If Bolton did not write a monograph on his ideas that scholars could analyze, at least this work allowed historians to "bring into clearer relief Bolton's broadening of the horizons of American history."[58]

The success of the "Epic" speech caused Bolton and others to re-evaluate the original plans to write and publish a textbook on the Americas. In 1929, F. S. Crofts had been against the manuscript, but four years later he wrote, "I know it will be an outstanding book."[59] In the middle of discussions over the essays, Lingelbach revived the idea of a full-blown history of the Americas. Bolton had first developed his detailed syllabus in 1928 and revised it in 1935. Over the years he had developed an elaborate set of notes that could easily be turned into a text. Lingelbach was very interested in Bolton's ideas, and with his contacts at Appleton-Century he was in a position to promote such a publication, which he did with enthusiasm through 1938.[60] Characteristically, Bolton was busy with other major projects, and those who sought a textbook from him could only hope and wait.

In the summer of 1938, there was a faint hope that Bolton would complete the long-awaited monograph. During a visit with John W. Caughey (Ph.D. 1928), he tentatively suggested that the two of them collaborate on a proposed textbook, *The Western Hemisphere.* Caughey was delighted with the prospect of working with his mentor on such an important project, and thought that this was Bolton's "major duty and opportunity" because he had completed the research for such a work and had an outline for it as well. Caughey further noted that such a work would help to promote the course because there were many teachers interested in presenting it. But unless they apprenticed under Bolton, they were unsure of what technique and approach to use, and most lacked adequate library resources.[61] Characteristically, nothing came of this proposal.

After World War II, Lingelbach tried to restart textbook negotiations with Bolton. He wrote in 1946: "We want your wisdom and scholarship in a book which I am confident will have more influence in moulding correct public opinion on the history and relations of the Americas than millions spent by good-will agencies. You just must do it!"[62] This would be Lingelbach's last unsuccessful attempt to get Bolton, who was seventy-six years of age and deeply involved in the Coronado biography, to write his tome.

Publishers were eager for a textbook on the history of the Americas during the 1930s and 1940s because at that time the course was taught to thousands of students throughout the United States and Canada. In 1935 the cultural division of the Pan-American Union (now the Organization of American States) commissioned a survey of United States institutions teaching a course on the history of the Americas. Because we do not know how many institutions were contacted, the study is flawed; however, twenty-nine institutions returned questionnaires yielding the following results. The majority (55.17%) of colleges and universities were located in the trans-Mississippi West, with California accounting for 37.5 percent of the total. East Coast schools followed with 20.68 percent and then the Midwest with 17.24 percent. South of the Ohio River, the University of Kentucky and the University of Puerto Rico taught the history of the Americas. The enrollment varied from as high as five hundred to one thousand in Bolton's Berkeley classes, to as low as ten, with the average being seventy-seven students. The types of colleges and universities teaching the Americas were fairly evenly divided among Catholic-sponsored colleges (20.68%), state teachers' colleges (27.58%), state universities (27.58%), and private colleges (24.13%).[63]

A dozen years later, the Pan-American Union brought forth a new report.[64] At this juncture, 899 institutions reported their Latin American offerings; eighty-two (9%) were teaching the history of the Americas, and a smaller number offered specialized Americas-oriented courses in art, architecture, geography, native peoples, and the Spanish Borderlands. These, however, were insignificant compared with the Americas offerings. By the 1948-1949 academic year, 42.68 percent of the institutions reporting were located west of the Mississippi River, with California still dominating this figure (71.42%, or 30.48% of the national total). The Midwest followed with 30.48 percent, the East Coast came in with 19.51 percent, and the South again trailed with 7.31 percent.

The Americas approach was not limited to colleges and universities. Junior and community colleges, especially in the West, created History 8 courses following Bolton's tradition. Since a text was non-existent at that time, Bolton's syllabus was the required book for the course; students referred to it as "the little green book." Many students liked the course because it provided them with a "broad overview which was extremely helpful." Others felt that although this course did not advance scholarship, it provided immature students with a wider horizon of hemispheric history and departed from the traditional narrow nationalism.[65]

In 1936 J. Manuel Espinosa noted that the "'Americas' approach...has influenced the teaching of 'American' history even in the high schools in some parts of the country." Catholic schools especially favored this approach, because the study of the history and influence of Catholicism in the colonial period could easily be combined with this new concept. These schools used Father S. K. Wilson's American history textbook, which greatly assisted the course. This approach was presented in the parochial schools of the archdiocese of San Francisco as late as the mid-1950s.[66]

Throughout the United States, interest in the Americas approach caused archives, libraries, museums, and associations to be established with Hispanic studies components. In addition, numerous institutions developed publication programs producing journals and monographs.[67]

Until 1932 only Bolton's syllabus was available to teachers. In the above-mentioned survey some 68 percent of the teachers used *History of the Americas: A Syllabus*, and another 9 percent used it in conjunction with additional texts. Another 27 percent used a variety of Latin American texts as supplemental reading.[68]

In the 1930s other textbooks began to appear on the market. In 1932 Wallace Thompson published *Greater America: An Interpretation of Latin America in Relation to Anglo-Saxon America*, which filled the demand for a supplemental textbook.[69] Stephen Duggan, the author of the next text with an Americas approach, was the Director of the Institute of International Education, and a lecturer in political science at the College of the City of New York and on international relations at Columbia University. In 1934, prior to publication of the monograph, *The Two Americas: An Interpretation*,[70] Duggan asked two Boltonians — Charles W. Hackett (Ph.D. 1917) of the University of Texas and Charles E. Chapman (Ph.D. 1915) of the University of California, Berkeley — to review the manuscript. He wrote the book primarily to dispel the misconceptions, based on ignorance and prejudiced sources, that Latins and Anglo-Saxons have of each other. Duggan contrasted the regions according to their geography and history, then examined the resulting political and social institutions. Next he proceeded to look at international relations, problems, and solutions that have affected the United States and Latin America, and then he closed with "a consideration of the methods of improving those relations."[71]

Five years later, Robert S. Cotterill attempted to reduce the mass of the history of the Americas into a textbook titled *A Short History of the Americas* (revised in 1945). Cotterill developed the monograph because he believed that teachers wanted to broaden their traditional United States history course to include the Americas, and because "there is certainly as much unity in the history of America as in the history of Europe." He emphasized that "in recent years the interrelations of the American nations have become so important that it is now hardly possible to view one of them in isolation."[72]

Besides these better-known monographs, by the end of the decade other studies had been published for the United States market, one of them written specifically for elementary schools.[73] Leland D. Baldwin wrote a readable account of this history, *The Story of the Americas*, which was published early in the 1940s.

Throughout Latin America, both individual and multiple-volume histories were written. Between 1932 and 1947 four works were published in Mexico.[74] Argentina's Ricardo Levene published his fifteen-volume edited set, *Historia de América*, along with Luis Germán Burmester's set of volumes. Other volumes on the history of the Americas were published in Santiago and Lima, and on the eve of the Spanish Civil War, Antonio Ballesteros y Beretta published his first volume in Spain.[75]

At this time, Vera Brown Holmes at Smith College, one of the proponents of the concept on the East Coast, introduced a course on the history of the Americas. Her actions were typical of many professors throughout the nation, but her importance lies in the fact that in 1950 she pioneered her own text on the subject. She was born in Fredericton, New Brunswick, in 1890 and received the A.B. (1912) and M.A. (1913) from McGill University. She received her Ph.D. from Bryn Mawr College in 1922 and two years later gained an appointment at Smith College, where she remained until her retirement in 1958.[76]

Holmes provides a review of how she became interested in the history of the Americas. Originally she did her research in eighteenth-century Anglo-Spanish relations, but she also did some work in Canadian and British history at McGill University. Later, at Bryn Mawr College, she took a minor in United States history and researched Latin American history under Clarence H. Haring. With this varied background she naturally developed her interest in the history of the Americas. This process typified what non-Boltonians had to do to prepare to work in this new field.[77]

Between the fall of 1924 and 1935, Holmes[78] taught one or more courses in Latin American history. Then she began to develop her Americas approach—an approach she felt had been neglected by historians. On February 22, 1935, Dr. Holmes presided over a departmental meeting and discussed her proposed course, "History 13: History of the Americas." In the discussion, a number of influential American historians made statements about the course's value. Merle Curti "thot [sic] that the history of the U.S. included all the movements to be found in the older civilizations and some more besides, but that the history of the Americas was broader and, in that way, better." Professor Scramuzza explained:

As an American who had given up a rich heritage and gladly adopted the United States as his country, he thot [sic] that the History of the Americas was the *best* way to show the true greatness of the United States, for it would show how the South American republics and even Canada got their independence only thru the influence of the United States, and that it was only by studying the history of the Western Hemisphere that we could understand our leadership, extend our trade, and increase our domination in Central America.[79]

Others felt that the course would strengthen the field of American history at Smith College. The course passed with a unanimous vote, and would be taught beginning in the fall semester. It was a two-part course. The first covered the colonial era to the international rivalry of the eighteenth century; the second covered independence through the 1930s. The three credits were divided between two hours of lectures and one hour of discussion. Holmes taught it "with the cooperation of Mr. Curti, Mr. Faulkner and others."[80] She continued to teach the course until her retirement.

The question of Canadian involvement with the Americas concept remained unanswered until the 1940s. Professor Reginald Trotter's broader historical and national outlook now focused on Canadian-Latin American affairs and Canada's potential role in the Pan-American Union. His files are filled with newspaper clippings on the subjects, advertisements for study trips to South America, and information on conferences held in Canada dealing with Canada and the Americas. Besides gathering these materials, he presented papers and published articles. In 1941 he presented a paper titled "Role of Canada in Western Hemispheric Solidarity," and six years later he read one titled "Canada and the Americas: Their Relations to the Rest of the World" at the Sixth Annual Drake University Institute of Pan-American Relations.[81]

Throughout Trotter's papers and correspondence, there is little direct mention of the study of the history of the Americas in Canada; however, he did discuss the matter in 1933. He noted that McGill University in Montreal had the best-developed course on the Bolton concept, but the course had made some headway in other Canadian institutions as well. Trotter concluded that Canada's membership in the British Commonwealth and in the League of Nations gave Canadian history close ties with the history of the Old World.[82]

Between October 1939 and January 1940, two Canadian scholars, Percy E. Corbett and Trotter, raised the question of Canadian participation in the Pan-American Union, stressing the Anglo ties represented in the British Commonwealth of Nations rather than an Americas identity.[83] Although the question of the Americas was raised, the conclusion of both men was that Canada would not be a member of the Union in the immediate future. However, it is important to note that at last Canadians recognized and established their place within the hemisphere.[84] Trotter concluded: "Canada is indubitably an American community, but one cannot by talking of 'Canada's essential Americanism' thereby dismiss other facts in the Canadian situation."[85]

At the same time the Canadians were questioning their role in the hemisphere and their participation in the Pan-American Union, others, including the United States, realized the lack of information available about Canada. In 1940 John MacCormac noted the irony of this fact:

They [citizens of the United States] know little about Canada because they have taken her for granted as a country half British, half American, and yet one-third French, lighted by the aurora borealis and the midnight sun and populated chiefly by the Indians, the Royal Canadian Mounted Police, and the Dionne quintuplets.[86]

Two responses came from Mexico. The history faculty of the National Autonomous University of Mexico perceived the value of the history of the Americas, and in 1936 courses were inaugurated. Within the department of the Secretary of Public Instruction, Luis Alvarez Barret and Antonio Rangel's *Historia de América* was prepared for use in the Mexican primary schools.[87]

Also from Mexico were the historian Silvio Zavala and the philosopher Leopoldo Zea, who in the coming years would study, analyze, and write about the Americas in historical and philosophical contexts. Zavala, the greatest Latin American promoter of the Americas concept, became involved with the Pan-American Institute of Geography and History, and the development of a journal and books on the concept of hemispheric history.[88] At approximately the same time Zea began his theoretical studies of the Americas, focusing on their role in world affairs. In 1949 he published "The Interpretation of the Ibero-American and North American Cultures;" later his ideas would reach publication through numerous additional articles and monographs.[89]

In Brazil, movement toward an Americas approach began to re-develop in the 1930s and 1940s. In 1931, after a long line of proposals to include the history of the Americas in the Brazilian national curriculum, the Minister of Education, Francisco Campos, promoted educational reform in the secondary schools, and Brazil finally allotted time to the history of the Americas. Within a decade this reform spread to the university level with the establishment of history of America chairs in schools responsible for the training of "intellectuals to engage in the highest cultural activities of a general or technical nature, of those who want to teach in secondary and *normal* schools and to conduct research on the subjects they teach."[90]

During the 1940s, Hélio Vianna, Brazilian historian and professor of the history of America at the Catholic Pontifical University of Rio de Janeiro, actively promoted the concept. He provided an important overview of the history of the Americas from a Brazilian point of view and looked at the sociological aspects of the creation of America.[91] In 1943 members of the Faculty of Philosophy, Sciences, and Letters at the University of São Paulo inaugurated a series "História da Civilização Americana."

Through conferences, international organizations were an important means of bringing together historians and scholars from other disciplines throughout the Americas. The International Congress of Americanists had been around for nearly a century and took a comparative approach in its quadrennial meetings. Because of his significant reputation, Bolton received a special invitation from G. Marañón, President, and José María Torroja,

Secretary, to attend the 1935 meeting in Seville. Four years later he received a similar invitation to attend the 27th International Congress of Americanists in Lima.[92]

The National Academy of History, headquartered in Buenos Aires, organized the Second International Congress of the History of America. Held in Buenos Aires, July 5-14, 1937, it commemorated the 400th anniversary of the founding of the city. The United States was well represented at the conference.[93] The Pan-American Columbianist Society of Havana actively held meetings in the 1930s.[94] In 1940 the Eighth American Scientific Congress, held in Washington, organized the Inter-American Statistical Institute. Scholars became active, and in 1941 the first round table conference was held with United States and Mexican scholars. Also in 1941 the Instituto Indígena Interamericano/Inter-American Indigenist Institute was established to coordinate indigenous affairs throughout the Americas. Its subjects ranged in scope from anthropological and archaeological to historical.

The most famous of these inter-American organizations was most likely the Pan-American Union with its active Pan-American Institute of Geography and History. From its Mexico City headquarters, the Institute took an active role in promoting hemispheric studies. In 1935, it began a publication program that has released several hundred titles covering a broad range of topics from natural history and resources to folklore, history, geography and linguistics. In 1938 Professor Silvio Zavala of the College of Mexico established the *Revista de historia de América*. He thought the timing was appropriate, given the research of scholars in the field and the popular interest in the concept. The editors of the *Revista* believed that a broader study of the Americas would lead to the development of more accurate national histories, an appreciation of the parallels and differences in the Americas, and a better understanding of the evolution of continental history. They also noted that the field had matured quickly and was ready for this new publication. Published under the auspices of the Pan-American Institute of Geography and History, the *Revista* would appear in the official languages of the Institute: Spanish, Portuguese, English, and French. Over the years the journal has lived up to the expectations of its founder.[95]

Not satisfied with only a journal to promote the Americas approach, the Institute initiated the Project for a General History of America in 1943. This began an odyssey lasting several decades. The First Conference of the Ministers and Directors of Education of the American Republics resolved that, given the fact of hemispheric unity, writers and historians should edit a text dealing with a history of all of America; however, nothing came of this resolution.[96]

The Commission on History of the Pan-American Institute was organized in October 1947. Its purpose was to stimulate, coordinate, and pub-

lish studies of the history of the Americas through the cooperation of scholars and institutions. In 1950 Silvio Zavala, chair of the Commission, stated
that the history of the Americas was still in a formative stage, and expressed his hope for its development:

The study of the parallel history of the American peoples should not, in my opinion, be undertaken with the sole object of pointing out resemblances and differences. An equally important purpose should be to create the habit of observing
and meditating on the historical phenomena of the New World within a broader
and at the same time more precise framework, for the history of each of its nations
will be enriched by the light derived from the experiences of the others.[97]

Although all of these organizations had newsletters, bulletins, and journals, a number of them were outstanding in the breadth of their thematic
approach. The Inter-American Indigenous Institute inaugurated the journal *América indígena* in 1941; it continues as the only multi-language journal devoted to the indigenous peoples of the Americas. Anthropologists
founded the inter-American review *Acta Americana*, which the Inter-American Society of Anthropology and Geography sponsored. Yale University
held the first Inter-American Congress on Philosophy in May 1943. Scholars of the Americas published in journals and served as visiting professors in the field of Latin American studies, which influenced the Americas
theme.[98]

The Pan-American Institute of Geography and History not only published *Revista de historia de América* out of Mexico City, but also the *Boletín
bibliográfico de antropología americana* and, after 1941, the *Revista geográfica*.
Continuing with this inter-American approach, in December 1940 the Division of Intellectual Cooperation of the Pan-American Union inaugurated
its "Points of View" series, whose objective was to present varying "aspects of cultural development...and the status and role of the intellectual
worker in a changing world."[99] Between December 1940 and September
1947, ten works were issued, dealing with a variety of inter-American
topics.[100]

In Washington, DC, the federal government and private institutions
promoted a new sense of the role of the Americas. The government dedicated the Hispanic Reading Room in the Library of Congress in 1939; the
director, Lewis Hanke, would play a prominent role in promoting the concept of the history of the Americas. The reading room served as a center to
orient and assist researchers who wished to use the Luso-Hispanic materials located throughout the Library of Congress.

Across Washington, a group of Franciscan scholars inaugurated the
Academy of American Franciscan History on April 18, 1944. The Academy was concerned with the development of the field of inter-American
historical research. Three months later, it published the premier issue of
The Americas: A Quarterly Review of Inter-American Cultural History. The
editor stated, "With this issue *The Americas* is launched upon a career which

it hopes will be of real service to the scholarship and cultural relations of all the American Republics."[101] Five years after its foundation, Bolton visited the Academy of Franciscan History to receive the Americas Award and noted that "among the common bonds between all the Americas, from Canada to Argentina and Chile, are the Catholic faith and Catholic culture. They form an obvious approach to inter-American history."[102] In its early years the journal stressed inter-American news, history, and themes.

Despite all of this interest in the Americas concept both inside and outside the classroom in the 1930s and 1940s, an ominous sign appeared at Berkeley. Bolton's course, History 8, had been the mainstay of the History Department for many years. As an elective course, it continued to attract hundreds of students per semester. However, during the late 1930s members of the United States history faculty looked at History 8 "with a bit of envy and resentment because of its and Dr. Bolton's drawing power." Once, when the faculty tried to curtail the course by not allowing it to count for United States history credit, Bolton threatened to drop the course and they backed off. It continued to be one of the most popular courses in the department, and possibly on campus.[103]

In the late 1930s lectures that were sponsored to promote the Good Neighbor Policy had the dual effect of promoting the Americas concept. In 1937 the University of California formed the Committee on International Relations in Berkeley and Los Angeles. The result was a series of lectures dealing with Latin America fostered by the increased interest manifested in the United States for "the other America." Three professors each from Berkeley and Los Angeles presented the lectures, titled "The Civilization of the Americas," weekly between April 4 and May 9, 1938. All of the lectures took an inter-American approach.[104]

As part of the Good Neighbor policy, the State Department became increasingly concerned with fostering and strengthening cooperative "relations with the Latin American countries through long-term, two-way, person-to-person communication."[105] As a result of this concern, in 1938 the State Department created the Division of Cultural Relations. Because of Bolton's experience and reputation, he was tapped on a number of occasions to work with the Director of the Division of Cultural Relations. When World War II began, the United States was in an excellent position to promote hemispheric solidarity. For several years Bolton escorted Latin American visitors to the San Francisco Bay area when they visited under the auspices of the State Department.[106] In July 1939 he aided the State Department with an important conference, "Inter-American Cultural Relations," held on the Berkeley campus.[107] In November 1939, at the invitation of Secretary of State Cordell Hull, Bolton was one of the keynote speakers at a special national conference on inter-American relations held in Washington. Hundreds of educators and leaders in the professional, intellectual, and cultural life of the nation attended.[108] Here Bolton presented an important paper that outlined the historical forces and common experiences which united the Americas and stressed the cultural aspects. This point was not included in his "Epic" address, an absence for which Edmundo O'Gorman and others had criticized him.[109] Bolton was also involved in the State Department's professor exchange program and taught some short courses in Mexico.[110]

If academic and governmental circles were interested in Latin American and Americas affairs, it was only natural that between 1935 and 1940, popular culture, art, and cinema would also focus in this direction. The theme and architecture of the California Pacific International Exposition held in San Diego in 1935-1936 had a decidedly Hispanic-American emphasis.[111] In 1939-1940, Latin American nations promoted themselves at the San Francisco Golden Gate International Exposition[112] and the New York World's Fair.[113] During the San Francisco exposition, Mexican muralist, Diego Rivera, was commissioned to create what was then his largest fresco, titled, "Pan-American Unity."[114] Rivera believed this fresco most clearly represented his theory of Pan-Americanism.[115] He said, "American art has to be the result of a conjunction between the creative mechanism of the North and the creative power of the South coming from the traditional deep-rooted Southern Indian forms."[116] Rivera's combination of art, culture, and history united the indigenous cultures of ancient Mexico with the industrial cultures of the United States.[117]

Hollywood continued to bring the inter-American theme to American audiences. In 1940, Brazilian actress Carmen Miranda appeared in her first American movie, *Down Argentine Way*. In the following years she appeared in other movies and, stereotyped or not, created a Latin American presence in American movie theaters. The movie *Springtime in the Rockies*, released in 1942, included Carmen Miranda and was set in the Canadian Rockies.

Walt Disney, cut off from European markets by World War II, sought to beef up his hemispheric market sales. South America had charmed Disney, and under State Department auspices he toured South America with a camera team, planning to develop a series of short cartoons for each nation. This proved to be shortsighted, and Disney instead united four shorts into a movie called *Saludos Amigos*, which was released in 1942 and was popular in both the United States and Latin America. Another cartoon, *The Three Caballeros*, dealing with hemispheric topics was not released until 1945. Less propagandistic than the first, it was warmly received.[118]

Public lectures with the Americas approach continued in coming years. In the summer of 1941, a series of lectures was given on an Americas theme. This was important because World War II had begun and there was a concern for solidarity in the Western Hemisphere. Scholars from throughout the Americas delivered lectures that dealt with hemispheric commonality, defense, trade and commerce, culture, Pan-Americanism, raw materials, and inter-American solidarity.[119]

As Bolton approached his seventieth year, retirement became manda-
tory, and the question for many was what would happen to the history of
the Americas. During the 1939-1940 academic year, Bolton cut back on his
teaching load and prepared for his retirement in 1940. Former students
were ready to take over. Bolton gave History 8 to Lawrence Kinnaird and
promoted Engel Sluiter's name to assist with the course.[120] It was divided
into two sections and taught during 1940-1941 and 1941-1942. However,
with the onset of World War II, the younger teachers were called into government service. Kinnaird went off to serve as Cultural Attaché in Santiago,
Chile, and Sluiter spent 1942-1943 as a Rockefeller Foundation Fellow in
Latin America.

With the removal of these two instructors from the faculty, the university re-appointed Bolton as a lecturer on January 1, 1942. In an interview
with the *Daily Californian* on January 30, 1942, it was obvious that Bolton
was happy to be back and, except for the chairship of the department, he
was working at full capacity, holding the position of Director of Bancroft
Library and serving as the editor of the "California Centennial History"
series.

Bolton taught a full schedule of classes for five consecutive regular terms,
including the summer session of 1942. He continued to teach "History of
the Americas" (History 8A-B), assisted by John Rydjord; "History of the
Pacific Coast and the Southwest" (History 189A-B); and a seminar (History 281A-B); and he continued to oversee the work of his Ph.D. students.[121]
He retired again in March 1944.

With Bolton detached from History 8, his students would again continue to carry the torch. In 1944 Sluiter returned to the faculty, Vernon J.
Puryear joined him, and History 8 was taught by both men. Throughout
the war years and until the mid-1950s the course prospered. Sluiter recalled that his section had several hundred students per semester with
three or four teaching assistants and felt that the other section was comparable.[122]

However, the field of Latin American history and its sub-area of the
Americas, which Bolton, Chapman, and Priestley had cultivated, would
go through some important changes. Retirement and death had removed
key players, and Bolton was no longer available to defend his course. In
August 1944 the department chair, Frederic L. Paxson, presented a ten-
year survey for the department. In his report he noted that in the past the
history of Europe, the United States, and the Americas had all attracted
large enrollments. Paxson also noted that in the past, California's Spanish
heritage had influenced the university's promotion of Hispanic American
history, but now the situation had changed. The position of United States
history had recently been altered. John D. Hicks, a new addition to the
department who specialized in United States history, held the newly cre-

ated Morrison Chair. To complement this development, the university inaugurated a new lower-division course, History 17A-B, a United States survey course. According to Paxson, this was a long-needed development that a growing demand for the subject had accelerated. He concluded that Hispanic American history, a "field upon which much of the reputation of the Department has been built, has suffered crushing losses in recent years with the retirement of Professor Herbert E. Bolton (1940), the death of Professor Charles E. Chapman (1941), and the illness and retirement of Professor Herbert I. Priestley (1941)."[123]

In early 1945 the history faculty voted to require all history majors to take History 4 ("Western Civilization"); they could elect to take either History 8 or History 17, "according to the intention of the student to concentrate in Hispanic or United States history."[124] This development shows that the faculty perceived the history of the Americas as a Latin American-oriented course rather than the general hemispheric course that Bolton had hoped for. At that time Kinnaird, Sluiter, and James F. King taught History 8; John D. Hicks and Lawrence A. Harper taught History 17.[125]

The causes of the decline of History 8 and the Latin American emphasis within the University of California history department at this time is subject to debate. The decline set in for a number of reasons. First, there were university and departmental requirements unfavorable to the continued success of the course. Students preparing to be history majors were required to take History 4 ("History of Western Civilization") as either freshmen or sophomores. Many other departments required or strongly recommended that their students take these courses. State and university requirements that every student had to take a course in United States history and institutions — History 17 — or pass a written examination further injured History 8 because it did not satisfy the "history and institution" requirement. However, in the early 1950s the University did allow History 8B, and as a result, History 8 became an elective with declining enrollments.[126]

Bolton's narrative style, personality, knowledge, and especially his enthusiasm were important ingredients in the success of the course at Berkeley. Standing in front of specially drawn maps, Bolton paced the stage in Wheeler Auditorium and made history come alive for people. With his retirement and other factors influencing the course of events, enrollment dropped in 1948-1949 to 150 people. By the time of Bolton's death in 1953, History 8 had gone into serious decline, but the concept of the history of the Americas was alive and being promoted by organizations and periodicals throughout the Americas.

Two years prior to his death, Bolton reflected on the development of his interest in the Spanish in the New World and the "ultranational" United States historians' hostility to this type of history. In an introduction to his collection of papers, he wrote:

When I went to [the University of] Texas, [George P.] Garrison and [Eugene C.] Barker were doing splendid work in the history of that area, beginning with the Anglo American occupation, on which their interests were definitely centered. The Spanish background of the Southwest and the Pacific Coast was new to me except in the most general sense, and I did not know a dozen words of the Spanish language. All my professors and all my text-books had dismissed the history of Spanish America in a few paragraphs dogmatically asserting that "Spain failed," but in what the failure consisted they never specified. This dictum seemed to them as axiomatic as two plus two equals four, and was neither questioned nor explained. A vast continent, two-thirds of which was colonized by Spain and Portugal, and still is inhabited and ruled by Spanish and Portuguese, who have developed great American nations, had little meaning for ultranational historians, and consequently it did not enlist their curiosity. The explanation of this myopic view is that they limited American history to the United States, which in area is less than one-fourth of America. The other three-fourths of the Continent, including Canada and Latin America, did not count in their synthesis.[127]

NOTES

1. John Francis Bannon, *Herbert E. Bolton: The Historian and the Man, 1870-1953* (Tucson: University of Arizona Press, 1978), 183-184.

2. George Peter Hammond, Charles W. Hackett, J. Lloyd Mecham, William C. Binkley, Cardinal Goodwin, and J. Fred Rippy eds., *New Spain and the Anglo-American West: Historical Contributions to Herbert Eugene Bolton*, 2 vols. (Los Angeles: privately printed, 1932), 1:x.

3. Ibid., 1:v.

4. Bannon, *Herbert Eugene Bolton*, 184.

5. Herbert E. Bolton, "The Epic of Greater America," in *Bolton and the Spanish Borderlands*, ed. John F. Bannon (Norman: University of Oklahoma Press, 1964), 302.

6. Herman Ausubel, *Historians and Their Craft: A Study of the Presidential Addresses of the American Historical Association, 1884-1945* (New York: Columbia University Press, 1950), 91.

7. Herbert E. Bolton, "The Epic of Greater America," *American Historical Review* 38 (1933): 448-474; also Bannon, *Bolton and the Spanish Borderlands* 301-332.

8. Ibid., 302.

9. Ibid., 307.

10. Ibid., 308-313.

11. Ibid., 313-319.

12. Ibid., 325.

13. Ibid., 326.

14. Ibid., 327-329.

15. Ibid., 331.

16. No accurate record was made of the length of the talk, but a count of the words of the address places its length at approximately eighty minutes.

17. Writing of Bolton after his death, Theodore E. Treutlein said, "Bolton apparently did not think consciously with respect either to fields of inquiry or to theories of history. He could appear to be the most naive of historical philoso-

phers or at the same time, as he unfolded a story, the most profound." See Treutlein's "Necrologías: Herbert Eugene Bolton (1870-1953)," *Revista de historia de América* 37-38 (1954): 299.

18. Bolton to Walter Sage, 01/31/1933, and to Eugene Barker, 02/01/1933, Bolton Papers, Out.

19. William E. Lingelbach to Bolton, 01/05/1933, Bolton Papers, In.

20. Sage to Bolton, 03/24/1933, Bolton Papers, In.

21. Reginald Trotter to Bolton [12/1932], Bolton Papers, In.

22. John B. Brebner to Bolton, 04/04/1933, Bolton Papers, In.

23. Curtis Putnam Nettels to Bolton, 09/08/1933, Bolton Papers, In.

24. J. Manuel Espinosa, "Bolton: History of the Americas," *Historical Bulletin* (St. Louis University) 14 (1936): 81-82. This is one of the first articles devoted to Bolton's role in the development of the history of the Americas.

25. Espinosa to Bolton, 03/25/1936; 10/02/1938, Bolton Papers, In.

26. Vito Alessio Robles to Bolton, 02/05/1934, Bolton Papers, In.

27. Silvio Zavala, review of *La epopeya de la máxima América*, by Herbert E. Bolton, *Revista de historia de América* 1 (1938): 81.

28. Carmen Alessio Robles, "Proposición que presenta ante el segundo Congreso Mexicano de Historia reunido en la Ciudad de Mérida, estado de Yucatán," 11/21/1937, Bolton Papers, In.

29. Alessio Robles to Bolton, 09/19/1937, Bolton Papers, In.

30. Bolton, *La epopeya de la máxima América*, trans. Carmen Alessio Robles, publication no. 30, Instituto Panamericano de Geografía e Historia (México, DF: Instituto Panamericano de Geografía e Historia, 1937).

31. Also included in *Wider Horizons* were three other of Bolton's most notable essays: "The Mission as a Frontier Institution in the Spanish-American Colonies," "Defensive Expansion and the Significance of the Borderlands," and "The Black Robes of New Spain."

32. Arthur P. Whitaker, review of *Wider Horizons of American History*, by Herbert E. Bolton, *Mississippi Valley Historical Review* 26 (1939): 459.

33. Edmundo O'Gorman, *Do the Americas Have a Common History?* trans. Angel Flores, Points of View no. 3 (Washington, DC: Pan-American Union, Division of Intellectual Cooperation, 1941).

34. Edmundo O'Gorman to Bolton, 04/22/1939, Bolton Papers, In.

35. Bolton to William C. Binkley, 12/22/1941, Bolton Papers, Out.

36. Herbert E. Bolton, "Cultural Coöperation with Latin America," National Education Association, *Journal* 29 (1940): 1-4. This article, sometimes under slightly different titles, was translated and published in Latin American newspapers and magazines. It also appeared in other United States periodicals, including the following: *Hispanic American Historical Review* 20 (1940): 3-11; *International Quarterly* 4 (1940): 21-24, 59; and *Southwest Review* 25 (1940): 115-125.

37. Peter M. Dunne to Bolton, 04/16/1940, Bolton Papers, In.

38. Hanke's interest in the subject can be traced back to the early 1920s, when he studied under an early Americanist, Isaac J. Cox, at Northwestern University. In 1923, at the annual meeting of the American Historical Association in Columbus, Ohio, he met Bolton. See David Bushnell and Lyle N. McAlister, "An Interview with Lewis Hanke," *Hispanic American Historical Review* 68 (1988): 655.

39. Curtis P. Nettels to Bolton, 01/21/1941, Bolton Papers, In.

40. Nettels to Bolton, 07/23/1941, Bolton Papers, In.

41. Although Bolton originally agreed to participate in the session, on August 12 he suddenly withdrew. The relevant correspondence is missing, but some speculations can be made. Bolton was seventy years of age, and throughout 1941 he was involved in a series of speaking engagements around the country. For instance, on November 11, 1941, he traveled across San Francisco Bay and presented a talk entitled "Some Bases for Hemispheric Understanding." This was the fifth and last of a series presented by the University of San Francisco on "Hispanic America."

42. Bolton to Nettels, 03/05/1941, Bolton Papers, Out.

43. The addresses by the various participants were published as a unit: George W. Brown, ed., "Have the Americas a Common History?" *Canadian Historical Review* 23 (1942): 132-139.

44. Binkley regretted that Bolton would not participate but noted that he and other Bolton students "have caught something of your vision and...we will do our best to show its validity as well as its significance." Binkley to Bolton, 12/15/1941, Bolton Papers, In.

45. William L. Sachse, "Echoes from Chicago," *American Historical Review* 47 (1942): 481-482. The entire session was published as Brown, "Have the Americas a Common History?"

46. Silvio Zavala, *El mundo americano en la época colonial*, 2 vols. (1962; México, DF: Editorial Porrúa, 1990), 1:xiii-xvi.

47. Charles C. Griffin, *A Program of the History of the New World Coordinator's Summary Reports*. Vol. 3, *The National Period in the History of the New World: An Outline and Commentary*. Publication no. 103 (México, DF: Instituto Panamericano de Geografía e Historia, 1961. Repr. New York: Greenwood Press, 1990).

48. Victoria Ocampo, ed., *Is America a Continent? A Round Table Discussion*, trans. Angel Flores, Points of View no. 2 (Washington, DC: Pan-American Union, Division of Intellectual Cooperation, 1941). Participants in the discussion included Raúl Arrarás Vergara; Eduardo E. Krapf; Amado Alonso, Spanish scholar; Germán Arciniegas, Colombian essayist; Carlos A. Erro, Argentine philosopher; Edith Helman, professor at Simmons College; Pedro Henríquez Urena, Dominican writer; María Rosa Oliver, Argentine literary critic; and Arnaldo Orfila Reynal, Argentine educator.

49. Enrique de Gandía, "Pan-Americanism in History," in *Do the Americas Have a Common History?*, ed. Lewis Hanke (New York: Knopf, 1964) 130, 132-133.

50. Luis Alberto Sánchez, *The Presence of Tradition* (Washington, DC: Pan-American Union, 1941).

51. Sánchez, "A New Interpretation of the History of America," *Hispanic American Historical Review* 23 (1943): 446ff.

52. Luis Quintanilla, *A Latin American Speaks* (New York: Macmillan, 1943), 3-88.

53. Philip C. Brooks, "Do the Americas Share A Common History?," 1949, p. 3, Bolton Papers, In. This was later published in Lewis Hanke. ed. *Do the Americas Have a Common History?* (New York: Knopf, 1964) 134-140. The following section is drawn from this material.

54. Brooks, "Do the Americas," 6.

55. William Lingelbach to Bolton, 12/23/1935, Bolton Papers, In.

56. Lingelbach to Bolton, 05/08/1936, 02/26/1937, 04/21/1937, Bolton Papers, In.

57. Lingelbach to Bolton, 09/24/1938, Bolton Papers, In. This small book continued to be published by Appleton-Century until it was picked up by the University of Notre Dame Press and published until the late 1980s.

58. Unsigned review of *Wider Horizons of American History*, by Herbert E. Bolton, *Pacific Historical Review* 9 (1939): 361.

59. F. S. Crofts to Bolton, 04/30/1929, 04/07/1933, Bolton Papers, In.

60. Lingelbach to Bolton, 02/26/1937, 04/21/1937, 09/24/1938, Bolton Papers, In.

61. John W. Caughey to Bolton, 09/04/1938, Bolton Papers, In. It should be emphasized that Bolton used many readings placed on reserve; the University of California was willing to finance this practice because of the large classes and the revenue generated, but this was not the case for other institutions.

62. Lingelbach to Bolton, 12/13/1946, Bolton Papers, In.

63. *Latin American Studies in American Institutions of Higher Learning, Academic Year, 1935-36* (Washington, DC: Pan-American Union, Division of Intellectual Cooperation, 1936).

64. Estellita Hart, comp. *Courses on Latin America in Institutions of Higher Education in the United States, 1948-1949* (Washington, DC: Pan-American Union, Division of Education, Department of Cultural Affairs, 1949).

65. Interview with Stephen B. Barnwell, Marquette, MI, 01/24/1992, Magnaghi Papers, In; Edith E. Ware, ed., *The Study of International Relations in the United States, Survey for 1934* (New York: Columbia University Press, 1935) 282-283.

66. Espinosa, "Bolton," 82; the author recalls the course (1955-56) through class notes. The social studies class started with Canada, stressing the people, life, provinces, and industries, then moved south to Latin America, where the geography and peoples were followed by regional studies: Central America, Mexico, Andean and southern countries and Brazil, and concluded with a detailed study of the United States. Interview with J. Manuel Espinosa, 11/03/1992, Magnaghi Papers, In.

67. Ronald Hilton, *Los estudios hispánicos en los Estados Unidos*, trans. Lino Gómez Canedo, O.F.M. (Madrid: Ediciones Cultura Hispánica, 1957).

68. The following texts were used for the history of the Americas: William W. Sweet, *History of Latin America*; Charles E. Chapman, *Colonial Hispanic America*; William S. Robertson, *History of the Latin-American Nations*; Mary W. Williams, *The Peoples and Politics of Latin America*; J. Fred Rippy, *Historical Evolution of Hispanic America*.

69. Wallace Thompson, *Greater America: An Interpretation of Latin America in Relation to Anglo-Saxon America* (New York: E. P. Dutton, 1932).

70. Stephen Duggan, *The Two Americas: An Interpretation* (New York: Scribner's, 1934).

71. Ibid., xi.

72. Robert S. Cotterill, *A Short History of the Americas* (1939; New York: Prentice-Hall, 1945), ix (Preface to 1st ed.).

73. Wallace Thompson, *The Civilization of the Americas* (Berkeley: University of California Press, 1938); Victor L. Webb, Edna Fay, and William L. Nida, *The New World, Past and Present: A Unified Course in History and Geography for Elementary*

Schools (Chicago: Scott Foresman, 1938); Delia Goetz and Varian Fry, *The Good Neighbors: The Story of the Two Americas* (New York: Foreign Policy Association, 1939).

74. José R. Millán, *Compendio de historia americana* (Buenos Aires: A. Kapelusz, 1932); Luis Alvarez Barret and Antonio Rangel, *Historia de América* (México, DF: Talleres de "El Nacional," 1938); Afranio Peixoto, *Pequeña historia de las Américas* trans. Pedro González-Blanco (México, DF: Botas, 1946); Teja Zabre, *Dinámica de la historia y frontera intramericana* (México, DF: Botas, 1947).

75. Luis Germán Burmester, *Historia americana*, vol. 1 (Buenos Aires: n.p., 1939); Ricardo Levene, *Historia de América*, 15 vols. (Buenos Aires: W. M. Jackson, 1940-1951); Carlos Pereyra, *Breve historia de América*, 2 vols. (1939; Santiago de Chile: Zig-Zag, 1946); Atilio Sivirichi, *Historia de América* (Lima: D. Miranda, 1939); Antonio Ballesteros y Beretta, *Historia de América y de los pueblos americanos*, 2 vols. (Barcelona: Salvat, 1936).

76. Data on Vera Brown Holmes from Maida Goodwin, Archives Specialist, College Archives, Smith College, Northampton, MA (hereafter: CA, Smith College) (especially helpful searching for the useful primary sources); and "Obituaries, Vera Brown Holmes," *Smith Alumnae Quarterly* 72 (1981): 51-52.

77. Vera Brown Holmes, "A Note Concerning My Research and Teaching" (1957), Papers of Vera Brown Holmes, CA, Smith College.

78. Professor Brown was married in 1936 and thus the name change. For simplicity I have used her better-known married name throughout the study.

79. History Department minutes, 02/22/1935, CA, Smith College.

80. "The Committee on the Departmental Offering Submits...," February 13, 1935, CA, Smith College.

81. Folder 27, "A Survey of Canadian-American Relations"; folder 64, "Study Trip to South America" (1940); folder 67, "Canada and the Americas"; folder 68, newspaper clippings on the Pan-American Union; folder 85, "Canada and the Americas"; folder 102, "Role of Canada in Western Hemispheric Solidarity," Trotter Papers, Queen's University Archives (hereafter: QUA).

82. Edith Ware to Trotter, 04/23/1933; Trotter to Ware, 04/26/1933, Folder 6, Trotter Papers, QUA.

83. Although it does not directly relate to the Bolton concept, Trotter promoted the study of United States-Canadian affairs through conferences and publications. See "Some American Influences upon the Canadian Federation Movement," *Canadian Historical Review* 5 (1924): 213-227; *Conference on Canadian-American Affairs* (Canton, NY: St. Lawrence University Press, 1935; Kingston, ON: Queen's University Press, 1937; Canton, NY: St. Lawrence University Press, 1939; Kingston, ON: Queen's University Press, 1941).

84. Percy E. Corbett, "Canada and Pan-Americanism," *Quarterly Journal of Inter-American Relations* 1.4 (1939): 30-34; Reginald Trotter, "More on Canada and Pan-Americanism, A Reply to Professor Corbett," *Inter-American Quarterly* 2 (1940): 5-10.

85. Trotter, "More on Canada," 9.

86. John MacCormac, *Canada: America's Problem* (New York: Viking, 1940), 14.

87. Luis Alvarez Barret and Antonio Rangel, *Historia de América* (México, DF: Talleres de "El Nacional," 1938).

88. *Biobibliografía de Silvio Zavala* (México, DF: Colegio Nacional, 1993).

89. Leopoldo Zea, "The Interpretation of the Ibero-American and North American Cultures," *Philosophy and Phenomenological Research* 9 (1949): 538-543; Gustavo Vargas Martínez, comp., *Bibliografía de Leopoldo Zea* (México, DF: Fondo de Cultura Económico, 1992).

90. Hélio Vianna, "Ensino e conceito de história da América," in his *Estudos de história colonial* (São Paulo: Companhia Editora Nacional, 1948), 18-19.

91. Ibid., 14-15.

92. G. Marañón and José María Torroja to Bolton, 04/12/1935; Rubén Vargas Ugarte, S.J., to Bolton, 08/10/1939, Bolton Papers, In.

93. The United States delegation consisted of Clarence H. Haring, Roscoe P. Hill (National Archives), María de Maeztu (Columbia University), Percy A. Martin (Stanford University), A. P. Nasatir (San Diego State College), Frank Tannenbaum (Columbia University), and Arthur P. Whitaker (University of Pennsylvania).

94. Havana was home to a number of inter-American institutions, such as the Pan-American Public Library, the American Periodical Library, the Inter-American Union of the Caribbean, the Casa de las Américas, the Inter-American Institute of Municipal and Institutional History, the Inter-American Archival Committee, and the Ministry of Education (which oversaw the Pan-American Columbianist Society).

95. Zavala, review of *La epopeya* 81; Silvio Zavala, Francisco Monterde, and Felipe Teixidor, eds., "Propósitos," *Revista de historia de América* 1 (1938): v-vi.

96. Guillermo Morón, "Informe sobre proyecto de historia general de América," *Revista de historia de América* 90 (1980): 61-62.

97. Silvio Zavala, "The Commission on History of the Pan-American Institute of Geography and History," *The Americas* 6 (1950): 489.

98. Lewis Hanke, "The Development of Latin American Studies in the United States, 1939-1945," *The Americas* 4 (1947): 38-39.

99. Américo Castro, *On the Relations Between the Americas*, trans. Angel Flores (Washington, DC: Pan-American Union, Division of Intellectual Cooperation, 1941), i.

100. No. 1, Américo Castro, *On the Relations Between the Americas* (1940); no. 2, Victoria Ocampo, ed., *Is America a Continent? A Round Table Discussion* (1941); no. 3, Edmundo O'Gorman, *Do the Americas Have a Common History?* (1941); no. 4, Luis Alberto Sánchez, *The Presence of Tradition* (1941); no. 5, Ernesto Nelson, *A Problem for the Americas* (1942); no. 6, *Mr. MacLeish, We Are Not Irresponsible* (1943); no. 7, Fernando Ortiz, *On the Relations between Blacks and Whites* (1943); no. 8, Mariano Picón-Salas, *On Being Good Neighbors* (1944); no. 9, Moisés Sáenz, *The Indian, Citizen of America* (1946); no. 10, Juan Oropesa, *Contrasting Philosophies of Education, North and South* (1947).

101. "Inter-American Notes," *The Americas* 1 (July 1944): 111.

102. Herbert E. Bolton, "The Confessions of a Wayward Professor," *The Americas* 6 (January 1950): 359-362.

103. Donald Worcester to Magnaghi, 06/05/1992, Magnaghi Papers, In.

104. *The Civilization of the Americas: Lectures Arranged by the University of California at Los Angeles, Committee on International Relations, Delivered in the Spring of 1938* (Berkeley: University of California Press, 1938).

105. Espinosa, *Inter-American Beginnings of U.S. Cultural Diplomacy, 1936-1948*

(Washington, DC: Bureau of Educational and Cultural Affairs, U.S. Department of State, 1976), vii

106. Rafael Belaúnde, Jr., to Bolton, 04/15/1935; U.S. Department of State, Division of Cultural Relations, Richard Pattee, to Bolton, 11/16/1942, 05/25/1943, Bolton Papers, In.

107. U.S. Department of State, Division of Cultural Relations, Ben M. Cherrington to Bolton, 03/28/1939, 05/25/1939, 06/15/1939, 06/18/1939, 07/08/1939, Bolton Papers, In.

108. Espinosa, *Inter-American Beginnings*, 142-144; U.S. Department of State, Division of Cultural Relations, Cherrington to Bolton, 06/15/1939; Cordell Hull to Bolton, 09/30/1939, Bolton Papers, In; *Evening Star* (Washington, DC), 11/08/1939.

109. Herbert E. Bolton, "Cultural Coöperation with Latin America," *Hispanic American Historical Review* 20 (1940): 3-11.

110. U.S. Department of State, Division of Cultural Relations, Pattee to Bolton, 03/12/1940, Bolton Papers, In; Espinosa, *Inter-American Beginnings*, 303.

111. Florence Christman, *The Romance of Balboa Park*, 4th ed. revised (San Diego: San Diego Historical Society, 1985), 81-97.

112. The exposition was held on Treasure Island in San Francisco Bay in view of the University of California and Bolton's route to his History 8 course in Wheeler Auditorium.

113. Germán Arciniegas, "Latin America at the San Francisco Exposition," *Bulletin of the Pan-American Union* 73.10 (October 1939): 549-561; Stanley Applebaum, *The New York World's Fair, 1939-1940* (New York: Dover, 1977), 122-124; "All Aboard! American Republics at the New York World's Fair," *Bulletin of the Pan-American Union* 73.7 (July 1939): 387-412. The nations included at these expositions included Argentina, Brazil, Canada, Chile, Columbia, Ecuador, El Salvador, Guatemala, Mexico, Peru, and Venezuela.

114. Rivera originally called his fresco, "Marriage of the Artistic Expression of the North and South on this Continent." The fresco, which measures 22½ feet by 44¼ feet, was originally commissioned for the San Francisco City College campus. Today it is located in the lobby of the school's theatre.

115. Diego Rivera (with Gladys March), *My Art. My Life: An Autobiography* (New York: Citadel Press, 1960; reprint New York: Dover, 199), 144.

116. Artists on Parade, *Time* 35 (June 24, 1940): 69.

117. Works that provide insight into Rivera's frescoes include Bertram D. Wolfe, *The Fabulous Life of Diego Rivera* (New York: Stein and Day, 1963), 363-366; "Fifth Columnists Beware," *Time* 37 (January 6, 1941): 32-33; "Diego Rivera, His Amazing New Mural Depicts Pan-American Unity," *Life* 10 (March 3, 1941): 52-56. The *Life* article includes color photographs of the frescoes.

118. Leonard Maltin, *The Disney Films* (1973; New York: Popular Library, 1978), 124-131, 140-148.

119. Walter H. C. Laves, ed., *Inter-American Solidarity* (Chicago: University of Chicago Press, 1941).

120. In the late 1930s Engel Sluiter (Ph.D. 1937) greatly expanded the Americas concept with the idea of introducing Dutch colonial history and Pacific Basin studies. Although he did little with these concepts, the latter has become an important part of modern historiography. Sluiter to Charles E. Chapman, 07/16/1937, Bolton

Papers, In.

121. In the year of his retirement, six students completed their work; in 1942-1944 another five received Ph.D.s, along with a larger number of M.A.s.

122. Engel Sluiter to Magnaghi, 07/30/1992, Magnaghi Papers, In.

123. Ibid.; Frederic L. Paxson to History Department, July 7, 1944, Bolton Papers, In.

124. History Department meeting, 01/12/1945, Bolton Papers, In.

125. *General Catalogue...1940-1941* (Berkeley: University of California Press, 1940), 270; *General Catalogue...1942-1943* (Berkeley: University of California Press, 1942), 293.

126. Sluiter to Magnaghi, 07/30/1992; Woodrow W. Borah to Magnaghi, 07/21/1992, Magnaghi Papers, In.

127. Herbert E. Bolton, *The Bolton Collection – Manuscript Materials for the History of the Pacific Coast and the Southwest* (Berkeley: Bancroft Library, 1951).

5

The Concept After Bolton, 1953-1970

The concept of the history of the Americas developed in the first half of the twentieth century and matured in the later decades. Since Bolton's death in 1953 the history of the Americas has gone through a number of significant developments. Although the concept entered American historiography, it was surrounded by controversy. Due to zealots who tried to create a commonality, with which Bolton disagreed, and the creation of the label "the Bolton thesis," many historians throughout the hemisphere attacked the concept. As a result, it has struggled to retain a tenable position among historians. One of the major problems with the Americas concept was that neither Bolton nor his students were intellectual historians who sought to define the concept according to a philosophical approach based on comparative history. Due to this problem and the influence of other factors, the Americas concept as a part of a college-university curriculum has fallen into disfavor in the United States although it thrives in Canada.

Those who come into contact with the concept still appreciate its merits. In recent years, the comparative theme of the history of the Americas has found its way into journal articles and monographs. As the Americas are tied together through broad economic initiatives such as the North American Free Trade Agreement (NAFTA), there is a growing demand for organizations to create links and programs that will join the Americas. When the Bolton concept is presented to young teachers and historians, they are fascinated that such a concept exists, but they have no idea who Bolton is or what the origins of the concept are.

To understand its recent historiographic context, it is necessary to review the critiques of historians familiar with the history of the Americas concept. In 1950 Herman Ausubel wrote about the importance of Bolton's

"Epic" speech:

Yet if Bolton simply repeated in "The Epic of Greater America" a point of view for which he had long been pioneering, there can be no question that the situation in the early thirties justified the repetition. For few historians had the courage to do what Bolton had done: to depart from the way of treating United States history that he had learned as a student of Turner and McMaster. Few historians had learned what Bolton had discovered early in his career, that a study undertaken in United States history would frequently defy present-day national boundaries.[1]

Two years later, H. Hale Bellot wrote:

The Southwestern and California school, of which the leader is Professor H. E. Bolton, working in the area in which the social foundations are Spanish, finds itself driven to make of American history more than the history of the United States.[2]

In 1957, for Charles Gibson and Benjamin Keen, Bolton's concept was "the only over-all interpretation of Hispanic American history ever devised in this country." Calling it the "celebrated unitary hemisphere thesis of Herbert E. Bolton," the authors continued:

and his "Epic of Greater America" presented the doctrine of hemispheric homogeneity. Argued principally in terms of the colonial materials of his specialization and resembling to some degree the Turner thesis of frontier history..., the unitary hemisphere thesis depended for its acceptance..., upon selected levels of generalization, and upon a philosophical interpretation of unity and diversity in history..., in which Bolton...was not profoundly interested.

Thus though the followers of Bolton accepted the doctrine of American unity, they did not in their monographic writing..., explore the Hispanic portion of the hemisphere.... Neither did the Bolton thesis receive that detailed critical reexamination.... It is symptomatic of the condition of American history in the 1920's and 1930's that the major critiques of the Bolton thesis came from Latin America itself.[3]

In the 1960s Lewis Hanke's name became linked with the Americas concept. In 1964 he edited *Do the Americas Have a Common History? A Critique of the Bolton Theory*, the first study to look at the subject in-depth.[4] Although there are some deficiencies in the work, it remains the standard. Two years later Hanke gave the Charles Wilson Hackett Memorial Lecture at the University of Texas and left some interesting insights. He called for a course titled "History of Latin American Civilization" in which more emphasis would be placed on art, literature, and philosophy rather than on the traditional political approach. Furthermore, Hanke suggested that as a way to "challenge and interest our students," a hemispheric comparative course should be experimented with. He further added that United States history textbooks should not merely present Columbus and then "discuss the Pilgrims and the first Thanksgiving," but should include the intervening hemispheric story. Later in life, Hanke continued to point out that "the influence of parochialism in the writing and study of history is so widespread that it should not surprise us that some of our historians have displayed what has been called a certain "condescension" toward Latin America.[5]

John F. Bannon (Ph.D. 1939), one of the more active Boltonians, conducted some important work. He is known for writing the Americas textbook and a modern version of Bolton's *Spanish Borderlands*. However, Bannon ultimately proved to be an enigma.

At the time of Bolton's death in 1953, Bannon sent a condolence letter to Mrs. Bolton that promised, "I will do all I can to see that his greatest contribution to American historiography, 'the Americas approach,' will be carried on to enjoy the understanding, appreciation, and acceptance which it deserves."[6] Bannon taught the history of the Americas for over thirty years and produced a textbook, thereby keeping his promise to perpetuate the concept.

By the early 1960s, several East Coast historians seemed to tie Bolton's place in American historiography to the "common history of the Americas," which they labeled "the Bolton thesis." This frustrated Bannon, who decided to give Bolton his proper place in American historiography.[7]

Unfortunately, over the years Bannon did not fully analyze and interpret the Americas concept, and in the early 1960s he decided to focus on one aspect of Bolton's scholarship. In 1964 he edited and published *Bolton and the Spanish Borderlands*. He introduced Bolton as "first and foremost the scholar who opened up the Spanish Borderlands, integrating them into the broader understanding of American history."[8]

Given the nature of his study, Bannon proceeded to downplay Bolton's role as the historian of the Americas. For him "there never was a 'Bolton thesis'" because all Bolton did was "prepare a broader approach to American history." Bannon finally labeled the history of the Americas "the controversial field of historical synthesis." He did a disservice to the Americas approach by not balancing Bolton the Borderlands historian with the larger image of Bolton the Americas historian.[9]

At the same time, Woodrow W. Borah (Ph.D. 1940) of the University of California made some observations in a book review of Lewis Hanke's *Do the Americas Have a Common History?* Borah commented on Bolton's "Epic" address: "It is, on the whole, a modest essay of limited claims." He went on to note that Bolton "was too wise" to advance the "Bolton theory." Borah contended that Bolton never adequately defined the term "common history." Borah asked, if Europe had a common history, then "Is the theory to mean that the Americas have that kind of unity, or is it to mean something else?" His final question was not whether the Americas had a common history but "whether they have a history that distinguishes them as more than a sub-area of European culture soon to be submerged in a global civilization."[10]

John Higham was another historian who was critical of Bolton. He noted in 1965 that "Bolton lacked the analytical ability to make his concept fruitful; he gave a specious appearance of significance to a program of fragmentary research."[11]

In 1980, Latin American historian Charles Gibson developed an insightful overview of the Bolton position. He noted that although "Boltonism successfully sloughed off many of the prejudices of the earlier interpretations...it never stimulated the scholarly response for which its author hoped." Gibson concluded that "In practice the Greater America idea was confined to introductory college courses, courses that attracted students but did little or nothing to develop the new field of scholarship envisaged by Bolton." He felt that the best works in the field to date "were comprehensive textbooks." Gibson found the intensive work of the Pan-American Institute had produced meager results. Of the scholars involved in the project, "None...was willing to argue that the similarities took precedence over the differences." Gibson also noted that in response to Hanke's anthology, *Do the Americas Have A Common History?* the answer from most readers was "No, they do not."[12]

Over the years Michael Krause has updated his work on American history and historians. In his 1985 revision, he recognized Bolton's role in the development of the Americas concept:

Going beyond his preceptors, McMaster and Turner, Bolton proclaimed the epic of greater America in which the essential unity of American history, North and South, has been stressed; his was literally a history of the Americas, not merely the story of the expansion of thirteen colonies into a nation.

Unfortunately, Krause and his associate David D. Joyce continued to identify Bolton as a frontier and sectional historian of the United States.[13]

In the 1990s the question of multiculturalism and the history of the Americas can be treated. Robert F. Berkhofer, Jr., provides some inferential insights through his comments about Frederick Jackson Turner's frontier interpretation of American history. For him, "the viewpoint underlying Turner's history is painfully enthnocentric and chauvinistic."[14] Since Bolton based his Americas approach on Turner's theories, the same can be said of Bolton's position. Trained in the late nineteenth century, Bolton never dealt with gender, race, ethnicity, or class. A review of his syllabus highlights the problem. For Bolton, "Settlers have transplanted European cultures to America, but those have become greatly modified by American environment and by contact with native peoples." Also, the native peoples are marginal to his story of "Spain's ablest men," "bold adventurers," and "great captains."[15] A passage from his syllabus dealing with the conquest of Mexico is indicative of the problem:

The conquest was not wholly a work of destruction, but was one of construction as well. Wherever they went the Spaniards founded cities, built churches, developed industries, and set up Spanish political institutions. The Indians were exploited, but the missionaries worked nobly to Christianize and educate them. Nahua culture was badly shattered but not wholly destroyed, and many of its finest features are preserved today in the mixed race which has resulted from the conquest.[16]

He also noted that Canada "was a land of explorers, missionaries, fur-traders, peasant farmers, feudal lords, and royal officials."[17] Later four of his lectures dealt directly with the American West, in which he continuously referred to it as a nationalizing force. Bolton was a historian of the American mainstream who took the traditional Great Story into the Western Hemisphere. The most positive aspect of the history of the Americas in terms of multiculturalism is that educators can utilize the approach to present gender, race, ethnicity, and class through the vehicle of the Americas.

Historians observe that the major problem for acceptance of the history of the Americas concept lay in the fact that Bolton never analyzed and interpreted, nor did he fully develop, the concept; rather, he took the traditional approach to the various parts of the story. First there was the problem with presenting a theoretical rationale for the need for, and the efficacious nature of, such a concept. Bolton was essentially a narrative historian rather than a theoretical historian. Although there are numerous references in his unpublished and published writings, only a few will be mentioned here. Writing in 1920, Bolton made some observations about his new Americas concept: "So you see my thesis is not local history, but American history in the largest sense. The Spanish Borderlands are only a bit of the whole." He further revealed:

Of course the entire thesis is too vast for one person to master except in outline, but I believe I have had a vision which is destined to reconstruct our teaching. We shall have general courses in American history, and special courses in national history (United States, Canada, Mexico, etc.).[18]

In his published works Bolton presents plausible reasons for studying the history of the Americas. In his 1928 syllabus he stated, "The day of isolation is past. The increasing importance of inter-American relations makes imperative a better understanding by each of the history and culture of all. This is so patent that it needs no demonstration...."[19] At this point the discussion abruptly ends. In his 1932 "Epic" speech, Bolton expanded his ideas. "There is a need," he observed, "of a broader treatment of American history, to supplement the purely nationalistic presentation to which we are accustomed." Using part of his syllabus Preface, he augmented the catchwords of the course syllabus:

It is time for change. The increasing importance of inter-American relations makes imperative a better understanding by each of the history and the culture of all. A synthetic view is important not alone for its present day political and commercial implications; it is quite as desirable from the standpoint of correct historiography.

His first section concludes:

Our national historians, especially in the United States are prone to write of these broad phases of American history as though they were applicable to one country alone. It is my purpose, by a few bold strokes, to suggest that they are but phases common to most portions of the entire Western Hemisphere; that each local story will have clearer meaning when studied in the light of the others; and that much of what has been written of each national history is but a thread out of a larger strand.[20]

These statements sum up Bolton's thinking on the concept. Although he clearly defined what should be studied, he never revealed how or why it should be studied.

A number of Bolton's former students commented on his lack of theoretical ability. J. Fred Rippy (Ph.D. 1920) identified the origin of the problem facing an interpretative approach to the history of the Americas. According to Rippy, the problem was centered among the Latin American history faculty—Herbert Priestley, Charles Chapman, and Bolton. Of the three, Priestley was "more ready to generalize and philosophize," but in general the California history faculty "distrusted the philosophy of history so profoundly that they discouraged attempts at broad generalization and interpretation."[21] Writing about Bolton specifically, Rippy said he had the highest regard for Bolton as a personal friend, mentor, and "a very capable historian." However, he continued, "He [Bolton] was not much interested in theory and he had no decided flair for interpretation...."[22] John W. Caughey (Ph.D. 1928) observed, "Bolton never claimed to be a great philosopher or a deep thinker. He did boast that he had hit upon two or three majestic ideas. One was that history is best observed and best understood by reaching beyond the confines of a single nation."[23] John Francis Bannon wrote in 1964: "Actually, there never was a 'Bolton thesis.' Bolton did little more than propose a broader approach to American history, one which was not simply Anglo-oriented or limited to the study of the thirteen colonies to which three dozen and one states were added in time."[24] Irving A. Leonard (Ph.D. 1928) said of Bolton, "He was a wonderful teacher. I do not consider him to have been profound, but he was enthusiastic and always encouraging."[25]

Boltonians and those familiar with the early evolution of the course were sold on the idea of its importance and value to students. The only Boltonians who took an analytical approach to the concept were William Binkley (Ph.D. 1920) in 1942 and Philip C. Brooks (Ph.D. 1933) in 1949-1950. Brooks satisfactorily analyzed the strengths and weakness of the position, but unfortunately his work did not reach a major historical journal in the United States, and thus mainstream historians never became acquainted with the results.[26] Numerous octogenarian Boltonians, who were interviewed in 1992-1993, continued to give their unflagging support for the "Epic of Greater America" approach.[27] However, hundreds of other historians did not appreciate this new concept and did not see why they should re-train and introduce this new approach. How would the history of the Americas fit into elementary and secondary curricula, and why should a student training to teach traditional history go into this area of study? Many people, from historians and college administrators to state school board members, would have to be sold on the concept of comparative history of the Americas in order for it to gain a position in college courses.

Ultimately, what Bolton presented was comparative history in a hemispheric setting. The French historian Marc Bloch, a contemporary of Bolton, was an early pioneer of "comparative history." Coincidentally, Bloch first presented his ideas of comparative history in 1928. Unfortunately, over the years historians have not been completely won over to comparative history. In December 1973, there was a flicker of hope when the annual meeting of the American Historical Association devoted a session to comparative history, but the question of the role of comparative history continued to be controversial.[28] The concept of the history of the Americas was never properly interpreted, thus East Coast historians and others could not accept it.

Further complicating the question and acceptance of the history of the Americas was the debate over the commonality of this history. Lewis Hanke, at a session of the 1941 American Historical Association conference, introduced the idea. Bolton was not enamored of the catchy title of the session, "Do the Americas Have a Common History?," and hoped that another could be substituted because of the controversy it might generate. The fact that Bolton was unable to participate in the session did not help the situation. Ultimately Bolton was accurate; the title did create controversy. In 1964 Hanke edited a work titled *Do the Americas Have a Common History? A Critique of the Bolton Theory*. Although it is a fine study of the controversy, the circular argument concerning the commonality or lack of it in the history of the Americas remained unresolved. Hanke further introduced the idea of a "Bolton theory" or "Bolton thesis," neither of which Bolton would ever acknowledge.

It would have been bad enough if there were only unanswered questions of definition, interpretation, and the commonality of the concept. However, there was the question of the continuation of the course History 8, which was the driving engine of the concept. There were not enough Bolton-trained teachers to staff such a course in colleges and universities. Since there was no formal "History of the Americas" program at Berkeley, the first instructors of the history of the Americas were primarily Bolton's teaching assistants, who had received on-the-job-training in History 8.

There is no indication that Bolton's "round table" seminars actually delved into comparative Americas history. These graduate students usually took degrees in Latin American or American history, and when they were hired, they taught a section or two of the history of the Americas because it was in demand at their college or university.

Conceptually, the history of the Americas was never popular with either United States or European historians. The idea behind it was unorthodox, and it made many traditional historians uncomfortable. John Caughey and others pointed out that even among Bolton's Berkeley colleagues, History 8 was never seen as a good substitute for straight United States history. Usually the sheer force of numbers in Bolton's classes ended attempts to demote the course.

Other barriers, which returned to the problem of a lack of theoretical interpretation of the concept, hindered the expansion of the hemispheric course. Even if there had been a growing number of Americas-trained teachers, many historians and administrators felt that they were nonconformists and would not hire them to teach the Americas approach.[29] A general decline in the field of Latin American history throughout the United States paralleled the decline in interest in and study of the history of the Americas. By 1958 the number of universities offering Latin American history courses remained constant, but the number of students had declined, as had graduate work, because many no longer saw it as a serious field of study. Between 1947 and 1951, 10 percent of dissertations in history at American universities were on Latin American history, whereas between 1952 and 1956 the number had declined to only 5.6 percent of the total.[30]

There were numerous reasons for this decline in the field. First, the discipline no longer appeared to be useful in contributing to an understanding of contemporary Latin American society and its role in the modern world. Second, Latin American historians in the United States failed to show that their field offered real intellectual challenges within the framework of contemporary historical thought or in developing new currents of historical thought. Due to a lack of guides and bewildering political shifts, most of the studies prior to 1958 focused on the colonial through independence eras; there were few studies in the nineteenth and twentieth centuries. This was due to the fact that national Latin American historians had tended to overlook broader socio-economic forces of international significance. Finally it was expensive to travel to Latin America, and once the traveler was there, sources were poorly organized in archives or libraries, or they were inaccessible in private hands.[31]

A stronger reason for the decline of the history of the Americas concept is associated with the rise of Latin American history as a distinct field, beginning in the 1960s. In response to the rise of Fidel Castro in Cuba and his Communist revolution, the United States government poured research money into the field, creating major Latin American studies centers all over the nation. Thus many historians focused narrowly on a portion of Latin America, just as previous United States historians had remained myopically focused on small pieces of United States history. Ironically, this explosion of Latin American specialists further inhibited the spread of Bolton's view.

The history profession as a whole also bears responsibility because of its archaic, Balkanized structure. Departments continue to fill microhistory positions defined by very narrow geotemporal boundaries. This overspecialization militates against any scholar who seeks to paint on a broader canvas.

Despite these problems facing the Americas concept, courses on the history of the Americas continued to be taught into the 1970s. At Berkeley, History 8 was taught primarily by Boltonians until the mid-1960s. Between 1940 and 1947, with the exception of military service, Lawrence Kinnaird (Ph.D. 1928) taught History 8 six times. When he returned to Berkeley, Engel Sluiter (Ph.D. 1937) taught the course seventeen times, almost on an annual basis until 1960-1961, "which saw the end of History 8A-B as such."[31] Other instructors included James F. King (1945-1953, seven times; Ph.D. 1939) and Robert C. Padden, who taught it in 1961-1962 and 1963-1964, "but not in recognizable form." History 8 appeared in the *General Catalogue*, and in 1965-1966, Cornelis C. Goslinga taught it for the last time.[32] "History 18: Latin American History," taught by King, replaced it.[33]

Other colleges and universities throughout the United States replicated this process. St. Louis University first offered the history of the Americas in 1934, and John F. Bannon continued to offer it from 1939 until his retirement in 1971.[34] At Smith College, where Vera Brown Holmes taught the Americas, it continued to be taught after her retirement (in 1958) until 1970.[35] On the West Coast, at San Diego State University, between 1929 and 1979 A. P. Nasatir (Ph.D. 1926) taught the history of the Americas to literally thousands of students.[36] In 1930, when John Caughey began teaching at the University of California, Los Angeles, he taught four sections of History 8.[37] The records show a similar experience for Theodore Treutlein (Ph.D. 1934) at San Francisco State University, Peter M. Dunne, S.J. (Ph.D. 1934), at the University of San Francisco, and Russell Ewing (Ph.D. 1934) at the University of Arizona, to highlight a few examples.[38]

Unfortunately, Bolton never inaugurated a special Americas program to train future instructors, and this practice continued with his students. Bannon's experience at St. Louis University was a typical example. As Bolton had done, Bannon taught the undergraduate Americas course to large classes of students with two graduate assistants. He took special pride in teaching undergraduates and tended to avoid graduate seminars. If a student sought to develop an Americas emphasis, it had to be done around colonial American history, strengthened by fields in United States and Latin American history. Since the demand for Americas teachers was declining, this approach was probably the wisest way to obtain a doctorate.[39]

If Boltonians did not train a new generation of faculty to teach, publish, and promote the history of the Americas, most of them also were derelict in developing comparative studies and analyzing the concept of the Americas. One of the few to take a more positive approach was William Binkley, who wrote to Bolton in 1945, "I suspect that you have no idea how far your influence reaches in the activities of your former students in the historical profession."[40] Philip C. Brooks (Ph.D. 1933), another former student, also dealt with an analysis of the concept. However, this was not the direction for many.

The root of the problem went back to the 1945 festschrift *Greater America*, purported to be a:

common contribution to the history of the Americas as broadly viewed by Professor Bolton himself. They are component parts of the complex epic of the opening of the New World by peoples of the Old, and of the development of closely related new societies in the human and physical environment of the Americas.[41]

In his review of the work, Lewis Hanke made some critical observations on the "younger crop of Boltonites [who] ranged far beyond the rim of Christendom" and wrote of Potosí, Patagonia, and African slavery in New Granada, yet no one had written "on the history of that vast and variegated world" of Brazil. Hanke pointed out that the introduction stated, "A major purpose of this volume is to present in the bibliographical section concrete evidence of Bolton's influence in creating a school of Western Hemisphere Historians." Yet there is not one essay that expounds, analyzes, or evaluates the concept of "Western Hemisphere History." Hanke hoped that the next generation of historians Bolton had influenced during his "retirement" would tackle the problem, but that was not the case.[42]

Few Boltonians or their successors developed comparative studies of the Americas either in theory or topically, even though in his "Epic" speech Bolton had provided future Americanists with a list of topics for research and publication.[43] They usually went into Latin American history, Western American history, or the Spanish Borderlands. John Francis Bannon's comparative study, *Colonial North America — A Short History*, was published with limited distribution.[44] One of the first academic descendants of Bolton was Stafford Poole, C.M., who received his doctorate under Bannon in 1961. In 1992 he contributed a section on the Spanish to a work entitled *Christianity Comes to the Americas, 1492-1776*.[45]

The course in the history of the Americas had its heyday in United States college curricula between 1950 and 1970. Although hundreds of students took the course, an adequate textbook had not been published.

Then three historians emerged — John Francis Bannon, Vera Brown Holmes, and Harold E. Davis — who would produce books to meet the demand.

On February 16, 1948, John Francis Bannon, S.J. took the initiative and laid before Bolton the idea of co-authoring a history of the Americas with the master or getting "permission" to write his own history. Bannon felt that without a textbook on the subject, all of Bolton's work in the field would be lost to future generations.[46] Although the correspondence does not exist, Bolton must have given Bannon, one of his "boys" from the round table, his blessing to do what the mentor was unable to do. In the 1952 preface Bannon acknowledged Bolton as the "'granddaddy of the Americas approach,' for the inspiration from which this effort springs."[47] After the 1952 publication of the *History of the Americas*, Bannon wrote to Bolton:

I hope that you will find that it measures up in some small way to the great historical concept which you fathered and through your students over the years had a hand in propagating beyond the confines of Wheeler Aud[itorium] and the Campus at Berkeley. When you note its inadequacy, or better inadequacies, lay the blame on a lesson poorly learned, not on a lesson poorly taught. However, as I note in the Preface, I will be most happy if my little effort helps to perpetuate the great Americas approach to the forgotten half of Western civilization history.[48]

Bannon's two-volume *History of the Americas* was a successful narrative history that filled the demand for a textbook.[49] His volume on the colonial era followed the Bolton format and developed easily. Unfortunately for the Americas concept, there was truth in Bannon's statement "I am more of a synthesizer than a scholar." Although he was an excellent synthesizer, he did not analyze or conceptualize the concept of the Americas. Without interpretative analysis, Bannon ran into trouble with the second volume, which focused on the national era. He wrote that he "was never wholly comfortable with" the volume and referred to the fact that the integration of material did not take place even after a careful revision of the 1963 edition.[50] In the revised edition Bannon noted, as Bolton had done in the past, that he was waiting "until the day when another, with the touch of the genius-synthesizer, can make *American* history as well-integrated a story as *European* history has become."[51]

Vera Brown Holmes, professor of history at Smith College, was the second of the trio of Americas textbook historians. She began researching and teaching the history of the Americas in 1935, and fifteen years later she published her text, *A History of the Americas: From Discovery to Nationhood*. There was a fourteen-year hiatus before she published a second volume, *A History of the Americas: From Nationhood to World Status*. Her theme was that colonial Americans "were engaged in the experiment of applying the precepts and practices of western European civilization to the conditions of an Indian America."[52]

Professor Holmes wrote the book for a number of audiences. It was primarily designed for students in her college courses, and she hoped that it would "also have correlative value in courses devoted to the United States, Canada, and Latin America, providing some of the larger perspectives within which these national histories have evolved." It was "also meant for the general reader who desires an introduction to hemispheric problems." Holmes sought to trace "the origins and early growth of the political and social foundations that underlie everyday life and international relationships in the Americas of the present time."[53]

The third author of an Americas history textbook was Harold E. Davis, professor of history and director of Inter-American Studies at the American University. In 1953 he published his one-volume work, *The Americas in History*. In the Preface he noted that the American nations "shared many common experiences in one of the greatest ventures of the human spirit — the creation of a New World." He felt that his textbook could be "used with discrimination" to "teach the history of the United States in its broad hemispheric setting." However, although he thought positively of the concept, he noted that historians had been slow to develop this synthetic history. In the Acknowledgments he noted:

It is therefore the author's special duty to acknowledge his great obligation to Professor Herbert E. Bolton, an inspiring teacher and friend whose scholarly spirit did much to quicken the realization among historians that the history of this country is part of a larger, hemispheric experience.[54]

In Canada during the post-war years, the "Spotlight on Canada" series envisioned and developed three works: *Canada and the Commonwealth*, *Canada and the Americas*, and *Canada and the World*. Ontario schools approved *Canada and the Americas* as a textbook. George W. Brown edited the text, assisted by University of Toronto colleagues J. M. S. Careless and Gerald M. Craig, and Eldon Ray, principal of the Kenner Collegiate Institute in Peterborough, Ontario. Brown wrote the reason for the text in the Preface:

the two continents present a fascinating study in contrasts while at the same time they are linked in a common American pattern. In spite of differences these twenty-two countries all stem from the culture of Western Europe and are all stamped indelibly by the environment of the New World.[55]

In this volume Brown and his colleagues stressed that the American environment had influenced all of the nations of the Western Hemisphere, "and all of them in greater or less degree have felt the influence of the expanding New World frontier and the use of modern industrialism." Brown pointed out that Canada shared these similarities but differed in others ways, such as her peaceful development to nationhood. He concluded that "in this constant interplay of similarities and differences can be found many illuminating suggestions which may encourage a greater understanding between Canada and her American neighbours."

By mid-century, and even after the English-language Americas text-books, historians of the Americas thought that an acceptable textbook did not exist.[56] The perceived problem was that individual historians did not have the necessary training and background to write on such a broad topic. Furthermore, most historians were trained in national rather than continental history. Spanish historians primarily wrote works that, although they had the Americas vision, were shaped by their European orientation.

As a result, the First Conference of American Ministers of Education, meeting in Panama in October 1943, decided to open a competition for a book on the history of the Americas. Among the considerations discussed were a common American origin, the indigenous tradition, and the unifying force of its discoverers, colonizers, and liberators that affirmed its common destiny. The ministers hoped that such a work would replace nationalistic rivalries and suspicions with more positive attitudes among the people of the New World. Unfortunately, no one expressed interest in the project.

In 1947 the Pan-American Institute of Geography and History established the Commission on History, which first met as a consulting body in Mexico in October. At that time the Committee of the History of America Program began to function. The general scope and nature of the project were set forth, and it was duly noted that this project would be the work of individuals and would not have any "official character." Finally, the Committee hoped that the completed project would be written for the general public and could be used by educational institutions.

At the second meeting, in Santiago, Chile, in 1950, the Commission approved plans to carry forth the project, by dividing the history into three periods: indigenous, colonial, and national. They reiterated their concern for bringing this completed project to the teaching community. The Committee hoped that in the process of developing this project, inter-American scholars would have opportunities for intellectual exchanges and "that it might effect a first crossing of the bibliographical frontiers of the different areas."[57]

The project obtained a grant from the Rockefeller Foundation, and the chair of the Commission on History, Silvio Zavala, organized work groups. Initially, Juan Comas headed the Native Period; following his resignation, he was replaced by Pedro Armillas. Zavala took the Colonial Period, and Charles C. Griffin was placed in charge of the National Period. During this first phase, the Commission concentrated on utilizing specialists in various fields to develop and publish First Contributions.[58]

Early in 1953, the Commission on History and the Committee for the Centennial Commemoration of the Birth of José Martí organized a meeting in Havana. The results of previous studies were published in the First Contributions, funded by the Martí Committee, and discussions were conducted. Also at this time the Commission made Comas, and then Armillas,

Zavala, and Griffin, officially responsible for coordinating and preparing Summary Reports on the various periods. There was a meeting of anthropologists at Mexico City in late 1954, as well as a meeting of historians in New York City. Later the three coordinators met in Poughkeepsie, New York, to discuss the progress of the project. In March 1956 a third meeting of the participants was held at the Library of Congress, Washington, DC, to discuss results, problems, and future directions. In an interesting development, in December 1957 the Pan-American Union, the Library of Congress, and the Academy of American Franciscan History co-sponsored a meeting at the Academy, in Washington, DC. The theme of the meeting was the history of religion during the Colonial Period. Chapter X of the Summary Report on the Colonial Period, which had been translated into English and circulated, served as the discussion paper. Arthur P. Whitaker, a national member for the United States on the Commission on History, organized three sessions at the annual meeting of the American Historical Association in 1952, 1954, and 1956, where the project was discussed by two dozen historians with varying backgrounds.[59]

The result of the publications, meetings, conferences, and seminars was three volumes in the Program of the History of America, which was considered the second phase of the Commission's plan for a comparative history of the Americas. The first monograph was Pedro Armillas' *The Native Period in the History of the New World*. Based on archaeological and historical records, it is divided into fifty themes and organized into ten chapters. Eight of the chapters focus on the pre-Columbian period and two on the post-Columbian period. The Mexican concept that Indians had an influence on the post-Conquest world served as a basis for the development of the latter topic. The bibliography contains a valuable, though dated, selection of English and Spanish sources.

Critics of the work pointed out that it fell short of the primary objectives of the Program, had an uneven presentation, and could not be used for undergraduate teaching purposes. It also did not provide any new theoretical insights of significance for the study of New World history. Finally, critics opined that the work was merely a descriptive inventory of topics to be used in a more comprehensive study in the future.[60]

Silvio Zavala's *The Colonial Period in the History of the New World*[61] is the result of an immense task that required developing a wealth of information. The study had to deal with the European background and the varying colonial experiences throughout the hemisphere, as well as and the role of Asia and Africa.

One of the shortcomings of the work was the fact that there is no information about what was left out in the abridged translation. Critics also did not like its encyclopedic approach. Stanley J. Stein noted, "Whatever the reasons, this is only an annotated outline of a summary of syntheses, lacking the insight and craftsmanship that Zavala displayed in his *Estudios indianos.*"[62] The last of the three volumes is Charles C. Griffin's *The National Period in the History of the New World.*[63] The work is divided into four parts: (1) independence movements; (2) period of national consolidation (1826-1870); (3) economic and political development (1870-1918); and (4) changes down to the mid-twentieth century (1918-1950). This move into periods contrasted with Zavala's work. Dexter Perkins believed that this volume was particularly important because the United States public needed to know the role of Latin America's world position.[64]

All of the volumes were praised for their extensive, multi-language bibliographies. However, after their publication, many historians felt that the original agenda of the Program had not been met. As a result of the May 1971 meeting at Lima, the Inter-American Council for Education, Science, and Culture of the Organization of American States (OAS) recommended the development of a general history of the Americas. In January 1973 Javier Malagón Barceló, director of the Department of Cultural Affairs of the OAS, named Guillermo Morón, professor at Simón Bolívas University in Caracas and Venezuelan historian, director of the project. Simón Bolívar University and the National History Academy of Venezuela funded the project, which was developed by a multi-national corps of scholars. The first volume of this multi-volume series was issued in 1983. Since 1983 over thirty volumes dealing with specific geographical areas and themes have been published. The project is scheduled to end in 1999-2000.[65]

There were other series of works that treated American history in a broader manner. The "New American Nation" series, which began in 1954, took its cue for a more inclusive view of United States history from the earlier "American Nation" series.[66] A number of volumes of text and readings dealt with the French and Spanish experiences in the Americas.[67] In the 1960s, Ray Allen Billington edited the "Histories of the American Frontier" series for Holt, Rinehart, and Winston. Within this series were monographs on the Spanish Borderlands, Mexican, Canadian, Latin American, and Pacific Basin frontiers.[68] The series took a broad and ultimately comparative approach to the frontiers of the Americas.

The development of the history of the Americas ended in the 1970s. The course History 8 was declining with the death and retirement of Boltonians. If only this course was focused on, then the end was near. However, there were other developments under way that would see the concept revived in the last quarter of the twentieth century.

NOTES

1. Herman Ausubel, *Historians and Their Craft: A Study of the Presidential Addresses of the American Historical Association, 1884-1945* (New York: Columbia University Press, 1950), 91-92.

2. H. Hale Bellot, *American History and American Historians* (Norman: Univer-

sity of Oklahoma Press, 1952), 36.

3. Charles Gibson and Benjamin Keen, "Trends of United States Studies in Latin American History," *American Historical Review* 62 (1957): 859-860.

4. Lewis Hanke, ed., *Do the Americas Have a Common History? A Critique of the Bolton Theory* (New York: Knopf, 1964).

5. David Bushnell and Lyle N. McAlister, "An Interview with Lewis Hanke," *Hispanic American Historical Review* 68 (1988): 669.

6. John F. Bannon to Mrs. Bolton, 02/02/1953, Bolton Papers, In.

7. John F. Bannon, "JFB, Historian: A Touch of Autobio," ca. 1982, 16, St. Louis University Archives and Magnaghi Papers, In.

8. John F. Bannon, ed., *Bolton and the Spanish Borderlands* (Norman: University of Oklahoma Press, 1964), xii.

9. Ibid., 3-4, 301.

10. Woodrow W. Borah, review of *Do the Americas Have a Common History?*, by Lewis Hanke, *Hispanic American Historical Review* 45 (1965): 101-103.

11. John Higham, *History* (Englewood Cliffs, NJ: Prentice-Hall, 1965), 41.

12. Charles Gibson, "Latin America and the Americas," in *The Past Before Us: Contemporary Historical Writing in the United States*, ed. Michael Kammen (Ithaca, NY: Cornell University Press, 1980), 201.

13. Michael Krause and David D. Joyce, *The Writing of American History*, rev. ed. (Norman: University of Oklahoma Press, 1985), 278-279.

14. Robert F. Berkhofer, Jr., *Beyond the Great Story: History as Text and Discourse.* (Cambridge, MA: Harvard University Press, 1995), 172.

15. Herbert E. Bolton. *History of the Americas: A Syllabus with Maps* (Boston: Ginn, 1928), 3, 20, 23.

16. Ibid., 19.

17. Ibid., 81.

18. Bolton to Mr. Glasgow, 11/06/1920, Bolton Papers, Out.

19. Bolton, *History*, iii.

20. Herbert E. Bolton, "The Epic of Greater America," *American Historical Review* 38 (1933): 448-449.

21. J. Fred Rippy, *Bygones I Cannot Help Recalling: The Memoirs of a Mobile Scholar* (Austin, TX: Steck-Vaughn, 1966), 100, 112.

22. Ibid., 110.

23. John W. Caughey, "Herbert Eugene Bolton," in *Turner, Bolton, and Webb: Three Historians of the West* by Wilbur R. Jacobs, John W. Caughey, and Joe B. Franz (Seattle: University of Washington Press, 1963), 54.

24. Bannon, *Bolton and the Spanish Borderlands*, 3.

25. John J. TePaske, "An Interview with Irving A. Leonard," *Hispanic American Historical Review* 63 (1983): 238.

26. Philip C. Brooks, "Do the Americas Share a Common History?" *Revista de historia de América* 33 (1952): 75-83.

27. Donald E. Worcester to Magnaghi, 07/01/1992; Woodrow W. Borah to Magnaghi, 07/21/1992; Engel Sluiter to Magnaghi, 07/30/1992; J. Manuel Espinosa to Magnaghi, 09/23/1992; Ursula Lamb to Magnaghi, 10/23/1992; Mary O'Callaghan, R.S.C.J., to Magnaghi, 06/30/1993, Magnaghi Papers, In.

28. Raymond Grew, "The Case for Comparing Histories," *American Historical Review* 85 (1980): 763-778; Alette Olin Hill and Boyd H. Hill, Jr., "Marc Bloch and

Comparative History," *American Historical Review* 85 (1980): 828-857.

29. Jacobs, Caughey, and Franz, *Turner, Bolton, Webb*, 52-53.

30. Howard F. Cline, ed., *Latin American History: Essays on Its Study and Teaching, 1898-1965*, 2 vols. (Austin: University of Texas Press, 1967), 1:6-16; American Council of Learned Societies and the Newberry Library, *Latin American Studies in the United States* (Chicago: ACLS, 1958), 30.

31. Ibid., 31-32; Sluiter to Magnaghi, 07/30/1992, Magnaghi Papers, In.

32. Much of this information can be found in the *General Catalogue...1942-1943* (Berkeley: University of California Press, 1942), 293; *Announcement of Courses...* (Berkeley: University of California Press, 1944), 117; 1948, 339; 1951, 337; 1959, 223.

33. *Announcement of Courses...*, 1964, 392; 1965, 403; 1966, 311. Among those who taught after Bolton's retirement were Lawrence Kinnaird, Engel Sluiter, John Rydjord, Vernon J. Puryear, James F. King, and Cornelis C. Goslinga.

34. Russell M. Magnaghi, *The History of the Americas at Two Jesuit Universities: St. Louis University and the University of San Francisco* (Marquette, MI: Belle Fontaine Press, 1994).

35. Maida Goodwin to Russell M. Magnaghi, Northampton, MA, April 30, 1993, Magnaghi Papers, In.

36. A. P. Nasatir, review of *Herbert E. Bolton: The Historian and the Man, 1870-1953*, by John F. Bannon, *Hispanic American Historical Review* 50 (1979): 499.

37. John Caughey to Bolton, 11/14/1930, Bolton Papers, In.

38. For a in-depth study of two of these universities, see Magnaghi, *The History of the Americas at Two Jesuit Universities.*

39. For a detailed study of this problem, see ibid.

40. William C. Binkley to Bolton, 01/04/1945, Bolton Papers, In.

41. Adele Ogden and Engel Sluiter, eds., *Greater America: Essays in Honor of Herbert Eugene Bolton* (Berkeley: University of California Press, 1945), iii.

42. Lewis Hanke, review of *Greater America: Essays in Honor of Herbert Eugene Bolton*, edited by Adele Ogden and Engel Sluiter, *American Historical Review* 52 (1946): 205.

43. Bolton highlighted a variety of topics that could be studied: "Who has written the history of the introduction of European plants and animals into the Western Hemisphere as a whole, or of the spread of cattle and horse raising from Patagonia to Labrador? Who has written on a Western Hemisphere scale the history of shipbuilding and commerce, mining, Christian missions, Indian policies, slavery and emancipation, constitutional development, arbitration, the effects of the Indian on European cultures, the rise of the common man, art, architecture, literature, or science? Who has tried to state the significance of the frontier in terms of the Americas?" Bolton, "The Epic of Greater America," 473.

44. Bannon, *Colonial North America — A Short History* (St. Louis: St. Louis University Press, 1946).

45. Charles H. Lippy et al., *Christianity Comes to the Americas, 1492-1776* (New York: Paragon House, 1992).

46. Bannon to Bolton, 02/16/1948, Bolton Papers, In.

47. John F. Bannon. *History of the Americas*, vol. 1. *The Colonial Americas* (New York: McGraw-Hill, 1952), viii.

48. Bannon to Bolton, 08/21/1952, Bolton Papers, In.

49. Bannon noted that through the years McGraw-Hill sold well over 50,000 copies of the book.

50. John F. Bannon, "JFB, Historian," 12. For another autobiographical statement, see "A Western Historian — How He Got That Way," *Western Historical Quarterly* 1 (1970): 246.

51. John F. Bannon, *History of the Americas*, rev. ed. 2 vols. (New York: McGraw-Hill, 1963), 2:vi.

52. Vera Brown Holmes, *A History of the Americas: From Discovery to Nationhood*, 2 vols. (New York: Ronald Press, 1950-1964), 1:v.

53. Ibid.

54. Harold E. Davis, *The Americas in History* (New York: Ronald Press, 1953), v.

55. George W. Brown, J.M.S. Careless, Gerald M. Craig, and Eldon Ray, eds., *Canada and the Americas* (Toronto: J. M. Dent, 1953), vi.

56. Two extremely useful studies on the work of the Pan-American Institute of Geography and History that were used in this section are Héctor José Tanzi, "Historiografía americana," *Revista de historia de América* 104 (1987): 102-108; and Pedro Armillas, *A Program of the History of the New World Coordinator's Summary Reports*. Vol. 1, *The Native Period in the History of the New World*, trans. Glenda Crevenna and Theo Crevenna, assisted by Eric Wolf, Publication no. 108 (México, DF: Pan-American Institute of Geography and History, 1962), vii-x.

57. Armillas, *The Native Period*, viii.

58. The researchers for the first phase included the following: Native Period — Miguel Acosta Saignes, Ignacio Bernal, Henry B. Collins, James B. Griffin, Fernando Márquez Miranda, Gerardo Reichel-Dolmatoff, Luis E. Valcárcel, Emilio Willems, and Hannah M. Wormington; the Colonial Period — Mariano Picón Salas, José Honório Rodrigues, Max Savelle, Charles Verlinden, and Silvio Zavala; the National Period — John W. Caughey, Américo Jacobina Lacombe, Enrique Ortega Ricaurte, Eugenio Pereira Salas, and María del Carmen Velásquez.

59. Sidney Painter, "The Washington Meeting, 1952," *American Historical Review* 58 (1953): 758; Richard P. McCormick, "The New York Meeting, 1954," *American Historical Review* 60 (1955): 735; Charles Gibson, "Pan-American Institute of Geography and History," *Hispanic American Historical Review* 37 (1957): 146-149. Historians who presented papers or commented at the AHA session on the Americas program were John F. Bannon, S.J.; Samuel F. Bemis; Harold A. Bierck; Robert N. Burr; Ernest Burrus, S.J.; John W. Caughey; Howard F. Cline; Merle Curti; Harold E. Davis; Bailey Diffie; Charles Gibson; William H. Grey; Charles C. Griffin; Vera Brown Holmes; Roland D. Hussey; Roy F. Nichols; J. H. Parry; Max Savelle; Alfred B. Thomas; and Arthur P. Whitaker.

60. Woodrow W. Borah, review of *The Native Period in the History of the New World*, by Pedro Armillas, *American Historical Review* 69 (1964): 851-852; William Madsen, review of *The Native Period in the History of the New World*, by Pedro Armillas, *Hispanic American Historical Review* 44 (1964): 405-407.

61. Silvio Zavala, *A Program of the History of the new World Coordinator's Summary Reports*. Abr. ed. Vol. 2, *The Colonial Period in the History of the New World*, trans. Max Savelle, Publication no. 102 1962 (Westport, CT: Greenwood Press, 1983).

62. Stanley J. Stein, review of *The Colonial Period in the History of the New World*, by Silvio Zavala, *American Historical Review* 68 (1963): 757-758; J. Preston Moore,

review of *The Colonial Period in the History of the New World*, by Silvio Zavala, *Hispanic American Historical Review* 43 (1963): 546-547.

63. Charles C. Griffin, *A Program of the History of the New World Coordinator's Summary Reports*. Vol. 3, *The National Period in the History of the New World: An Outline and Commentary*, Publication no. 103 (New York: Greenwood Press, 1990).

64. Dexter Perkins, review of *The National Period in the History of the New World*, by Charles C. Griffin, *American Historical Review* 69 (1964): 467-468; Donald E. Worcester, review of *The National Period in the History of the New World*, by Charles C. Griffin, *Hispanic American Historical Review* 43 (1963): 144-145.

65. Guillermo Morón, "Informe sobre proyecto de historia general de América," *Revista de historia de América* 90 (1980), 61-66; Guillermo Morón to Magnaghi, Magnaghi Papers In, 01/21/98.

66. This series began under the editorship of Henry Steele Commager and Richard B. Morris.

67. Texts: Charles Gibson, *Spain in America* (New York: Harper & Row, 1966); W. J. Eccles, *France in America* (New York: Harper & Row, 1972); David B. Quinn, *North America from Earliest Discovery to First Settlements: The Norse Voyages to 1612* (New York: Harper & Row, 1977). Documentary readers: Charles Gibson, ed., *The Spanish Tradition in America* (New York: Harper & Row, 1968); Yves F. Zoltvany, ed., *The French Tradition in America* (New York: Harper & Row, 1969); David B. Quinn, ed., *North American Discovery, Circa 1000-1612* (New York: Harper & Row, 1971).

68. These volumes were originally published by Holt, Rinehart and Winston; later, rights were turned over to the University of New Mexico Press. See John F. Bannon, *The Spanish Borderlands Frontier, 1513-1821* (New York, 1970); Alistair Hennessy, *The Frontier in Latin American History* (Albuquerque, 1978); W. J. Eccles, *The Canadian Frontier, 1534-1760* (rev. ed., Albuquerque, 1983); David J. Weber, *The Mexican Frontier, 1821-1846: The American Southwest Under Mexico* (Albuquerque, 1982); and A. H. Gibson and John S. Whitehead, *Yankees in Paradise: The Pacific Basin Frontier* (Albuquerque, 1993).

6

The Concept Flourishes

The period since the 1970s has not been one of unbroken decline for Boltonians or comparative historians. In fact, the opposite is true. The idea of American "exceptionalism" — an exaggerated sense of uniqueness "not just as different, but as specially or providentially blessed" — has been questioned. Since the 1960s, Europe and the United States have closed in on the standard of living and degrees of freedom and democratic political stability. Furthermore, the Vietnam conflict had many people questioning American moral character. As a result, historians began to move away from purely nationalistic history whose goals were to inculcate patriotism and national identity.[1] Something of a comparative history renaissance began in the 1980s. Terms such as "ultranational historians"; "global, transnational, and world history"; and "American exceptionalism" are commonly found in mainstream historical journals. There is a growing interest in and awareness of the need for studying history both comparatively and on a hemispheric level. Throughout the Americas, this interest has been realized and developed among scholars and educators, academic institutions and organizations, and publishers and governmental agencies.

A focus on comparative history goes back to the 1950s and 1960s when historians rethought the role of this concept.[2] By 1958 there was enough interest in the field for the establishment of the journal *Comparative Studies in Society and History*. Throughout the 1960s comparative studies developed in the field of slavery in the Americas. Within the decade a number of edited works blossomed. There was Lewis Hanke's *Do the Americas Have A Common History?*; Louis Hartz edited *Founding New Societies*; and C. Vann Woodward followed with *The Comparative Approach to American History*. In 1969 Robert F. Berkhofer, Jr., wrote *A Behavioral Approach to*

Historical Analysis, which addressed some of the theoretical aspects of comparative historical analysis.

As the 1970s passed, the interest in comparative history continued. In 1974 Richard P. McCormick presented an insightful review of the comparative method as it is applied to American history.[3] This was an important development in the fieldbecause at the time many of the educators working the Americas field were passing from the scene.

The revival began in earnest in 1980. George M. Fredrickson led the way with a study titled "Comparative History." For him there "is a relatively small but significant body of scholarship that has *as its main objective* the systematic comparison of some process or institution in two or more societies that are not usually conjoined within one of the traditional geographical areas of historical specialization."[4] Much of what Fredrickson postulated fits the Boltonian concept. The October 1980 issue of the *American Historical Review* was devoted to comparative history, a topic that had been the focus of a program during the 1978 meeting of the American Historical Association. In December 1982 Peter Kolchin joined the discussion in an article titled "Comparing American History." He closed his study optimistically: "The comparative consciousness that now exists is in itself a major sign of progress and explicit comparison has yielded positive results in a number of areas."[5]

In December 1983, in his American Historical Association presidential address, Philip D. Curtin attacked the narrow specialization that plagues historians in the late twentieth century. He called for a broader synthesis of history to enable students to better understand the world they live in. Curtin concluded with a strong Boltonian position: "It can be argued that the fullest understanding of New World history requires a comparative study...." He was reaffirming the views presented in 1945 by a predecessor, Carleton J. H. Hayes.[6]

For decades there had been a debate over the question of the role and value of American exceptionalism, transnational history, and comparative history.[7] This debate blossomed in the 1980s and 1990s. In 1985 Raymond Grew argued that American historiography was more parochial than others. He was followed by A. A. Van Den Braembussche, who provided an excellent discussion of the varieties of comparative history.[8] In October 1991 the prestigious American Historical Association took up the "questions of comparative history and explore[d] the ways in which ideas originating in one part of the world affect and give conceptual shape to events (and perception of events) taking place elsewhere." In the *AHR Forum,* Australian scholar Ian Tyrrell and Indiana University professor Michael McGerr dealt with American exceptionalism and transnational history. This was followed in 1993 by Michael Kammen's in-depth reconsideration of the matter.[9] John Higham has looked at multiculturalism, the role of transnational history, and future directions to be taken by American historians.[10] In 1995 Michael Geyer and Charles Bright discussed "world history in a global age," going far beyond national limitations.[11]

If some historians are interested in a global outlook, others are concerned with comparative hemispheric history. Latin American historian Magnus Mörner and two graduate students, Julia Fawaz de Viñuela and John D. French, provided an insightful look at comparative history in general and how it relates to Latin America. The work is a useful synthesis and provides ideas for further study.[12] Several years later, Professor Tyrrell acknowledged the legacy of Bolton. He wrote that Bolton had "treated, on a slightly smaller scale, the transnational interaction of cultures in the Spanish borderlands and went on to propose a hemispheric approach to American studies." Unfortunately, this "grand transnational historiography" failed because it fell between United States and Latin American history, and Bolton's colonial emphasis was avoided by historians focused on the national historical tradition. Tyrrell concluded that further historical investigation could be directed toward "the impact of the United States on Latin America, the comparative history of revolution and state making in the New World, and the cultural interchange between Hispanic America and the United States in the 'borderlands' region from Texas to California," and the continental focus of Canadian-American studies.[13]

Richard Maxwell Brown issued another clarion call for comparison in his presidential address to the Western Historical Association in 1992. He noted that the development of the American West could be studied comparatively in Canada, Mexico, Chile, or Argentina.[14] Richard W. Slatta, who took his direction from Bolton's 1932 call for a comparative study of the cattle frontier from "Patagonia to Labrador," developed a monograph, *Cowboys of the Americas*, thus proving Brown correct in his assessment.[15] This work is typical of many developed during the 1990s that treat specific topics in a comparative approach.

Clearly, neo-Boltonians are still alive and well. Albert L. Hurtado and David J. Weber, among others, continue to promote the incorporation of the Hispanic story into United States history, which is an aspect of the history of the Americas.[16] In the spring of 1993 Weber, the dean of the Spanish Borderlands historians, lamented that the Hispanic focus on United States history remained "fuzzy." Too few academic historians were working in the field of Spanish North American history, and new scholarship had not yet been integrated into history texts. As Weber saw it, "Although the United States has always been a multi-cultural society, in American popular culture and in most general histories, the American past has been understood as the story of English America rather than as the stories of the diverse cultures that make up our national heritage."[17]

The analysis of a comparative approach to national and hemispheric history, especially in response to the emphasis on multiculturalism among historians and educators, was not limited to neo-Boltonians. Colonial historian James Axtell, of the College of William and Mary noted that historians had failed to reconstruct early America as it actually looked and was perceived by the colonists. "One way to do this is to serve not only as *American* colonial historians but as historians of *colonial America* by enlarging our perspective beyond anachronistic political boundaries."[18] Further, these colonies and later nations were extensions of Europe and its culture and mores, and were "sustainers and mature models for comparison." Historians should shift their focus to cultural forces, and frontiers should be seen as anthropologists see them: "as fluid points of human contact between culture-bearing ethnic groups." Axtell stressed the importance of using ethnohistory, which "provides an invaluable key to the interlocking histories of American's colonial frontiers."

Joyce Appleby raised the question of internationalizing American history in her 1992 presidential address, "Recovering America's Historic Diversity: Beyond Exceptionalism," which was presented before the Organization of American Historians.[19] This was followed by an extensive round table discussion, "Toward the Internationalization of American History," which includes comments from a group of multinational historians.[20] Two years later, in his article, "Why the West Is Lost," Professor James A. Hijiya of the University of Massachusetts, Dartmouth called for a broader approach in the teaching of American history.[21] The forum that followed provided critical insights into Hijiya's concerns and stimulated further debate on the subject.[22]

Taking a different position, William F. Sater, of California State University, Long Beach, called for the integration of Latin American history into the teaching of world history. In order to best accomplish this, Dr. Sater recommended that the comparative approach be used for certain themes, such as slavery.[23] In writing about a new approach in teaching American history as directed by the Bradley Commission, Thomas Bender, of New York University, discussed the problem of a strictly national history and called for relating and integrating the parts to the whole. Professor Bender thought that such an approach would provide wider meaning and significance to particular events, institutions, and objects in national history.[24] And Natalie Zemon Davis, professor emeritus at Princeton, developed a series of articles in the American Historical Association newsletter, *Perspective* in which she discussed "Who Owns History?" In the course of her comments about the introduction of new concepts into the teaching of history, she reflected Bolton's comments on "ultranational historians" when she wrote about how "Established national traditions resent interlopers...."[25]

If the Boltonian history of the Americas course is no longer popular, many colleges and universities in the United States do offer comparative approaches to topics in history, and a select number of institutions still teach the history of the Americas or aspects of this concept.[26] Today, more colleges and universities are seeking historians to teach comparative history than in the past.[27]

Comparative history has become popular in other academic settings. Since 1991 the University of South Florida in Tampa has offered a biennial conference whose theme is "Culture, Technology and Change in the Americas." Harvard University's Charles Warren Center for Studies in American History has been offering seminars since 1996. Young, multinational historians engaged in creative research on aspects of Atlantic history are invited to attend ten day seminars and present papers, discuss, and exchange ideas with peers and senior scholars. The Renaissance Studies Conference at the City University of New York had as its 1997 theme "Early Modern Trans-Atlantic Encounters: England, Spain, and the Americas." The Rockefeller Foundation, through its Humanities Fellowships for 1997-1999, supported "scholars and writers engaged in research on transnational social and cultural issues, non-Western cultures, and the diverse cultural heritage of the United States." Assisting in this direction are a number of centers that take a comparative approach. At the University of Toronto, the Centre for the Study of Religion promotes a comparative approach to the subject. The Indigenous Research Center of the Americas at the University of California, Davis, has an "interdisciplinary and interdepartmental research program which is committed to the study of and by indigenous people and to the understanding of their politics within the growing process of globalization." The Center believes that its "unique hemispheric methodological approach focuses on the historical and spatial dimensions that provide a thorough comprehension of the cultural and social complexity of contemporary indigenous people."[28] In 1944 the Institute of Early American History and Culture in Williamsburg, Virginia diversified its fifty year old agenda to embrace a larger range of colonial subjects in it programs and publications. The University of Iowa has a Center for International and Comparative Studies, Johns Hopkins has long had a program in Atlantic History and Culture, and the John Carter Brown Library, with the largest collection of printed material related to the colonial Americas has developed a Center for New World Comparative Studies. The idea of comparative programs and symposia dealing with the hemisphere has become a reality. For instance, in October 1996 the Library of Congress sponsored a symposium titled "Imaging the City in the Americas: Washington, DC, and Mexico City, 1910." Scholars from a variety of backgrounds looked at the urbanization of both capitals. In April 1998 the Henry Huntington Library at San Marino, California offered its second biennial meeting, "The Forum on European Expansion and Global Interaction." In November 1999, the Tenth Meeting of the Conference of Mexican, United States, and Canadian Historians will meet at Dallas-Forth Worth, with the theme "Migration in North American History."

Other organizations are striving to promote the study of the hemisphere.

The Resource Center, which was established in the early 1980s and is based in Minneapolis, has as its goal helping Americans grasp the intricate connections between peoples of the Americas. This non-profit organization of more than 1,300 members provides educational resources, links individuals and grass roots groups across national borders, and reveals relations within and between the Americas.[29]

The University of Miami established the North-South Center in 1984. Congressman Dante Fascell, a University of Miami Law School graduate who represented this district, sought to create a center modeled on the East-West Center located in Honolulu, which receives federal funding. In 1991 the North-South Center greatly expanded its operations with funding from the U.S. Congress aimed at improving inter-American relations. Unfortunately, since that time budget austerity has cut the funding. "The mission of the North-South Center is to promote better relations and serve as a catalyst for change among the United States, Canada, and the nations of Latin America and the Caribbean by advancing knowledge and understanding of the major political, social, economic, and cultural issues affecting the nations and peoples of the Western Hemisphere." The Center published the first issue of its journal, *North-South: The Magazine of the Americas,* in 1990, and it has created the North-South Center Press. Its thrust is a broad approach to affairs throughout the Americas in terms of trade, international relations, and foreign policy.[30]

Cornell University's American Indian Program has taken a broad approach and presents the indigenous people of the Americas. Since the spring of 1984 its Akwe:kon Press has published *Akwe:kon, A Journal of Indigenous Issues.* In the spring of 1995 the title of the journal to *Native Americas* to accurately reflect that approach.

A careful survey uncovers many services and organizations that deal with a broader approach to the hemisphere. The journal *Locus,* a University of North Texas Press publication, specializes in articles "that deal with regional or local history of the Americas." Organizations like Turning Tide Productions of Wendell, Massachusetts, are creating videos dealing with multi-cultural and social issues throughout the Americas.[31]

The federal government in the United States has stressed the idea of hemispheric unity going back to the Monroe Doctrine. In December 1994, President Bill Clinton hosted the Summit of the Americas in Miami, which leaders from throughout the hemisphere attended. Prior to the Summit, Vice President Al Gore hosted an *encuentro* of cultural leaders from throughout the hemisphere, titled "A New Moment in the Americas." It was held in Washington, DC, and promoted the concept of closer relations with the United States' neighbors in the hemisphere.[32]

During 1930-1998 there was an outpouring of publications, both journals and monographs, dealing with the history of the Americas and comparative history in general.[33] They have included everything from general histories to topical and interpretative studies.[34] The two largest categories are general studies or textbooks and interpretative works. Three other topics, averaging twenty-three items each were Africans/slavery, economy, and Indians. During the 1990s a plethora of books and articles have been published on the Americas theme. This was especially true at the time of the commemoration of the Columbian Quincentennial in 1992. (See Table 6.1.)

Table 6.1
Americas-Related Publications

Years	Numbers
1553-1795	9
1812-1898	25
1903-1907	3
1910-1919	15
1920-1929	8
1930-1939	30
1940-1949	49
1950-1959	40
1960-1969	58
1970-1979	70
1980-1989	55
1990-1998	125

Three works are models of the types of broadly based studies available to American educational institutions that provide a comparative historical approach. The *Encyclopedia of the North American Colonies* gives the student of United States colonial history a better appreciation of the multifaceted nature of this portion of national history.[35] In 1996, Lester D. Langley published *The Americas in the Age of Revolution, 1750-1850*, which followed Bolton's 1932 call for a comparative approach to hemispheric topics. It is a model for a relatively untouched theme in hemispheric history— revolution and nation-building. In a attempt to bring a comparative approach into United States history survey classes, Houghton Mifflin published Carl J. Guarneri's two-volume reader, *America Compared: American History in International Perspective*. Its goal is to present United States history in a global context based on comparative readings on key issues.[36]

In Canada, policy toward the Americas has gone through changes since the late 1950s. Initially Canada was not a member of the Organization of American States, and interest in Latin American affairs was minuscule. As a result of immigration, Canada has a population with varied ethnic and cultural background and experiences. This national diversity has led historians away from the nation-building approach. It has been replaced by a focus on the board Canadian experience that "has produced a continent-wide entity identifiable in its very pluralism, constraints, and compromises."[37] Today Canadian historians are writing about the European community, the United States, and the Third World and their relationship to Canada.

Prior to the end of the Cold War in 1989, for business, security, and other reasons, Canada remained disengaged from Latin America. The public perception of the region was best summed up by the "four "Ds": debts, dictatorships, drugs, deforestation. Then a reversal in attitude occurred; interests and policy began with Canada's entry into the Organization of American States in 1990, and within a year negotiations began among Canada-Mexico-United States that led to the signing of the North American Free Trade Agreement (NAFTA). The activation of NAFTA on January 1, 1994, consolidated Canada's position vis-à-vis the nations south of the United States, "a region of growth and potential rather than economic and political crisis." Subsequently the partnership linking Canada and Mexico has been the object of newspaper articles and public interest.[38]

Interest in the history of the Americas has survived in Canadian collegiate classrooms. One of the original Canadian historians teaching the history of the Americas from the Bolton era was Professor Edward E. Adair, at McGill University in Montreal. He taught "General History of North and South America" until the early 1950s.[39] Professor Hereward Senior continued to teach the course at McGill until 1964-1965. After that time, it was split into two sections, and Dr. Senior taught the South American section until 1977. In 1958-1959, Dr. Senior taught the course at Memorial University in St. John's, Newfoundland.[40]

In 1972, Canadian representatives on the History Commission of the Pan-American Institute of Geography and History promoted a seminar with an inter-American theme. Held at Laval University in Quebec City in March, the seminar dealt with "Colonial Institutions in the Americas of the 18th Century."[41]

The noted historian Professor W. J. Eccles stated that Adair's course influenced him to go into the history of New France. His many influential articles and monographs left a mark on the French colonial story. Because many of these were written in English, they were available to scholars south of the Canadian border. Prior to his retirement from the University of Toronto, Eccles and a colleague, W. H. Nelson, promoted a comparative historical approach. Graduate students who chose English or French colonial history as a topic for their thesis prepared to be examined in both fields at their comprehensive examinations. Both professors hoped that eventually New Spain and Brazil would be included in the sequence, but this was never realized.[42]

A 1993 survey of higher education institutions throughout Canada showed that interest in comparative history was alive and well. Of the thirty-four institutions surveyed,[43] eighteen (52.9%) taught some type of comparative history course dealing directly with the Americas and 23.5 percent taught a topical hemispheric course. This interest in the Americas approach is surprising, given Canada's previous limited focus in the hemisphere.

Canada has taken steps to bridge the gap between herself and the countries of Latin America and the Caribbean. An agreement between the University of Ottawa and the National University of Rosario in Argentina led to the publication *Les discours du Nouveau Monde au XIXᵉ siècle au Canada français et en Amérique Latine* in 1995. This publication presents comparative history dealing with topics in Argentina, Brazil, Canada, Chile, and Mexico.[44]

The Canadian Foundation of the Americas (FOCAL), an independent, non-profit organization based in Ottawa, was founded in 1990. Through its regional offices in Fredericton, New Brunswick; Ste. Foy, Quebec; and Calgary, Alberta, it has formed outreach programs that host conferences and disseminate information in order to maintain dialogue at the economic and political levels. In cooperation with Carleton University Press, through its "Changing Americas Series,"[45] FOCAL is publishing monographs dealing with Canadian-oriented inter-American topics; the organization also publishes *FOCAL Papers* and *FOCAL Update*. More specialized organizations include the Inter-American Organization for Higher Education and the Inter-American Institute for Cooperation on Agriculture. For a nation that was reluctant to get involved in the affairs of the Americas, Canada has made a rapid turnaround in its outlook.

The study of the history of the Americas in Latin America has paralleled North American developments. In the 1950s during the hemispheric heyday of the history of the Americas, Bolton's syllabus remained an indispensable source. In 1950, Francisco Morales Padrón sought permission to translate the syllabus into Spanish so that it could be used throughout Latin America. The project seemed to have died when Morales wanted Ginn & Company to publish the Spanish edition without the company having the necessary marketing ability.[46]

In Mexico, a course in the history of the Americas has been all but nonexistent since it was taught in the 1930s-1940s at the National Autonomous University of Mexico. Usually the issue is divided between Latin American and Anglo American history. However, the appropriately named University of the Americas in Puebla does have such a course focused on the colonial era.[47]

If teaching of hemispheric history has declined, interest in it is still strong among Mexican scholars. The historian Silvio Zavala and the philosopher Leopoldo Zea remain leading authorities in the field. Professor Zavala has played a pivotal role through his work with the Pan-American Institute of Geography and History and as the founder of *Revista de historia de América*, whose goal it was to develop a broad interpretation of hemispheric history.[48] Professor Zea, Mexico's most distinguished philosopher, has looked at the intellectual aspects of the Americas. In 1957 he published his seminal work, *América en la historia*, which explores the significance of the Americas in relation to universal history. It was translated into English thirty-five years later.[49]

The National Autonomous University of Mexico has been the site of colloquia that presented comparative themes. In 1994 the 17th International Colloquium on Art History's theme was "Art History and Identity in America: Comparative Visions," which was subsequently published.[50]

Elsewhere in Latin America, the presentation of this broad approach to the history of the hemisphere depends on the nation. In the 1990s Venezuela's elementary and secondary schools do not teach the history of the Americas as a separate topic. When it does appear, it is presented in a chapter on nineteenth- and twentieth-century developments in the "universal history" program. Two undergraduate history programs exist, one at the Central University of Venezuela in Caracas and the other at the University of the Andes in Mérida; both include an option in the "History of the Americas.

The other two options are "universal" and "Venezuelan" history. Two master's degree programs include an option in the "History of the Americas." One is available at the Institute of Hispanic-American Studies at the Central University of Venezuela and the other at the Catholic University Andrés Bello. Some years ago, the Institute for Historical Investigation was established at the latter, and it has developed a master's program concentrating on the history of the Americas.[51] In Chile, where there is a long historic connection with hemispheric history, the history of the Americas is taught only in teacher education schools.[52] The Catholic Pontifical University and the University of San Marcos in Peru teach courses on the history of America as well.[53] Argentina has seen a rise and decline in the history of the Americas as a requirement in secondary and college experiences. Since the 1860s, the history of America and Argentina has been a popular course. However, this course has primarily stressed national history; the American portion has been limited to the themes of discovery and independence in Latin America and the United States. Variations on this theme continue into the present, and comparative history is stressed in the department of United States Studies at the University of Palermo in Buenos Aires.[54]

In the 1960s the Bolton concept received little attention among Brazilian historians although they were sympathetic to the concept even if they did not know it by name. Hélio Vianna of the University of Brazil published a statement in 1932 titled "Bases sociológicas da formação americana." In it he insisted that despite certain political and social similarities in historical evolution, the English-, Portuguese-, and Spanish-speaking peoples of America are fundamentally different from one another.[55]

Brazil is interested in comparative history not only in the hemisphere but topically throughout the world. The Center for North American Studies at Cándido Mendes University in Rio de Janeiro promotes such an effort. In 1994 the Center had workshops, conferences, and research programs directed toward issues related to Brazilian-North American relations. Professors at the Federal Fluminense University in Niterói, Brazil are undertaking studies of a comparative nature, such as indigenous uprisings in the United States and Brazil. The Catholic Pontifical University, Rio de Janeiro, is undertaking a comparative study of slavery, and professors are following a similar course in comparative history.[56]

A few titles illustrate the fact that specialized themes within the Americas concept are being published in Latin America and Spain. In 1985 Hebe Clementi wrote a classic four-volume study, *La Frontera en América*, which focuses on the role of the frontier throughout the Americas.[57] The idea of a monumental, traditional, four-volume *Historia de las Américas* was realized in 1991 by the Spanish through the generosity of the University of Seville, the Alhambra Longman publishing house, and the State Society for the Quincentenary.[58] This work, running over 3,000 pages, covers the history of the Americas "from Columbus to the present and from pole to pole," to quote Bolton. Arturo Chavolla looked at the idea of America in European thought from Oviedo to Hegel in his work *La idea de América*, published in 1993.[59]

Besides the nations of the Western Hemisphere, a number of other nations have been focusing on the Americas concept. In Spain, the study of the Americas is centered in Seville, the colonial gateway to the New World and the home of the Archives of the Indies. Although such studies preceded the Columbian Quadcentennial in 1892, this event acted as a catalyst for the development of American studies. During the twentieth century, numerous Hispanic America centers and institutes have been established in the city.[60] Scholars have produced a wealth of journal articles and monographs, and other centenary events have been commemorated with symposia, congresses, and round tables. Seville remains at the forefront of Americas studies in Spain.[61]

In Italy, the Italian Society of the History of the Americas was founded in 1978 at the University of Turin. This national organization, with some thirty member institutions where the history of either North or Latin America is taught, coordinates teaching, colloquia and publications on the Americas. The Society also publishes *Rivista di storia delle Americhe* (Review of the History of the Americas). The University of Genoa is home to the non-profit Euro-Atlantic Center. The Center's multidisciplinary interests are organized around broad topics: federalism, citizenship, ethnicity, collective identity and multiculturalism in Canada, the United States, and Europe. Its doctoral program in the history of the Americas is the only one offered in Italy. In Chengdu, China, the Southwest Jiaotong University is home to the Center for American Cultural/Cross-Cultural Studies, which stresses comparative or cross-cultural communications.[62]

In the 1990s, scholars from the Americas and the world at large have written about the concept of the Americas and its differences. S. N. Eisenstadt, professor of sociology at Hebrew University in Jerusalem, looked at the great divergence of economic patterns throughout the Americas and based the difference on religious factors. Aníbal Quijano, from the University of San Marcos, Peru, and Immanuel Wallerstein, from SUNY Binghamton, developed a thoughtful analysis of the Americas and their role in the future. Finally, writing in the *Australasian Journal of American Studies*, Jim Levy and Peter Ross made a comparative analysis of the economy of the Americas, the politics of industrialization, the military, and the Indian "problem." Interest in the concept of the Americas is alive among scholars around the world, although few of them know of Bolton, his earlier work, or his promotion of the Americas concept.[63]

Bolton's idea of exchanges of students and professors among academic institutions throughout the Americas continued to be pursued. Between 1992 and 1996, three meetings were held with educators from the United States, Canada, and Mexico. The United States called the first meeting and pushed for trilateral programs in which faculty and students would be exchanged by academic institutions. Unfortunately, economic problems in Mexico and Canada, a downsizing of government spending by the U.S. Congress, and a lack of interest by American educators, brought the proposal to a halt. When the educators met in April 1996, out of 1000, only 125 were from the United States. The idea was to seek funding from private sources and push ahead with the concept.[64]

On the eve of the twenty-first century, Bolton's course on the history of the Americas has all but vanished from most colleges, except in Canada. Even his name as the father of the Americas concept is recognized by few younger historians. However, all of the evidence shows that the comparative approach to the history of the Western Hemisphere is alive and thriving in a variety of historical venues. With renewed vigor, historians around the world are seriously discussing the question of comparative hemispheric history. The concept has gained a flourishing new life through publications, symposia, institutional programs, and other formats. As educators prepare new teachers to deal with multiculturalism, transnational, and global history, this hemispheric approach should find an expanded life in the twenty-first century, reaching far beyond the dreams of Bolton. In the words of C. Vann Woodward, this is "one of the most exciting periods of American historical scholarship for a century."[65]

NOTES

1. Gordon S. Wood, "Doing the Continental," *The New York Review of Books* 44.18 (November 20, 1997): 51; Carl J. Guarneri, "Reconsidering C. Vann Woodward's *The Comparative Approach to American History*," *Reviews in American History* 23.3 (September 1995): 552-563.

2. For a historiography of the works produced in comparative history, see the Appendix.

3. Richard P. McCormick, "The Comparative Method: Its Application to American History," *Mid-America* 56 (1974): 231-247.

4. George M. Fredrickson, "Comparative History," in *The Past Before Us: Contemporary Historical Writing in the United States*, ed. Michael Kammen (Ithaca, NY: Cornell University Press, 1980), 457-473.

5. Peter Kolchin, "Comparing American History," *Reviews in American History* 10 (1982): 64-81.

6. Philip D. Curtin, "Depth, Span, and Relevance," *American Historical Review* 89 (1984): 1-9; Carlton J. H. Hayes, "The American Frontier—Frontier of What?" *American Historical Review* 51 (1946): 199-216.

7. American exceptionalism is the idea that the United States historical experience, based on the merger of the republican and millennia traditions, is special and exists "outside" the norms of historiography. Transnational history is based on the idea that "national boundaries have been subordinated to the analysis of regional economies and viewpoints that reflect the local environment" (see Tyrrell, "American Exceptionalism," 1038, in notes).

8. Raymond Grew, "The Comparative Weakness of American History," *Journal of Interdisciplinary History* 16 (1986): 87-101; A. A. Van Den Braembussche, "Historical Explanation and Comparative Method: Towards a Theory of the History of Society," *History and Theory* 28 (1989): 1-24.

9. Ian Tyrrell, "American Exceptionalism in an Age of International History," and Michael McGerr, "The Price of the 'New Transnational History,'" *American Historical Review* 96 (1991): 1031-1055, 1056-1072; Michael Kammen, "The Problem of American Exceptionalism: A Reconsideration," *American Quarterly* 45 (1993): 1-43.

10. John Higham, "Multiculturalism and Universalism: A History and Critique," *American Quarterly* 45 (1993): 195-219; "The Future of American History," *Journal of American History* 80 (1994): 1289-1307.

11. Michael Geyer and Charles Bright, "World History in the Global Age," *American Historical Review* 100 (1995): 1034-1060.

12. Magnus Mörner, Julia Fawaz de Viñuela, and John D. French, "Comparative Approaches to Latin American History," *Latin American Research Review* 17 (1982): 55-89.

13. Tyrrell, "American Exceptionalism," 1039-1041.

14. Richard Maxwell Brown, "Western Violence: Structure, Values, Myth," *Western Historical Quarterly* 24 (1993): 13.

15. Richard W. Slatta, *Cowboys of the Americas* (New Haven: Yale University Press, 1990), 1.

16. Albert L. Hurtado, "Parkmanizing the Spanish Borderlands: Bolton, Turner, and the Historians' World," *Western Historical Quarterly* 26 (1995): 149-168; David J. Weber, "Turner, the Boltonians, and the Borderlands," *American Historical Review* 91 (1986): 66-81; *The Spanish Frontier in North America* (New Haven: Yale University Press, 1992).

17. David J. Weber, "Our Hispanic Past: A Fuzzy View Persists," *The Chronicle of Higher Education* 10 (March 1993): A44. Professor Weber has discussed the role of Borderlands history as part of United States history. See *The Spanish Frontier in North America*, 335-360.

18. James Axtell, "A North American Perspective for Colonial History," *History Teacher* 12.4 (1979): 550.

19. Joyce Appleby, "Recovering America's Historic Diversity: Beyond Exceptionalism," *Journal of American History* 79.2 (September 1992): 419-431.

20. "Toward the Internationalization of American History: A Round Table," *Journal of American History* 79.2 (September 1992): 432-532.

21. James A. Hijiya, "Why the West Is Lost," *The William and Mary Quarterly* 51.2 (April 1994): 276-292.

22. "Forum: 'Why the West Is Lost,'" *The William and Mary Quarterly* 51.4 (October 1994): 717-754.

23. William F. Sater, "Joining the Mainstream: Integrating Latin America into the Teaching of World History," *Perspectives* 33.5 (1995): 19-22, 37.

24. Thomas Bender, "Public Culture: Inclusion and Synthesis in American History," in *Historical Literacy: The Case for History in American Education*, ed. Paul Gagnon and the Bradley Commission on History in Schools (New York: Macmillan, 1989), 188-191.

25. Natalie Zemon Davis, "Who Owns History? History in the Profession," *Perspectives* 34.8 (November 1996): 1.

26. Recent developments in the teaching of the history of the Americas include the following: A straight history of the Americas course has been offered sporadically at Tulane University. After a twenty year hiatus, a history of the Americas course has been offered on a more regular basis at Northern Michigan University.

In 1988-1989 California State University, Hayward offered "Inter-American Relations," and in 1991-1992 Duke University offered a number of courses under the generic title, "Comparative Area Studies." Under this rubric, the following courses have been offered: "U.S. & Canadian Constitutional Issues;" "Atlantic Slave Trade;" "The Destruction and Aftermath of Slavery in America: A Comparative Perspective;" "Fugitive Slave (Maroon) Communities in New World Society;" "Slave Resistance and Social Control in New World Society;" "Slave Society in Colonial Anglo-America: The West Indies, South Carolina, Virginia;" and "History of Mexico and Spanish Caribbean in the 19th and 20th Centuries."

The University of Florida, Gainesville offered two general courses dealing with comparative history of the Americas: "Expansion of Europe: Exploration and Settlement, 1415-1650" and "Slavery in the New World: Comparative Perspectives." The University of California, Los Angeles no longer offers History 8; today only "Comparative Slavery Systems" remains. The same is true of the University of California, Santa Barbara, which offered "Comparative History of the

Americas," but in the fall of 1992 presented History 153, "Comparative Seaborne Empire, 1415-1700."

In the fall of 1996 the University of Michigan offered a new course, HS170, "New World's: Colonialism and Cultural Encounters," which broadly defined early American history and culture—encompassing Canada, the United States, Mexico and the Caribbean. A similar course is offered at Urbana College in Ohio. In 1997 Johns Hopkins University offered a post-doctoral fellowship in "Comparative Historical Development" under the auspices of the Sawyer Seminar Program of the Andrew W. Mellon Foundation. The inter-disciplinary seminar in comparative historical development was titled," National Cultures and the Construction of the Modern World." Students needed expertise in one or more of the following aspects of the Atlantic world (1500-1800): comparative colonization, formation of colonial cultures and societies, and evolution of diasporic communities. *Perspectives* 35 (May-June 1997): 45.

27. A review of the American Association's *Perspective* under "employment" best illustrates this new focus in academe. New York University sought a person in "Global" history, while the five institutions associated through Five Colleges, Inc.—Amherst College, Hampshire College, Mount Holyoke College, Smith College, and the University of Massachusetts at Amherst—desired "a crossdisciplinary comparativist in the study of the Americas...interested in such issues as migration, citizenship, and nation, and the intersections of these issues with changing definitions of class, race, ethnicity, gender, and sexuality." The Kellogg Institute for International Studies at Notre Dame University sought a comparative historian. The College of Liberal Arts and Sciences at the University of Kansas at Lawrence desired a director for their Indigenous Nations Studies Program. The individual would have to "direct a unique masters program focused on the indigenous peoples of the entire Western hemisphere." *Perspective* 36.1 (January 1998): 50, 52, 56-57.

28. Advertisements for the Rockefeller Foundation Humanities Fellowships, 1997-1999.

29. Over the years the Resource Center has developed the following publications: *Connection to the Americas* (1983), *Centroamérica: The Month in Review* (1985), *Latin American Resource Review* (1993), *Working Together: Labor Report on the Americas*, and *Educating about the Americas*.

30. Ambler H. Moss, Jr., to Magnaghi, 03/25/1996, Magnaghi Papers, In; *North-South Center, University of Miami* (Coral Gables, FL: North-South Center, 1996).

31. In a 1996 press release, Turning Tide Productions had the following video items in a partial list: *Columbus Didn't Discover Us*, which studies the impact of the Columbian legacy on the indigenous people from North, South, and Central America; *Futbolito: A Journey Through Central America*, a chronicle of five North American young people who travel through Guatemala and Nicaragua, waging peace with "Hacky Sack"; *Songs of the Talking Drum*, in which world beat musicians Tony Vacca and Tim Moran link contemporary jazz with its African roots, and African-American performance artist Andrea Hairston blends dramatic monologue, movement, and music to create a "jazz theater"; and *A Heritage Within*, which looks at the culture and heritage of Irish, French-Canadian, and Puerto Rican immigrants in one of America's first industrial mill towns.

32. Robert S. Leiken, ed., *A New Moment in the Americas* (New Brunswick, NJ:

Transaction, 1994), v-viii.

33. The Appendix is a Chrono-Bibliography that attempts to gather all of the works related to the concept of the history of the Americas in its broadest and narrowest senses. Although possibly incomplete, it does provide a sense of what has been published since the sixteenth century.

34. A review of the topics in publications published between 1930 and 1997 shows the following: African, agribusiness, Borderlands, boundaries, cattle/cowboys, church-state, comparative national studies, Conquest, culture, defense/solidarity, demography, dogs, drugs, economy, education, ethnicity, ethnogensis, Euro images, exploration, food, foreign relations, frontier, general works and texts, government/political theory, ideology, Indians, Indian slavery, interpretation, Jesuits, literature, medicine, music, Pan-Americanism, poverty, race, religion, revolution/liberation, society, travel, and urban development. Some topics could have appeared in several categories.

35. Jacob E. Cooke, ed., *Encyclopedia of the North American Colonies*, 3 vols. (New York: Scribner's, 1993).

36. Carl J. Guarneri, *America Compared: American History in International Perspective*, 2 vols. (Boston: Houghton Mifflin, 1997); "Out of Its Shell: Internationalizing the Teaching of United States History," *Perspectives* 35.2 (February 1997): 1, 5-8.

37. J. M. S. Careless, quoted in Carl Berger, *The Writing of Canadian History: Aspects of English-Canadian Historical Writing Since 1900* (Toronto: University of Toronto Press, 1986), 261-262.

38. *The Globe and Mail*, June 10, 1996; Alvina Ruprecht, ed., *The Reordering of Culture: Latin America, the Caribbean, and Canada in the Hood* (Ottawa: Carleton University Press, 1995), 3-11.

39. The course ran for two terms and covered New France to 1763, New Spain to 1821, England's thirteen American colonies, and the United States to the Civil War.

40. Hereward Senior to Magnaghi, 12/02/1993, Magnaghi Papers, In; Dr. Senior took the course, "General History of North and South America," in 1946-1947, and later, as a graduate student, served as a teaching assistant (1952-1953, 1953-1954).

41. *Les Institutions coloniales dans les Amériques au XVIIIᵉ siècle: Colloque / Colonial Institutions in the Americas of the 18th Century: Seminar.* Organized by the Canadian section of the historical commission of the Pan-American Institute of Geography and History. Laval University, March 6-10, 1972 (Mexico: L'Institut, 1974).

42. W. J. Eccles to Magnaghi, 03/13/1993, Magnaghi Papers, In.

43. Institutions surveyed: Bishop's University, University of British Columbia, University of Calgary, University of Cape Breton, Carleton University, Concordia University, Dalhousie University, Dawson College, University of Guelph, University College of Hearst, Lakehead University, Laurentian University, Laval University, Malaspina College, University of Manitoba, Moncton University, McGill University, University of Newfoundland, University of Ottawa, University of Prince Edward Island, University of Quebec at Three Rivers, Redeemer College, University of Regina, Royal Military College of Canada, Sainte-Anne University, University of Saskatchewan, St. Thomas University, Sherbrooke University, Wilfred Laurier University, University of Toronto, Trent University, University of Western

Ontario, Windsor University, and York University.

44. Marie Couillard and Patrick Imbert, eds., *Les Discours du Nouveau Monde au XIXe siècle au Canada français et en Amérique Latine* (New York: Legas, 1995).

45. FOCAL published its first volume, *Beyond Mexico*, in 1995, and others were planned. The purpose of the series is to explore the range and realities of Canada's involvement in the Americas. See: Jean Daudelin and Edgar J. Dosman, eds., *Beyond Mexico* (Ottawa: Carleton University Press, 1995), 2-11.

46. Richard H. Thornton to Bolton, 10/11/1950, 11/16/1950, Bolton Papers, In.

47. Felipe Castro to Magnaghi, 06/04/1996, Magnaghi Papers, In.

48. *Biobibliografía de Silvio Zavala* (Mexico City: El Colegio Nacional, 1993); Peter Bakewell, "An Interview with Silvio Zavala," trans. Dolores Gutiérrez Mills, *Hispanic American Historical Review* 62 (1982): 553-568.

49. Leopoldo Zea, *The Role of the Americas in History*, ed. Amy A. Oliver, trans. Sonja Karsen (Savage, MD: Rowman & Littlefield, 1992); see also Gustavo Vargas Martínez, comp., *Bibliografía de Leopoldo Zea* (Mexico City: Fondo de Cultura Económica, 1992).

50. Nikita L. Harwich to Magnaghi, 09/30/1993, Magnaghi Papers, In; Gustavo Curiel, Renato González Mello, and Juana Gutiérrez Haces, eds., *Arte, historia, e identidad en América: Visiones comparativas*, XVII Coloquio Internacional de Historia del Arte, 4 vols. (México, DF: Instituto de Investigaciones Estéticas, Universidad Nacional Autónoma de México, 1994).

51. Dirección General de los Estudios de Post-Grado, "Historia," 1990-91, Universidad Católica Andrés Bello, Magnaghi Papers, In.

52. Luis Celis Múñoz to Juan Ignacio González, 09/01/1993, Magnaghi Papers, In.

53. Oswaldo Holguín Callo to Magnaghi, 03/16/1994, Magnaghi Papers, In.

54. Augusto Montenegro González to Magnaghi, 07/02/1996, Magnaghi Papers, In.

55. Hélio Vianna, "Bases sociológicas da formação americana," *Espelho* (Rio de Janeiro) 8 (November 1935): 14-15.

56. A review of *Connections: American History and Culture in an International Perspective* 1 (1994) provides insights into the extent of comparative hemispheric historical studies under way at a variety of Latin American universities.

57. Hebe Clementi, *La Frontera en América: Una clave interpretativa de la historia americana*, 4 vols. (Buenos Aires: Editorial Leviatán, 1985).

58. Luis Navarro García, ed., *Historia de las Américas*, 4 vols. (Madrid: Alhambra Longman, 1991).

59. Arturo Chavolla, *La Idea de América en el pensamiento europeo de Fernández de Oviedo a Hegel* (Guadalajara: Universidad de Guadalajara, 1993).

60. Some of these institutions include Hispanic American University of Santa Maria de la Rábida; the Art Laboratory and the School of Hispanic American Studies at the University of Seville; Royal Hispanic American Academy of Cádiz; Studies Center of History of America; and Hispanic Cuban Institute of History of America.

61. José Antonio Calderón Quijano, *El Americanismo en Sevilla, 1900-1980* (Seville: Escuela de Estudios Hispano-Americanos de Sevilla, 1987), xxv-1.

62. *OAH Newsletter* 25 (May 1997): 22.

63. S. N. Eisenstein, "Culture, Religions and Development in North American

and Latin American Civilizations," *International Social Science Journal* 34 (1992): 593-603; Aníbal Quijano and Immanuel Wallerstein, "Americanity as a Concept, or the Americas in the Modern World-System," *International Social Science Journal* 34 (1992): 549-557; Jim Levy and Peter Ross, "A Common History? Two Latin Americans View the Writing of US History in Hemispheric Perspective," *Australasian Journal of American Studies* 12 (1993): 3-25.

64. Amy Magaro Rubin, "Trying to Revive a 3-Way Collaboration," *The Chronicle of Higher Education* 42 (May 17, 1996): A43 and A46.

65. C. Vann Woodward, *The Comparative Approach to American History* (Repr. New York: Oxford University Press, 1997), xiii.

Appendix: Chrono-Bibliography of the History of the Americas

1553

Münster, Sebastian. *A Treatyse of the Newe India*. Trans. Richard Eden. London: Edward Sulton, 1553.

1568

Thevet, Andrewe. *The New Found Worlde or Antarctike*. London: Henry Bynneman, 1568.

1582

Hakluyt, Richard. *Divers Voyages Touching the Discouerie of America and the Ilands Adiacent vnto the Same, Made First of All by Our Englishmen and afterward by the Frenchmen and Britons*. London: Thomas Woodcocke, 1582.

Popelinière, Lancelot Voisin, Sieur de La. *Les Trois Mondes*. Paris: Pierre L'Huillier, 1582.

1757

Burke, Edmund. *An Account of the European Settlements in America*. 2 vols. London: R & J. Dodsley, 1757. (Over the years, numerous editions were published.)

1776

Young, W. A. *The History of North and South America, with an Account of the West Indies and American Islands, to Which Is Prefized a Candid and Impartial Enquiry into the Present Disputes*. 2 vols. London: W. Lane, 1776.

1777

Robertson, William. *The History of the Discovery and Settlement of America*. 2 vols. Dublin: Messrs. Whitestone, 1777; Edinburgh: W. Strahan, 1777. (Numerous editions followed.)

1786-1789

Alcedo, Antonio de. *El diccionario geográfico histórico de las Indias Occidentales o América*. 5 vols. Madrid: Imprenta de B. Cano, 1786-1789.

1795

Winterbotham, William. *American Historical, Geographical, Commercial and Philosophical Views of the American United States and of the European Settlements in America and the West-Indies.* 4 vols. London: J. Ridgway, 1795.

1812-1815

Alcedo, Antonio de. *The Geographical and Historical Dictionary of America and the West Indies Containing an Entire Translation of the Spanish Work of Colonel Don Antonio de Alcedo with Large Additions and Compilations from Modern Voyages and Travels and from Original and Authentic Information.* Trans. G. A. Thompson. 5 vols. London: J. Carpenter, 1812-1815.

1820-1822

Compagnoni, Giuseppe. *Storia dell' America, in continuazione del compendio della storia universale del Sig. conte di Segur....* 28 vols. Milan: Fusi, Stella e Com., 1820-1822.

1821

Taylor, Isaac. *Scenes in America for the Amusement and Instruction of Little Tarry-at-Home Travellers.* London: Harris & Son, 1821.

1826-1844

Warden, David Baille. *Chronologie historique de l'Amérique.* 10 vols. Paris: A. Dupont et Roret, 1826-1844.

1827

Everett, Alexander H. *America or A General Survey of the Political Situation of the Several Powers of the Western Continent with Conjectures on Their Future Prospects.* Philadelphia: H. C. Carey and I. Lea, 1827.

1831

Warden, David Baille. *Bibliotheca Americana: Being A Choice Collection of Books Relating to North and South America and the West Indies....* Paris: Paul Renouard, 1831.

1834

Anonymous. *A General History of North and South America.* London: Mayhew, Isaac and Co., 1834.

1847

MacGregor, John. *The Progress of America: From the Discovery by Columbus to the Year 1846.* 2 vols. London: Whittaker and Co., 1847.

1850

Kottenkamp, Franz Justus. *Geschichte der Kolonisation Amerikas.* 2 vols. Frankfurt: Literarische Anstalt, 1850.

1852

Goodrich, Samuel G. *A Pictorial History of America: Embracing Both the Northern and Southern Portions of the New World.* Hartford, CT: House and Brown, 1852.

1864

Barra, Miguel de la. *La América.* Santiago de Chile: Imprenta Nacional, 1864.

1865

Barros Arana, Diego. *Compendio de historia de América.* 2 vols. Santiago, Chile: Imprenta del Ferrocarril, 1865. (Numerous editions followed.)

――― . *Compendio elemental de historia de América.* Santiago de Chile: Imprenta del Ferrocarril, 1865. (Numerous editions followed.)

1870

Mesa y Leopart, José. *Compendio de la historia de América desde su descubrimiento hasta nuestros dias.* 2 vols. Paris: Rosa y Bourte, 1870.

1878

Stephenson, L. M. *Chronology of the History of the Two Americas.* New York: H. S. Allen, 1878.

Headley, Phineas C., ed. *The History of Two Americas.* Chicago: A. S. L. Coburn & Co., 1878.

1879

Headley, Phineas C. *The Two Americas: Their Complete History from the Earliest Discoveries to the Present Day.* New York: H. S. Allen, 1879. (Reprints followed.)

1882

Mackenzie, Robert. *America: A History.* Repr. London: T. Nelson & Sons, 1882.

Scobel, Albert. *Nordamerika, Mexico, Mittelamerika und Westindien, kommerziell, politisch und statistisch.* Leipzig: Metzger & Wittig, 1882.

1884-1889

Winsor, Justin, ed. *Narrative and Critical History of America.* 8 vols. Boston: Houghton Mifflin, 1884-1889.

1888-1931

James G. Wilson and John Fiske, eds. *Appleton's Cyclopedia of American Biography.* 12 vols. New York: Appleton, 1888-1931.

1890

Thwaites, Reuben Gold. *The Colonies, 1492-1750.* New York: Longmans, Green, 1897.

1891

Blackmar, Frank W. *Spanish Institutions of the Southwest.* Baltimore: Johns Hopkins University Press, 1891.

1895-1896

Journal de la Société des Américanistes de Paris 1 (1895-1896).

1898

Moses, Bernard. "The Neglected Half of American History." *University Chronicle* (Berkeley) 1 (1898): 120-126.

1903+

University of California Publications in American Archaeology and Ethnography. (Series.)

1906

Bourne, Edward Gaylord. "The Relation of American History to Other Fields of Historical Study." In *Universal Exposition, St. Louis, 1904,* ed. Howard J. Rogers. *Congress of Arts and Science.* 2 vols. Boston: Houghton Mifflin, 1906.

1907

Bandelier, Adolph. "America." In *Catholic Encyclopedia* vol. 1, 1907. 409-416.

1910

Shepherd, William R. "The Contribution of the Romance Nations to the History of the Americas." In *Annual Report of the American Historical Association for the Year 1909*, 221-227. Washington, DC: Government Printing Office, 1910.

1910-1913

Navarro y Lamarca, Carlos. *Compendio de la historia general de América.* 2 vols. Buenos Aires: Angel Estrada, 1910-1913.

1911

Bartholomew, J. G. *A Literary and Historical Atlas of America.* New York: Dutton, 1911.

1913

Lauber, Almon W. *Indian Slavery in Colonial Times Within the Present Limits of the United States.* New York: Columbia University Press, 1913.

Oliveira Lima, Manuel de. *América latina e America ingleza: A evolução brazileira comparada com a hispano-americana e com a anglo-americana.* Rio de Janeiro: Livraria Garnier, 1913.

1914

Oliveira Lima, Manuel de. *The Evolution of Brazil Compared with that of Spanish and Anglo-Saxon America.* Stanford: Stanford University Press, 1914.

1915

Chase, Lew Allen. "The Last American Frontier." *History Teacher's Magazine* 6 (February 1915): 37-46.

Stearns, W. N. "Canadian History Next?" *History Teacher's Magazine* 6 (November 1915): 294.

1916

Chase, Lew Allen. "How the Furs Came Down from the North Country." *History Teacher's Magazine* 7 (February 1916): 44-46.

Cox, Isaac J. "European Background for the High School Course in American History." *History Teacher's Magazine* 7 (1916): 163-169.

1917

Cleven, N. Andrew N. "Latin American History in Our Secondary Schools." *History Teacher's Magazine* 8 (1917): 219-222.

Westergaard, Waldemar. "American Interest in the West Indies." *History Teacher's Magazine* 8 (1917): 249-253.

1919

Buffington, Arthur H. "British and French Imperialism in North America." *History Teacher's Magazine* 10 (1919): 489-496.

Robertson, James A. "A Symposium on the Teaching of the History of Hispanic America in Educational Institutions of the United States." *Hispanic American Historical Review* 2 (1919): 397-446.

Wittke, Carl. "Canada—Our Neglected Neighbor." *History Teacher's Magazine* 10 (1919): 485-488.

1920

Bolton, Herbert E., and Thomas M. Marshall. *The Colonization of North America, 1492-1783.* New York: Macmillan, 1920.

1923

Bolton, Herbert E. *History of the Americas: History 8A-8B, 1923-1924.* Berkeley: University of California Press, 1923-1924. (Other revisions.)

Morehouse, Frances. "Broadening the Historical Background." *Historical Outlook* 14 (1923): 220-222.

1927

Trotter, Reginald G. "Canadian History in the Universities of the United States." *Canadian Historical Review* 8 (1927): 190-207.

1928

Bolton, Herbert E. *History of the Americas: A Syllabus with Maps.* Boston: Ginn, 1928.

Sage, Walter N. "Some Aspects of the Frontier in Canadian History." In *Canadian Historical Association Report* 6 (1928): 62-72.

1929

Priestley, Herbert I. *The Coming of the White Man, 1492-1848.* New York: Macmillan, 1929.

Trotter, Reginald G. "Canadian Interest in the History of the United States." *Queen's Quarterly* 36 (1929): 92-107.

1930

Bartholomew, J. G. *A Literary and Historical Atlas of America.* Rev. ed. New York: Dutton, 1930.

1931

Brebner, John B. "Canadian and North American History." In *Canadian Historical Association, Annual Report* 9 (1931): 37-48.

1932

Millán, José R. *Compendio de historia americana.* Buenos Aires: A. Kapelusz, 1932.

Ruch, Gastão. *História da América.* Rio de Janeiro: F. Briguiet, 1932.

Thompson, Wallace. *Greater America: An Interpretation of Latin America in Relation to Anglo-Saxon America.* New York: Dutton, 1932.

1933

Bolton, Herbert E. "The Epic of Greater America." *American Historical Review* 38 (1933): 448-474.

Brebner, John B. *The Explorers of North America, 1492-1806.* New York: Macmillan, 1933.

1934

Duggan, Stephen. *The Two Americas: An Interpretation.* New York: Scribner's, 1934.

1935-1936

Zavala, Silvio. "Los conquistas de Canarias y América. Estudio comparativo." *Tierra firme* (Madrid) 1 (1935): 81-112; 2 (1936):89-115.

1936

Ballesteros y Beretta, Antonio. *Historia de América y de los pueblos americanos.* 2 vols. Barcelona: Salvat, 1936.

1937

Bolton, Herbert E. *La epopeya de las maxima América.* Trans. Carmen Alessio Robles. México, DF: Instituto Panamericano de Geografíca e Historia, 1937.

Dunne, Peter M., S.J. "The Americas and the Jesuits." *San Francisco Quarterly* 3 (1937): 1-15.

Lower, A.R.M. "Canada and the Americas." *Dalhousie Review* 17 (1937): 17-21.

Oswald, John C. *Printing in the Americas*. New York: W. F. Hall, 1937.

Verrell, A. Hyatt. *Foods America Gave the World*. Boston: L. C. Page, 1937.

Wayte, Raymond. *The Gold Coins of North and South America: An Illustrated Catalogue of All the Types with an Indication of Their Retail Value*. New York: Raymond Wayte, 1937.

Weddell, Alexander W. "A Comparison of the Executive and Judicial Powers Under the Constitutions of Argentina and the United States." *Bulletin of the College of William and Mary* 31 (1937): 37-84.

1938

Alvarez Barret, Luis, and Antonio Rangel. *Historia de América*. México, DF: Talleres de "El Nacional," 1938.

The Civilization of the Americas. Berkeley: University of California Press, 1938.

Webb, Victor L., Edna Fay, and William L. Nida. *The New World, Past and Present: A Unified Course in History and Geography for Elementary Schools*. Chicago: Scott Foresman, 1938.

1939

Bolton, Herbert E. *Wider Horizons of American History*. New York: Appleton-Century, 1939.

Burmester, Luis Germán. *Historia americana*. 1 vol. to date. Buenos Aires: n.p., 1939- .

Corbett, Percy E. "Canada and Pan-Americanism." *Quarterly Journal of Inter-American Relations* 1.4 (1939): 30-34.

Cotterill, Robert S. *A Short History of the Americas*. New York: Prentice-Hall, 1939.

Goetz, Delia, and Varian Fry. *The Good Neighbors: The Story of the Two Americas*. New York: Foreign Policy Association, 1939.

O'Gorman, Edmundo. "Hegel y el moderno panamericanismo." *Universidad de la Habana* 8 (1939): 61-74.

Pereyra, Carlos. *Breve historia de América*. 2 vols. Santiago de Chile: Letras, 1939.

Sivirichi, Atilio. *Historia de América*. Lima: D. Miranda, 1939.

Swigart, Beulah H. "The Americas as Revealed in the *Encyclopédie*." Diss. University of Illinois, Urbana, 1939.

Trotter, Reginald G. "The Appalachian Barrier in Canadian History." In *Canadian Historical Association Report* 6 (1928): 5-21.

1940

Alba, Pedro de. *Breve reseña histórica del movimiento panamericanista*. México, DF: E. Murguía, 1940.

Bolton, Herbert E. "Some Cultural Assets of Latin America." *Hispanic American Historical Review* 20 (1940): 3-11.

Castro, Américo. *On the Relations Between the Americas*. Trans. Angel Flores. Points of View no. 1. Washington, DC: Pan-American Union, Division of Intellectual Cooperation, 1940.

Roa Y Reyes, Jorge. *Positive and Negative Factors in Inter-American Relations*. Havana: Libros y Folletos, 1940.

Trotter, Reginald G. "More on Canada and Pan-Americanism, A Reply to Professor Corbett." *Inter-American Quarterly* 2 (1940): 5-10.

1940-1951

Levene, Ricardo. *Historia de América*. 15 vols. Buenos Aires: W. M. Jackson, 1940-1951.

1941

Chéradame, André. *Defense of the Americas*. Trans. George Swan Challies. Garden City, NY: Doubleday, 1941.

Laves, William H. C., ed. *Inter-American Solidarity*. Chicago: University of Chicago Press, 1941.

Ocampo, Victoria, ed. *Is America a Continent?* Trans. Angel Flores. Points of View no. 2. Washington, DC: Pan-American Union, Division of Intellectual Cooperation, 1941.

O'Gorman, Edmundo. *Do the Americas Have a Common History?* Trans. Angel Flores. Points of View no. 3. Washington, DC: Pan-American Union, Division of Intellectual Cooperation, 1941.

Rippy, J. Fred. *South America and Hemisphere Defense*. Baton Rouge: Louisiana State University Press, 1941.

Sánchez, Luis Alberto. *The Presence of Tradition*. Trans. Angel Flores. Points of View no. 4. Washington, DC: Pan-American Union, Division of Intellectual Cooperation, 1941.

1942

Binkley, William C. "Have the Americas a Common History?: A United States View." *Canadian Historical Review* 23 (1942): 125-132.

Brown, George W. "Have the Americas a Common History?: A Canadian View." *Canadian Historical Review* 23 (1942): 132-138.

Gandía, Enrique de. "El panamericanismo en la historia." *Boletín de la Academia Nacional del la Historia* (Buenos Aires) 5 (1942): 383-393.

"Have the Americas a Common History?" *Canadian Historical Review* 23 (1942): 125-156.

Nelson, Ernesto. *A Problem for the Americas*. Trans. Clarabel H. Wait. Points of View no. 5. Washington, DC: Pan-American Union, Division of Intellectual Cooperation, 1942.

O'Gorman, Edmundo. *Fundamentos de la historia de América*. México, DF: Universitaria, 1942.

———. "¿Tienen las Américas una historia común?" *Filosofía y letras* 6 (1942): 215-235.

Sánchez, Luis Alberto. *Historia general de América*. 2 vols. Santiago de Chile: Ercilla, 1942.

1943

Baldwin, Leland Dewitt. *The Story of the Americas*. New York: Simon & Schuster, 1943.

Hill, R. R. "A Latin American Speaks." *Hispanic American Historical Review* 23 (1943): 668-675.

Mr. MacLeish, We Are Not Irresponsible. Trans. Lloyd Mallan. Points of View no. 6. Washington, DC: Pan-American Union, Division of Intellectual Cooperation, 1943.

Ortiz, Fernando. *On the Relations Between Blacks and Whites*. Trans. Ben Frederick

Carruthers. Points of View no. 7. Washington, DC: Pan-American Union, Division of Intellectual Cooperation, 1943.

Otero, G. A. "El futuro de nuestra América." *Revista de Indias* 55 (1943): 64-93.

Pereira Salas, Eugenio. *Notas para la historia del intercambio musical entre las Américas antes del año 1940.* Washington, DC: Pan-American Union, Music Division, 1943.

———. *Notes on the History of Music Exchange Between the Americas before 1940.* Washington, DC: Pan-American Union, Music Division, 1943.

Quintanilla, Luis. *A Latin American Speaks.* New York: Macmillan, 1943.

Sánchez, Luis Alberto. "A New Interpretation of the History of America." *Hispanic American Historical Review* 23 (1943): 441-456.

1944

Picón-Salas, Mariano. *On Being Good Neighbors.* Trans. Muna Lee. Points of View no. 8. Washington, DC: Pan-American Union, Division of Intellectual Cooperation, 1944.

Whitaker, A. P. *Inter-American Affairs, 1943.* New York: Columbia University Press, 1944.

1945

Alvarez López, Enrique. "Las plantas de América en la botánica europea del siglo XVI." *Revista de Indias* 6 (1945): 221-288.

Brebner, John B. *North Atlantic Triangle: The Interplay of Canada, the United States, and Great Britain.* New Haven: Yale University Press, 1945.

Pereira Salas, Eugenio. *La influencia norteamericana en las primeras constitutiones de Chile.* Santiago de Chile: Gráficos Valdés, 1945.

1946

Bannon, John F., S.J. *Colonial North America: A Short History.* St. Louis: St. Louis University Press, 1946.

Magdaleno, Vicente. *Perspectivas del nuevo mundo.* México, DF: Editorial Inter-Continental, 1946.

Peixoto, Afranio. *Pequeña historia de las Américas.* Trans. Pedro González-Blanco. México, DF: Ediciones Botas, 1946.

Pereyra, Carlos. *Breve historia de América.* Santiago de Chile: Zig-Zag, 1946.

Sáenz, Moisés. *The Indian, Citizen of America.* Points of View no. 9. Washington, DC: Pan-American Union, Division of Intellectual Cooperation, 1946.

1947

"Acuerdo organizativo de la Comisión Panamericana de Historia." *Boletín de la Academia Nacional de la Historia* (Venezuela) 30 (1947): 362-381.

Diccionario enciclopédico de las Américas. Buenos Aires: Futuro, 1947.

Oropresa, Juan. *Contrasting Philosophies of Education, North and South.* Trans. George C. Compton. Points of View no. 10. Washington, DC: Pan-American Union, Division of Intellectual Cooperation, 1947.

Teja Zabre, A. *Dinámica de la historia y frontera intramericana.* México, DF: Ediciones Botas, 1947.

1948

Soward, F. H., and A. M. Macaulay. *Canada and the Pan-American System.* Toronto: Ryerson, 1948.

Vianna, Hélio. *Estudos de história colonial.* São Paulo: Companhía Editora Nacional, 1948.

1949

Duggan, Laurence. *The Americas: The Search for Hemispheric Security*. New York: Holt, 1949.

Muñoz Pérez, J. "Comentarios en torno a una historia general de América." *Estudios americanos* 1 (1949): 701-718.

Zea, Leopoldo. "The Interpretation of the Ibero-American and North American Cultures." *Philosophy and Phenomenological Research* 9 (1949): 538-543.

1949-1953

Cooper, John I. "The West Indies, Bermuda, and the American Mainland Colleges." *Jamaican Historical Review* 2 (1949-1953): 1-6.

1950

Holmes, Vera B. *A History of the Americas*. Vol. 1 *From Discovery to Nationhood*. New York: Ronald Press, 1950.

Jensen, Merrill, and Robert I. Reynolds. "European Colonial Experience: A Plea for Comparative Studies." *Studi di Gino Luzzatto* (Milan) 4 (1950): 75-90.

Zavala, Silvio. "The Commission on History of the Pan-American Institute of Geography and History." *The Americas* 6 (1950): 487-493.

1951

Brooks, Philip C. "Do the Americas Share a Common History?" *Revista de historia de América* 33 (1951): 75-83.

Griffin, Charles C. "Unidad y variedad en la historia americana." *Ensayos sobre la historia del Nuevo Mundo*, 97-123. Publication no. 31. México, DF: Pan-American Institute of Geography and History, 1951.

McInnis, Edgar, et al., eds. *Ensayos sobre la historia del Nuevo Mundo*. Publication no. 31. México, DF: Pan-American Institute of Geography and History, 1951.

Whitaker, Arthur P. "The Americas in the Atlantic Triangle." In *Ensayos sobre la historia del Nuevo Mundo*, 69-96. Publication no. 31. México, DF: Pan-American Institute of Geography and History, 1951.

1952

Bannon, John F. *History of the Americas*. 2 vols. New York: McGraw-Hill, 1952.

Griffin, Charles C. "Problems of the National Period." *Revista de historia de América* 34 (1952): 470-476.

Lobo, Eulalia Maria Lahmeyer. *Administração colonial luso-espanhola nas Américas*. Rio de Janeiro: Companhia Brasileira de Artes Gráficas, 1952.

Malagón, Javier. *Informe de la Comisión de Historia del I.P.G.H. (1950-1951)*. Publication no. 39. México, DF: Pan-American Institute of Geography and History, 1952.

Mosk, Sanford A. "Latin America Versus the United States." American Economic Association, *Papers and Proceedings* 40 (1952): 367-383.

Turner, Ralph E. "Comments on the Project on the History of America." *Revista de historia de América* 34 (1952): 486-489.

Zavala, Silvio. *El Instituto Panamericano de Geografía e Historia*. Publication no. 45. México, DF: Pan-American Institute of Geography and History, 1952.

1953

Brown, George W., J.M.S. Careless, Gerald M. Craig, and Eldon Ray, eds. *Canada and the Americas*. Toronto: J. M. Dent, 1953.

Davis, Harold E. *The Americas in History*. New York: Ronald Press, 1953.

Tinker, Edward Larocque. *The Horsemen of the Americas and the Literature They Inspired.* New York: Hastings, 1953.

Zavala, Silvio. "Colaboración internacional en torno de la historia de América." *Revista de historia de América* 35-36 (1953): 209-226.

1954

Cabot, John Moors. *Toward Our Common American Destiny.* Medford, MA: Fletcher School of Law and Diplomacy, 1954.

Menez, Joseph. "Presidents and Constitutions in the Americas." *Mid-America* 36 (1954): 3-38, 75-95.

Whitaker, Arthur P. *The Western Hemisphere Idea: Its Rise and Decline.* Ithaca, NY: Cornell University Press, 1954.

1955

Onís, José de. "The Americas of Herbert E. Bolton." *The Americas* 12 (1955): 157-168.

Río, A. del, ed. *Responsible Freedom in the Americas.* Garden City, NY: Doubleday, 1955.

Sharp, Paul F. "Three Frontiers: Some Comparative Studies of Canadian, American and Australian Settlement." *Pacific Historical Review* 24 (1955): 369-377.

1957

Boxer, C. R., and John Francis Bannon, S.J. "The 'Programa de Historia de America': Colonial and National Periods." *Inter-American Review of Bibliography* 7 (1957): 271-276.

Nichols, Roy F. "A United States Historian's Appraisal." *Revista de historia de América* 43 (1957): 144-158.

Whitaker, Arthur P. "Introduction to the Project for a History of America." *Revista de historia de América* 43 (1957): 141-144.

Wolf, Eric R., and Sidney W. Mintz. "Haciendas and Plantations in Middle America and the Antilles." *Social and Economic Studies* (Mona, Jamaica) 6 (1957): 380-412.

Wyman, W. D., and C. B. Kroeber, eds. *The Frontier in Perspective.* Madison: University of Wisconsin Press, 1957.

Zea, Leopoldo. *América en la historia.* México, DF, and Buenos Aires: Fondo de Cultura Económica, 1957.

1958

Eastlack, Charles L. "Herbert Eugene Bolton (1870-1953): His Ideas and Practice as a Historian of the Americas." Thesis, University of Texas, Austin, 1958.

Paddock, John. "The War of the Myths: Spanish and English Treatment of the Native Americans." *América indígena* 18 (1958): 281-292.

Redlich, Fritz. "Toward Comparative Historiography: Background and Problems." *Kyklos* 11 (1958): 362-389.

Ruiz, Ramón Eduardo. "Indifference South of the Border: Why Latin Americans Ignore Our History." *Southwest Review* 43 (1958): 54-60.

Thrupp, Sylvia L. "Editorial." *Comparative Studies in Society and History* 1 (1958): 1-4.

1959

Elkins, Stanley. *Slavery: A Problem in American Institutional and Intellectual Life.* Chicago: University of Chicago Press, 1959.

Gerhard, Dietrich. "The Frontier in Comparative View." *Comparative Studies in Society and History* 1 (1959): 205-229.

Mintz, Sidney. "Labor and Sugar in Puerto Rico and in Jamaica, 1800-1850." *Comparative Studies in Society and History* 1 (1959): 273-283.

Phelan, John L. "Free Versus Compulsory Labor: Mexico and the Philippines 1540-1648." *Comparative Studies in Society and History* 1 (1959): 189-201.

Zavala, Silvio. "International Collaboration in the History of America." *Comparative Studies in Society and History* 1 (1959): 284-287.

1960

Barros Arana, Diego. *Historia de América*. Ed. Álvaro Yunquel. Buenos Aires: Editorial Futuro, 1960.

Jennison, Peter S., and William H. Kurth. *Books in the Americas*. Washington, DC: Pan-American Union, 1960.

1961

Armillas, Pedro. *A Program of the History of the New World Coordinator's Summary Report*. Vol. 1, *The Native Period in the History of the New World*. Trans. Glenda Crevenna and Theo Crevenna. Publication no. 108. México, DF: Pan-American Institute of Geography and History, 1961.

Griffin, Charles C. *A Program of the History of the New World Coordinator's Summary Reports*. Vol. 3, *The National Period in the History of the New World: An Outline and Commentary*. Publication no. 103. México, DF: Pan-American Institute of Geography and History, 1961.

New York Public Library. Reference Dept. *Dictionary Catalog of the History of the Americas*. Boston: G. K. Hall, 1961.

Zavala, Silvio A. *Programa de historia de América. Coordinaciones finales*. Vol. 1, *Programa de historia de América en la época colonial*. Publicación no. 104. México, DF: Instituto Panamericano de Geografía e Historia, 1961.

———. "A General View of the Colonial History of the New World." *American Historical Review* 66 (1961): 913-929.

1962

Arciniegas, Germán. "Las cuatro Américas." *Cuadernos* 60 (1962): 1-9.

Ballesteros y Beretta, Antonio. *Historia de América y de los pueblos americanos*. 26 vols. Barcelona: Salvat, 1962.

Cline, Howard E. "Imperial Perspectives on the Borderlands." In *Probing the American West: Papers from the Santa Fe Conference*, 168-174. Ed. K. Ross Toole et. al. Santa Fe: Museum of New Mexico, 1962.

Guerrero Castillo, Julián N. *Historia de América*. Guatemala: Centro Editorial "José de Pineda Ibarra," Ministerio de Educación Pública, 1962.

Hartz, Louis. "American Historiography and Comparative Analysis." *Comparative Studies in Society and History* 5 (1962): 365-377.

Morales Padrón, F., ed. *Historia general de América*. 2 vols. Madrid: Espasa-Calpe, 1962.

Thompson, Lawrence S. "Bookbinding in the Americas." *Inter-American Review of Bibliography* 12 (1962): 253-268.

Zavala, Silvio A. *A Program of the History of the New World Coordinator's Summary Reports*. Vol. 2, *The Colonial Period in the History of the New World*. Trans. Max Savelle. Abr. ed. Publication no. 102. México, DF: Pan-American Institute of

Geography and History, 1962.

1963

Bannon, John F. *History of the Americas*, 2nd ed. 2 vols. New York: McGraw-Hill, 1963.

Hartz, Louis. "American Historiography and Comparative Analysis: Further Reflections." *Comparative Studies in Society and History* 5 (1963): 365-400.

Hernández Sánchez-Barba, Mario. *Historia universal de América*. 2 vols. Madrid: Ediciones Guadarrama, 1963.

Marbán Escobar, Edilberto. *Curso de historia de America*. 2 vols. New York: Minerva, 1963.

Sánchez, Luis Alberto. *Historia general de América*. 7th ed. 2 vols. Santiago de Chile: Ercilla, 1963.

1964

Chaunu, Pierre. *L'Amérique et les Amériques*. Paris: Armand Colin, 1964.

Driver, Harold, ed. *The Americas on the Eve of Discovery*. Englewood Cliffs, NJ: Prentice-Hall, 1964.

Hanke, Lewis, ed. *Do the Americas Have a Common History? A Critique of the Bolton Theory*. New York: Knopf, 1964.

Harris, Marvin. *Patterns of Race in the Americas*. New York: Walker, 1964.

Hartz, Louis. *The Founding of New Societies: Studies in the History of the United States, Latin America, South Africa, Canada, and Australia*. New York: Harcourt Brace & Jovanovich, 1964.

Holmes, Vera Brown. *A History of the Americas*. Vol. 2, *From Nationhood to World Status*. New York: Ronald Press, 1964.

1965

Aguilar, Alonso. *El panamericanismo de la doctrina Monroe a la doctrina Johnson*. México, DF: Cuadernos Americanos, 1965.

Sánchez, Luis Alberto. *Breve historia de América*. Buenos Aires: Losada, 1965.

Stanford, Henry K. "The Need for an Inter-American Approach." *Journal of Inter-American Studies* 7 (1965): 1-4.

Urbanski, Edmund S. *Angloamérica e Hispanoamérica: Análisis de los civilizaciónes*. Madrid: Studium, 1965.

1966

Fieldhouse, D. K. *The Colonial Empires: A Comparative Survey from the Eighteenth Century*. London: Weidenfeld and Nicolson, 1966.

Oliveira Lima, Manuel de. *The Evolution of Brazil Compared with That of Spanish and Anglo-Saxon America*. 1914. Ed. and intro. Percy Alvin Martin. Repr. New York: Russell & Russell, 1966.

1967

Alcedo, Antonio de. *Diccionario geográfico de las Indias...Occidentales o América*. 4 vols. Madrid: Atlas, 1967.

Bendix, Reinhard. "Tradition and Modernity Reconsidered." *Comparative Studies in Society and History* 9 (1967): 292-346.

Bolton, Herbert E. *Wider Horizons of American History*. 1939. New York: Appleton-Century, 1939. Repr. Notre Dame, IN: University of Notre Dame Press, 1967.

Hanke, Lewis. "Studying Latin America: The Views of an 'Old Christian.'" *Journal of Inter-American Studies* 9 (1967): 43-64.

Howell, Ellen D. "Continuity or Change: A Comparative Study of the Composition of the Cabildos in Seville, Tenerife and Lima." *The Americas* 24 (1967): 33-45.

Klein, Herbert S. *Slavery in the Americas: A Comparative Study of Virginia and Cuba.* Chicago: University of Chicago Press, 1967.

List, George, and Juan Arrego-Salas, eds. *Music in the Americas.* Bloomington: Research Center in Anthropology, Folklore, and Linguistics, Indiana University, 1967.

Pike, Frederick B. "Church and State in Peru and Chile Since 1840: A Study in Contrasts." *American Historical Review* 73 (1967): 30-50.

Sewell, William H., Jr. "Marc Bloch and the Logic of Comparative History." *History and Theory* 6 (1967): 208-218.

TePaske, John J., ed. *Three American Empires.* New York: Harper & Row, 1967.

Zavala, Silvio. *El mundo americano en la época colonial.* 1961. 2 vols. Repr. México, DF: Porrúa, 1967.

1968

Aguilar, Alonso. *Pan-Americanism from Monroe to the Present: A View from the Other Side.* Trans. Asa Zatz. New York: Monthly Review Press, 1968.

Eisenstadt, S. N. "Social Institutions: Comparative Study." *International Encyclopedia of the Social Sciences* 14 (1968): 421-428.

Holmes, John W. "Canada and Pan America." *Journal of Inter-American Studies* 10 (1968): 173-184.

Rokkan, Stein, ed. *Comparative Research across Cultures and Nations.* Paris: International Social Science Council, and The Hague: Mouton, 1968.

Woodward, C. Vann. "The Comparability of American History." In *The Comparative Approach to American History.* Ed. C. Vann Woodward. New York: Basic Books, 1968.

1968-1969

Baily, Samuel L. "The Italians and the Development of Organized Labor in Argentina, Brazil, and the United States, 1880-1914." *Journal of Social History* 2 (1968-1969): 123-134.

1969

Berkhofer, Robert F., Jr. *A Behavioral Approach to Historical Analysis.* New York: Free Press, 1969.

Curtin, Philip. *The Atlantic Slave Trade: A Census.* Madison: University of Wisconsin Press, 1969.

Foner, Laura, and Genovese, Eugene D., eds. *Slavery in the New World: A Reader in Comparative History.* Englewood Cliffs, NJ: Prentice-Hall, 1969.

Genovese, Eugene D. "The Treatment of Slaves in Different Countries: Problems in the Application of the Comparative Method." In *Slavery in the New World: A Reader in Comparative History.* Ed. Laura Foner and Eugene D. Genovese. Englewood Cliffs, NJ: Prentice-Hall, 1969.

Knowlton, Robert J. "Expropriation of Church Property in Nineteenth Century Mexico and Colombia: A Comparison." *The Americas* 25 (1969): 387-401.

Miller, Theodore R. *Graphic History of the Americas.* New York: John Wiley, 1969.

Peckham, Howard, and Charles Gibson, eds. *Attitudes of Colonial Powers toward the American Indian.* Salt Lake City: University of Utah Press, 1969.

Schwartz, Stuart B. "Cities of Empire: Mexico City and Bahia." *Journal of Inter-American Studies and World Affairs* 11 (1969): 616-667.

Worcester, Donald E. "The Spanish American Past—Enemy of Change." *Journal of Inter-American Studies and World Affairs* 11 (1969): 66-75.

1970

Alcedo, Antonio de. *The Geographical and Historical Dictionary of America and the West Indies Containing an Entire Translation of the Spanish Work of Colonel Don Antonio de Alcedo with Large Additions and Compilations from Modern Voyages and Travels and from Original and Authentic Information.* Trans. G. A. Thompson. 5 vols. 1812-1815. Repr. New York: Burt Franklin, 1970.

Genovese, Eugene D. "The Comparative Focus in Latin American History." *Journal of Inter-American Studies and World Affairs* 12 (1970): 317-327.

Gerlach, Arch C. *Pan-American Institute of Geography and History — PAIGH.* Publication no. 315. Washington, DC: Pan-American Institute of Geography and History, 1970.

Lobo, Eulalia Maria Lahmeyer. "Rio de Janeiro e Charleston, SC: As comunidades de mercadores no século XVIII." *Journal of Inter-American Studies and World Affairs* 12 (1970): 565-582.

1970-1971

Moran, Theodore. "The 'Development' of Argentina and Australia: The Radical Party of Argentina and the Labor Party of Australia in the Process of Economic and Political Development." *Comparative Politics* 3 (1970-1971): 71-92.

1971

Bastide, Roger. *African Civilizations in the New World.* Trans. Peter Green. New York: Harper & Row, 1971.

Davis, Harold E., and Harold A. Durfee. "Philosophy and the University of the Americas." *Inter-American Review of Bibliography* 21 (1971): 326-332.

Degler, Carl N. *Neither Black Nor White: Slavery and Race Relations in Brazil and the United States.* New York: Macmillan, 1971.

Garfin, Susan B. "Comparative Studies: A Selective, Annotated Bibliography." In *Comparative Methods in Sociology: Essays on Trends and Applications,* 423-467. Ed. Ivan Vallier. Berkeley and Los Angeles: University of California Press, 1971.

Hall, Gwendolyn M. *Social Control in Slave Plantation Societies: A Comparison of St. Domingue and Cuba.* Baltimore: Johns Hopkins University Press, 1971.

Hollingsworth, J. Rogers. "American History in Comparative Perspective." In J. Rogers Hollingsworth, ed. *Nation and State Building in America: Comparative Historical Perspectives.* Boston: Little, Brown, 1971.

1972

Brading, David A., and Cross, Harry E. "Colonial Silver Mining: Mexico and Peru." *Hispanic American Historical Review* 52 (1972): 545-579.

Burke, Edmund. *An Account of the European Settlements in America.* 2 vols. 1757. Repr. New York: Arno Press, 1972.

Cohen, David W., and Jack P. Greene, eds. *Neither Slave nor Free: The Freedman of African Descent in the Slave Societies of the New World.* Baltimore: Johns Hopkins University Press, 1972.

Ribeiro, Darcy. *The Americas and Civilization.* New York: E. P. Dutton, 1972.

Skidmore, Thomas E. "Toward a Comparative Analysis of Race Relations Since

Abolition in Brazil and the United States." *Journal of Latin American Studies* 4 (1972): 1-28.

1973

Arjona Colomo, Miguel. *Historia de América...en cuadros esquemáticos*. 2 vols. to date. Madrid: E.P.E.S.A., 1973- .

Arndt, Karl J. *The German Language Press of the Americas*. Munich: Verlag Dokumentation, 1973.

Saskatchewan Provincian Library. *Bibliographic Services Division. Indians of the Americas: History and Travel*. Regina: Saskatchewan Provincial Library, 1973.

Stewart, T. D. *The People of America*. New York: Scribner's, 1973.

Tipps, Dean C. "Modernization Theory and the Comparative Study of Society: A Critical Perspective." *Comparative Studies in Society and History* 15 (1973): 119-126.

1974

Bannon, John F. "Lewis and Clark Came Late." *South Dakota History* 4 (1974): 222-237.

Lombardi, John. "Comparative Slave Systems in the Americas: A Critical Review." In *New Approaches to Latin American History*. Ed. Richard Graham and Peter H. Smith. Austin: University of Texas Press, 1974.

McCormick, Richard P. "The Comparative Method: Its Application to American History" *Mid-America* 56 (1974): 231-247.

Mörner, Magnus. "Some Comparative Remarks on Colonial Mining in Lapland and Spanish America During the 17th Century." *Bulletin de l'Institut Historique Belge de Rome* (Brussels and Rome) 44 (1974): 423-435.

Sampablo, Raúl, dir. *América, que hermosa eres*. 3 vols. Barcelona: Mateu, 1974.

Toplin, Robert B., ed. *Slavery and Race Relations in Latin America*. New York: Greenwood, 1974.

1975

Barrett, Ward J., and Stuart B. Schwartz. "Comparación entre dos economías azucareras coloniales: Morelos, México y Bahía, Brasil," 534-572. In *Haciendas, latifundios y plantaciones en América Latina*. Ed. Enrique Florescano. México, DF: Siglo XXI, 1975.

Bowser, Frederick P. "The Free Person of Color in Mexico City and Lima: Manumission and Opportunity, 1580-1650." In *Race and Slavery in the Western Hemisphere*, 331-368. Ed. Stanley Engerman and Eugene Genovese. Princeton: Princeton University Press, 1975.

Bray, Warwick M., Earl H. Swanson, and Ian S. Farrington. *The New World*. Oxford: Elsevier-Phaidon, 1975.

Cardoso, Ciro F. S. "Historia económica del café en Centroamérica (siglo XIX): Estudio comparativo." *Estudios sociales centroamericanos* (San José, Costa Rica) 4 (1975): 129-151.

Engerman, Stanley, and Eugene Genovese, eds. *Race and Slavery in the Western Hemisphere. Quantitative Studies*. Princeton: Princeton University Press, 1975.

Jones, Peter d'Alroy. *Since Columbus: Poverty and Pluralism in the History of the Americas*. London: Heinemann, 1975.

Kammen, Michael G. "The Unique and the Universal in the History of New World Colonization." In *Eighteenth Century Florida and Its Borderlands*, 48-60. Ed. Samuel

Proctor. Gainesville: University of Florida Press, 1975.

Katzman, Michael T. "The Brazilian Frontier in Comparative Perspective." *Comparative Studies in Society and History* 17 (1975): 266-285.

Kirby, John. "On the Viability of Small Countries: Uruguay and New Zealand Compared." *Journal of Interamerican Studies and World Affairs* 17 (1975): 259-280.

Lang, James. *Conquest and Commerce: Spain and England in the Americas.* New York: Academic Press, 1975.

Mauro, Frederic. "Crecimiento urbano e industrial comparado de los países iberoamericanos: El caso de Brasil y de México." In *Estudios sobre la ciudad iberoamericana.* Ed. Francisco de Solano. Madrid: Instituto Gonzalo Fernández de Oviedo, CSIC, 1975.

Pérotin, Anne. "Deux situations révolutionnaires en pays colonial: La Guadeloupe (1793), Cuba (1809). Étude comparative des innovations institutionelles locales: Comités de surveillance et juntas de vigilancia." *Bulletin de la Société d'histoire de la Guadeloupe* (Basse-Terre) 24 (1975): 51-69.

Sánchez, Luis Alberto. *América desde la revolución emancipadora hasta nuestros días.* Madrid: EDAF, 1975.

Waterbury, Ronald. "Non-Revolutionary Peasants: Oaxaca Compared to Morelos in the Mexican Revolution." *Comparative Studies in Society and History* 17 (1975): 410-442.

1976

Boysse-Cassagne, Thérèse, and Tomás Gómez. "Sociétés indigènes et structures de colonisation. Études comparative de la société Muisca (Colombie) et des sociétés indigènes du Collao (Bolivie)." *Cahiers des Amériques latines* (Paris) ser. Sciences de l'Homme, no. 13/14 (1976): 5-32.

Cardoso, Ciro F. S. "Propriétés de la terre et techniques de production dans les colonies esclavagistes de l'Amérique et des Caraïbes au XVIIIᵉ siècle." *Cahiers des Amériques Latines* (Paris) ser. Sciences de l'Homme, no. 13/14 (1976): 129-151.

Chaunu, Pierre. *Les Amériques, 16ᵉ, 17ᵉ, 18ᵉ siècles.* Paris: A. Colin, 1976.

Crosby, Edward W. *A Chronology of Notable Dates in the History of Africans in the Americas and Elsewhere.* Kent, OH: Institute for African American Affairs, Kent State University, 1976.

Henry, Frances, ed. *Ethnicity in the Americas.* The Hague: Mouton, 1976.

Katz, Friedrich. "Comparación entre algunos aspectos de la evolución del d'Cuzco y Tenochtitlán." *Atti del XL Congresso Internazionale egli Americanisti* (Genoa) 4 (1976): 23-31.

Morris, Richard B., Josefina Zoraida Vazquez, and Elias Tribulse, eds. *Las revoluciones de independencia en México y en los Estados Unidos: Un ensayo comparativo.* 3 vols. México, DF: SepSetentas, 1976.

Smelser, Neil S. *Comparative Methods in the Social Sciences and Essays in Sociological Explanation.* Englewood Cliffs, NJ: Prentice Hall, 1976.

Vazquez, Josefina Z., and Richard Morris, eds. *Dos revoluciones: México y los Estados Unidos.* México, DF: Editorial Jus, 1976.

1977

Bushnell, David. "El proceso inicial del liberalismo en Colombia y en la Argentina: Un esquema comparativo." *Revista de historia* (Heredia, Costa Rica) 2 (1977):

77-91.

Farrell, David R. "Anchors of Empire: Detroit, Montreal and the Continental Interior, 1760-1775." *American Review of Canadian Studies* 7 (1977): 33-54.

Miller, David H., and Jerome O. Steffen, eds. *The Frontier: Comparative Studies.* Norman: University of Oklahoma Press, 1977.

Rouse, John E. *The Criollo: Spanish Cattle in the Americas.* Norman: University of Oklahoma Press, 1977.

Walton, John. *Elites and Economic Development: Comparative Studies on the Political Economy of Latin American Cities.* Austin: University of Texas Press, 1977.

1978

Barretta, Silvio, et al. "Civilization and Barbarism: Cattle Frontiers in Latin America." *Comparative Studies in Society and History* 20 (1978): 587-620.

Contreras, Remedios. *Catálogo de la colección de manuscritos sobre América de la Real Academia de la Historia.* Badajoz: Real Academia de la Historia, Institución "Pedro Valencia," 1978.

Hamnett, Brian R. *Revolución y contrarrevolución en México y el Perú: Liberalismo, realeza y separatismo, 1800-1824.* México, DF: Fondo de Cultura Económica, 1978.

Hardoy, Jorge Enrique, and María Elena Kangdon. "Desigualdades regionales en Hispanoamérica (1850-1930): Análisis histórico y estudios nacionales (Argentina, Costa Rica, Chile)." *Revista de Indias* (Madrid) 38 (1978): 11-133.

Jackson, W. Turrentine. "A Brief Message for the Young and/or Ambitious: Comparative Frontiers as a Field for Investigation." *Western Historical Quarterly* 9 (1978): 5-18.

Kinsbruner, Jay. "The Pulperos of Caracas and San Juan During the First Half of the Nineteenth Century." *Latin American Research Review* 13 (1978): 65-85.

Klein, Herbert S. *The Middle Passage: Comparative Studies in the Atlantic Slave Trade.* Princeton: Princeton University Press, 1978.

Mörner, Magnus. "The Impact of Regional Variety on the History of the Afro-Latin Americans." *SECOLAS Annals* 9 (1978): 1-13.

Simpson, George E. *Black Religions in the New World.* New York: Columbia University Press, 1978.

Urbanski, Edmund S. *Hispanic America and Its Civilizations: Spanish-Americans and Anglo-Americans.* Trans. Frances Kellam Hendricks and Beatrice Berler. Norman: University of Oklahoma Press, 1978.

Van Oss, A. C. "Comparing Colonial Bishoprics in Spanish South America." *Boletín de estudios latinoamericanos y del Caribe* (Amsterdam) 24 (1978): 27-68.

Wong, Bernard. "A Comparative Study of the Assimilation of the Chinese in New York City and Lima, Peru." *Comparative Studies in Society and History* 20 (1978): 335-358.

1979

Axtell, James. "A North American Perspective for Colonial History." *History Teacher* 12 (1979): 549-562.

Degler, Carl N. "Plantation Society: Old and New Perspectives on Hemispheric History." *Plantation Society* 1 (February 1979): 9-14.

Dyster, Barrie. "Argentine and Australian Development Compared." *Past and Present* (Oxford) 84 (1979): 91-110.

Hanke, Lewis. *Selected Writings of Lewis Hanke on the History of Latin America.* Tempe: Arizona State University, Center for Latin American Studies, 1979.

Hennessy, Alistair. *The Frontier in Latin American History.* Albuquerque: University of New Mexico Press, 1979.

Quinn, David B., ed. *New American World: A Documentary History of North America to 1612.* 5 vols. New York: Arno, 1979.

1979+

Plantation Society in the Americas. (Journal.)

1980

Burbach, Roger, and Patricia Flynn. *Agribusiness in the Americas.* New York: Monthly Review Press, 1980.

Detweiler, Robert, and Ramón Ruiz, eds. *Liberation in the Americas: Comparative Aspects of the Independence Movements in Mexico and the United States.* San Diego: Campanile, 1980.

Fredrickson, George M. "Comparative History." In *The Past before Us: Contemporary Historical Writings in the United States,* 457-473. Ed. Michael Kammen. Ithaca, NY: Cornell University Press, 1980.

Gibson, Charles. "Latin America and the Americas." In *The Past Before Us: Contemporary Historical Writing in the United States.* Ed. Michael Kammen. Ithaca, NY: Cornell University Press, 1980.

Grew, Raymond. "The Case for Comparing Histories." *American Historical Review* 86 (1980): 763-778.

Hammel, E. A. "The Comparative Method in Anthropological Perspective." *Comparative Studies in Society and History* 22 (1980): 145-155.

Morón, Guillermo. "Informe sobre proyecto de historia general de América." *Revista de Historia de América* 90 (1980): 61-66.

Wilhite, John F. "The Inter-American Enlightenment." *Inter-American Review of Bibliography* 30 (1980): 254-261.

1981

Bowden, Henry W. *American Indians and Christian Missions: Studies in Cultural Conflict.* Chicago: University of Chicago Press, 1981.

Dictionary of Indian Tribes of the Americas. 2nd ed. 4 vols. Newport Beach, CA: American Indian Publishers, 1981.

Rawley, James. The Transatlantic Slave Trade. New York: 1981.

Sweet, David G., and Gary B. Nash, eds. *Struggle and Survival in Colonial America.* Berkeley: University of California Press, 1981.

Walker, William O. *Drug Control in the Americas.* Albuquerque: University of New Mexico Press, 1981.

1982

Cuello, José. "Beyond the 'Borderlands' Is the North of Colonial Mexico: A Latin-Americanist Perspective to the Study of the Mexican North and the United States Southwest." Ed. Kristyna P. Demaree. *Proceedings of the Pacific Coast Council on Latin American Studies* 9 (1982): 1-34.

Dictionary of Daily Life of Indians of the Americas. 2 vols. Newport Beach, CA: American Indian Publishers, 1982.

Hernández Sánchez-Barba, Mario. *Historia de América.* Madrid: Universidad Nacional de Educación a Distancia, Departamento de Historia, 1982.

Kolchin, Peter. "Comparing American History." *Reviews in American History* 10 (1982): 64-81.

Mörner, Magnus, Julia Fawaz de Viñuela, and John D. French. "Comparative Approaches to Latin American History." *Latin American Research Review* 17 (1982): 55-89.

1983

Liss, Peggy K. *Atlantic Empire: The Network of Trade and Revolution, 1713-1826.* Baltimore: Johns Hopkins University Press, 1983.

Zavala, Silvio. *A Program of the History of the New World Coordinator's Summary Reports.* Vol. 2, *The Colonial Period in the History of the New World.* Trans. Max Savelle. Abr. ed. Publication no. 102. 1962. New York: Greenwood Press, 1983.

1983+

Morón, Guillermo, ed. *Historia general de América.* 32 vols. Caracas: Distribuidora Historica General de América, 1983+.

1984

Barbier, Jacques, and Allan J. Kuethe, eds. *The North American Role in the Spanish Imperial Economy, 1760-1819.* Manchester: Manchester University Press, 1984.

Biographical Dictionary of Indians of the Americas. 2 vols. Newport Beach, CA: American Indian Publishers, 1984.

Centro Editor de América Latina. *Historia de América en el siglo XX.* 4 vols. to date. Buenos Aires: Centro Editor de América Latina, 1984- .

Ortiz, Roxanne Dunbar. *Indians of the Americas: Human Rights and Self-Determination.* New York: Praeger, 1984.

Parry, John H., and Robert G. Keith, eds. *New Iberian World: A Documentary History of the Discovery and Settlement of Latin America to the Early 17th Century.* 5 vols. New York: Time Books, 1984.

Smith, Raymond T., ed. *Kinship Ideology and Practice in Latin America.* Chapel Hill: University of North Carolina Press, 1984.

1985

Clementi, Hebe. *La frontera en América: Una clave interpretativa de la historia americana.* 4 vols. Buenos Aires: Editorial Leviatán, 1985.

Davis, Harold E. "Hispanic American Independence: A Comparative View." *Revista de historia de América* 100 (1985): 63-78.

Greaves, Thomas, and William Culver, eds. *Miners and Mining in the Americas.* Dover, NH: Manchester University Press, 1985.

Grew, Raymond. "The Comparative Weakness of American History." *Journal of Interdisciplinary History* 16 (1985): 87-101.

Jarolimek, John. *American Neighbors.* New York: Macmillan; London: Collier Macmillan, 1985.

McNeill, John R. *Atlantic Empires of France and Spain: Louisbourg and Havana, 1700-1763.* Chapel Hill: University of North Carolina Press, 1985.

Rashad, Adib [James Miller]. *The History of Islam and Black Nationalism in the Americas.* Washington, DC: Privately printed, 1985.

The World, A Television History: The Americas Before the Europeans, 300-1500. 1985. Produced by Nicholas Barton. Goldcrest Television. Falls Church, VA: Landmark Films. Videocassette.

1986

Ardura, Ernesto. *América en el horizonte.* Miami: Universal, 1986.

Coe, Michael, et al. *Atlas of Ancient America.* New York: Facts on File, 1986.

Grant, Kenneth E. *UNICEF in the Americas: For the Children of Three Decades*. Paris: United Nations Children's Fund, 1986.

Meinig, D. W. *The Shaping of America: A Geographical Perspective on 500 Years of History*. Vol. 1, *Atlantic America, 1492-1800*. New Haven, CT: Yale University Press, 1986.

Thevet, André. *André Thevet's North America: A Sixteenth Century View*. Ed. and trans. Roger Schlesinger and Arthur P. Stabler. Kingston, ON: Queen's University Press; Montreal: McGill University Press, 1986.

1987

Axtell, James. "Europeans, Indians, and the Age of Discovery in American History Textbooks." *American Historical Review* 92 (1987): 621-632.

Canny, Nicholas, and Anthony Pagden, eds. *Colonial Identity in the Atlantic World, 1500-1800*. Princeton: Princeton University Press, 1987.

Lorenzo, José Luis. *Etapa lítica en Norte y Centroamérica sobre los orígenes del hombre americano*. Caracas: Academia Nacional de la Historia de Venezuela, 1987.

Lye, Keith. *The Americas*. "Today's World" series. New York: Gloucester Press, 1987.

Numbers, Ronald L., ed. *Medicine in the New World: New Spain, New France, and New England*. Knoxville: University of Tennessee Press, 1987.

Thompson, Vincent Bakpetu. *The Making of the African Diaspora in the Americas, 1441-1900*. New York: Longman, 1987.

1988

Fairfield, Sheila. *Peoples and Nations of the Americas: A Short History of Each Country in North, Central, and South America, and the Caribbean Sea*. Milwaukee: Gareth Stevens, 1988.

1989

Bray, Warwick M., Earl H. Swanson, and Ian S. Farrington. *The Ancient Americas*. 2nd ed. Oxford: Phaidon, 1989.

Hilton, Sylvia L. *El americanismo en España: Bibliografía, 1988-1989*. Madrid: Centro de Estudios Históricos, Departamento de Historia de América, Consejo Superior de Investigaciones Científicos, 1989.

Klein, Herbert S. *Slavery in the Americas: A Comparative Study of Virginia and Cuba*. Chicago: Elephant, 1989.

Langley, Lester D. *America in the Americas: The United States in the Western Hemisphere*. Athens: University of Georgia Press, 1989.

Morse, Richard M. *New World Soundings: Culture and Ideology in the Americas*. Baltimore: Johns Hopkins University Press, 1989.

Newcombe, Jack, ed. *Travels in the Americas*. New York: Weidenfeld & Nicolson, 1989.

Swanson, Earl H., et al. *The Ancient Americas: The Making of the Past*. New York: Peter Bedrick, 1989.

Van Den Braembussche, A. A. "Historical Explanation and Comparative Method: Towards a Theory of the History of Society." *History and Theory* 28 (1989): 1-24.

Walker, William O. *Drug Control in the Americas*. 1981. Albuquerque: University of New Mexico Press, 1989.

1990

Griffin, Charles C. *The National Period in the History of the New World: An Outline and Commentary.* 1961. Repr. Westport, CT: Greenwood Press, 1990.

Pérez Firmat, Gustavo, ed. *Do the Americas Have a Common Literature?* Durham, NC: Duke University Press, 1990.

Shannon, Don E. *Comparative History of the Americas.* Dubuque, IA: Kendall/Hunt, 1990.

Slatta, Richard W. *Cowboys of the Americas.* New Haven: Yale University Press, 1990.

1991

Alternative Concepts for Commemorating Spanish Colonization. Washington, DC: Department of the Interior, National Park Service, 1991.

Borah, Woodrow W. "Epidemics in the Americas: Major Issues and Future Research." *Latin American Population History Bulletin* 19 (Spring 1991), 2-13.

Fagan, Brian M. *Kingdoms of Gold, Kingdoms of Jade: The Americas Before Columbus.* London: Thames and Hudson, 1991.

Fitz, Earl E. *Rediscovering the New World: Inter-American Literature in a Comparative Context.* Iowa City: University of Iowa Press, 1991.

McGerr, Michael. "The Price of the 'New Transnational History.'" *American Historical Review* 94 (1991): 1056-1067.

Navarro García, Luis, ed. *Historia de las Américas.* 4 vols. Madrid: Alhambra Longman, 1991.

Rashad, Adib [James Miller]. *The History of Islam and Black Nationalism in the Americas.* 2nd ed. Beltsville, MD: Writers, Inc., 1991.

Sondrol, Paul C. "Totalitarian and Authoritarian Dictators: A Comparison of Fidel Castro and Alfredo Stroessner." *Journal of Latin American Studies* 23 (1991): 599-620.

Thomas, David Hurst, ed. *Columbian Consequences.* Vol. 3, *The Spanish Borderlands in Pan-American Perspective.* Washington, DC: Smithsonian Institution Press, 1991.

Tyrrell, Ian. "American Exceptionalism in an Age of International History." *American Historical Review* 96 (1991): 1031-1055.

Viola, Herman J., and Carolyn Margolis. *Seeds of Change: A Quincentennial Commemoration.* Washington, DC: Smithsonian Institution Press, 1991.

Weber, David J. "The Idea of the Spanish Borderlands." In *Columbian Consequences.* Vol. 3, *The Spanish Borderlands in Pan-American Perspective.* Ed. David H. Thomas. Washington, DC: Smithsonian Institution Press, 1991.

1992

Berger, Thomas R. *A Long and Terrible Shadow: White Values, Native Rights in the Americas, 1492-1992.* Seattle: University of Washington Press, 1992.

Boone, Elizabeth Hill, and Walter D. Mignolo, eds. *Writing Without Words: Alternative Literacies in Mesoamerica and the Andes.* Durham, NC: Duke University Press, 1994.

Butzer, Karl W. "The Americas Before and After 1492: An Introduction to Current Geographical Research." *Annals of the Association of American Geographers* 82 (1992): 345-368.

Dambrosio, Monica. *The Americas in the Colonial Era.* Trans. Mary Di Ianni. Austin, TX: Raintree Steck-Vaughn, 1992.

Denevan, William M. *The Native Population of the Americas in 1492.* Madison: University of Wisconsin Press, 1992.

Doggett, Rachel, ed. *New World of Wonders: European Images of the Americas, 1492-1700.* Washington, DC: Folger Shakespeare Library, 1992.

Eisenstadt, S. N. "Culture, Religions and Development in North American and Latin American Civilizations." *International Social Science Journal* 34 (1992): 593-603.

Faragher, John Mack. "Americans, Mexicans, Métis: A Community Approach to the Comparative Study of North American Frontiers." In *Under an Open Sky: Rethinking America's Western Past*, 90-109. Eds. William Cronan, George Miles, and Jay Gitlin. New York: Norton, 1992.

Fiedel, Stuart J. *Prehistory of the Americas.* New York: Cambridge University Press, 1992.

Foster, Nelson, and Linda S. Cordell. *Chilies to Chocolate: Foods the Americas Gave the World.* Tucson: University of Arizona Press, 1992.

Garavaglia, Juan Carlos. "Human Beings and the Environment in America: On 'Determinism' and 'Possibilism.'" *International Social Science Journal* 44 (November 1992): 569-577.

Herzog, Lawrence A., ed. *Changing Boundaries in the Americas: New Perspectives on the U.S.-Mexican, Central American, and South American Borders.* San Diego: Center for U.S.-Mexican Studies, University of California, 1992.

Heth, Charlotte, ed. *Native American Dance: Ceremonies and Social Traditions.* Washington, DC: National Museum of the American Indian, Smithsonian Institution/Starwood, 1992.

Jaggers, Keith. "War and the Three Faces of Power: War Making and State Making in Europe and the Americas." *Comparative Political Studies* 25 (April 1992): 26-62.

Johnson, Harmer. *Guide to the Arts of the Americas: Pre-Columbian American Indians.* New York: Rizzoli, 1992.

Karras, Alan L. *Sojourners in the Sun: Scottish Migrants in Jamaica and the Chesapeake, 1740-1800.* Ithaca, NY: Cornell University Press, 1992.

Karras, Alan L., and J. R. McNeill, eds. *Atlantic American Societies: From Columbus Through Abolition, 1492-1888.* London: Routledge, 1992.

Kullen, Allan S., comp. *The Peopling of America: A Timeline of Events That Helped Shape Our Nation: A Historical Perspective.* Beltsville, MD: Portfolio Project, 1992.

Kupperman, Karen Ordahl. *North America and the Beginnings of European Colonization. Essays on the Columbian Encounter.* Washington, DC: American Historical Association, 1992.

Lévine, Daniel. *Americas Lost, 1492-1713: The First Encounter.* n.p.: Bordas, 1992.

Lippy, Charles H., et al. *Christianity Comes to the Americas, 1492-1776.* New York: Paragon House, 1992.

Mullin, Michael. *Africans in America: Slave Acculturation and Resistance in the American South and the Caribbean, 1736-1831.* Urbana: University of Illinois Press, 1992.

Pagden, Anthony. *European Encounters with the New World: From the Renaissance to Romanticism.* New Haven: Yale University Press, 1992.

Quijano, Aníbal, and Immanuel Wallerstein. "Americanity as a Concept, or the Americas in the Modern World-System." *International Social Science Journal* 34 (1992): 549-557.

Quincentennial: A Critical Exploration (1492-1992). San Antonio, TX: Incarnate Word,

The College, 1992.

Randall, Stephen J., Herman Konrad, and Sheldon Silverman, eds. *North America Without Borders? Integrating Canada, the United States, and Mexico.* Calgary, Alberta: University of Calgary Press, 1992.

Rivera, Luis N. *A Violent Evangelism: The Political and Religious Conquest of the Americas.* Louisville, KY: Westminster/John Knox Press, 1992.

Romano, Ruggieri. "The Institutional Inheritance of the American Colonies." *International Social Science Journal* 44 (November 1992): 559-568.

Salisbury, Neal. "Religious Encounters in a Colonial Context: New England and New France in the Seventeenth Century." *American Indian Quarterly* 16 (1992): 501-509.

Serrill, Michael S. "The Americas: Struggling to Be Themselves." *Time*, November 9, 1992, 52-54.

Shaw, Elizabeth A. *Plants of the New World: The First 150 Years.* Cambridge, MA: Harvard College Library, 1992.

Verano, John W., and Douglas H. Ubelaker, eds. *Disease and Demography in the Americas.* Washington, DC: Smithsonian Institution Press, 1992.

Williams, Raymond L. ed. *The Novel in the Americas.* Niwot: University Press of Colorado, 1992.

Winn, Peter. *Americas.* New York: Pantheon, 1992.

Zavala, Silvio. *El mundo americano en la época colonial: suplemento bibliográfico: 1967-1991.* México, DF: Instituto Panamericano de Geografía e Historia, 1992.

Zea, Leopoldo. The Role of the Americas in History. Trans. Sonja Karsen. Savage, MD: Rowman and Littlefield, 1992.

1993

Abénon, Lucien-René, and John A. Dickinson. *Les Français en Amérique: Histoire d'une colonisation.* Lyon: Presses Universitaires de Lyon, 1993.

"Amazing Stories (spread of maize in the Americas)." *The Economist* 327 (May 8, 1993): 89-90.

Braun, Barbara. *Pre-Columbian Art and the Post-Columbian World: Ancient American Sources of Modern Art.* New York: Harry Abrams, 1993.

Chavolla, Arturo. *La idea de América en el pensamiento europeo de Fernández de Oviedo a Hegel.* Guadalajara: Universidad de Guadalajara, 1993.

Cohen, Martin A., and Abraham J. Peck, eds. *Sephardim in the Americas: Studies in Culture and History.* Tuscaloosa: University of Alabama Press, 1993.

Cooke, Jacob E., ed. *Encyclopedia of the North American Colonies.* 3 vols. New York: Scribner's, 1993.

Eltis, David. "Europeans and the Rise and Fall of African Slavery in the Americas: An Interpretation." *American Historical Review* 98 (1993): 1399-1423.

Haar, Jerry, and Edgar J. Dosman, eds. *A Dynamic Partnership: Canada's Changing Role in the Americas.* Miami: University of Miami, North-South Center, and New Brunswick, NJ: Transaction 1993.

Higham, John. "Multiculturalism and Universalism: A History and Critique." *American Quarterly* 45 (1993): 195-219.

Lemonick, Michael D. "Coming to America." *Time.* May 3, 1993, 60-62.

Levy, Jim, and Peter Ross. "A Common History?: Two Latin Americanists View the Writing of US History in Hemispheric Perspective." *Australian Journal of American Studies* 12 (1993): 3-25.

Maybury-Lewis, David. "The Indians in the Americas: A Shameful History, A Modest Proposal." *Dissent* 40 (Fall 1993): 505-512.

Meinig, D. W. *The Shaping of America: A Geographical Perspective on 500 Years of History.* Vol. 2, *Continental America, 1800-1867.* New Haven: Yale University Press, 1993.

Nessen, Susan. "Multiculturalism in the Americas." *Art Journal* 52 (Summer 1993): 86-91.

Payne, Johnny. *Conquest of the New World: Experimental Fiction and Translation in the Americas.* Austin: University of Texas Press, 1993.

Rogers, J. Daniel, and Samuel M. Wilson, eds. *Ethnohistory and Archaeology: Approaches to Postcontact Change in the Americas.* New York: Plenum, 1993.

Taylor, William B., and Franklin Pease, eds. *Violence, Resistance and Survival in the Americas: Native Americans and the Legacy of Conquest.* Washington, DC: Smithsonian Institution Press, 1993.

Voeltz, Peter M. *Slave and Soldier: The Military Impact of Blacks in the Colonial Americas.* New York: Garland, 1993.

Waszkis, Helmut. *Mining in the Americas: Stories and History.* Cambridge: Woodhead, 1993

Weber, David J. "Our Hispanic Past: A Fuzzy View Persists." *The Chronicle of Higher Education,* March 10, 1993, A-44.

Whitten, Dorothea S., and Norman E. Whitten, Jr., eds. *Imagery and Creativity: Ethnoaesthetics and Art Worlds in the Americas.* Tucson: University of Arizona Press, 1993.

Wiencek, Henry. "The Spanish Among Us." *American Heritage* 44 (1993): 52-62.

Williams, Jerry M., and Robert E. Lewis, eds. *Early Images of the Americas: Transfer and Invention.* Tucson: University of Arizona Press, 1993.

1994

Conniff, Michael L., and Thomas J. Davis. *Africans in the Americas: A History of the Black Diaspora.* New York: St. Martin's Press, 1994.

Crosby, Alfred W. *Germs, Seeds and Animals: Studies in Ecological History.* Armonk, NY: M. E. Sharpe, 1994.

Curiel, Gustavo, Renato González Mello, and Juana Gutiérrez Haces, eds. *Arte, historia, e identidad en América: Visiones comparativas.* XVII Coloquio Internacional de Historia del Arte. 4 vols. México, DF: Instituto de Investigaciones Estéticas, Universidad Nacional Autónoma de México, 1994.

Galenson, David W. "The Rise and Fall of Indentured Servitude in the Americas: Economic Analysis." *Journal of Economic History* 44 (March 1994): 1-26.

Haase, Wolfgang, and Meyer Reinhold, eds. *The Classical Tradition and the Americas.* Vol. 1, *European Images of the Americas and the Classical Tradition.* Part 1. Berlin: Walter de Gruyter, 1994.

Higham, John. "The Future of American History." *Journal of American History* 80 (1994): 1289-1307.

Larsen, Clark S. "In the Wake of Columbus: Native Population Biology in the Postcontact Americas." *American Journal of Physical Anthropology* 19 (1994) 54 pp. (Supplement.)

Leiken, Robert S., ed. *A New Moment in the Americas.* New Brunswick, NJ: Transaction, 1994.

MacFarlane, Anthony. *The British in the Americas, 1480-1815.* London: Longman,

1994.

Slatta, Richard W. *The Cowboy Encyclopedia*. New York: W. W. Norton, 1994.

Tomasi, Lydio, Piero Gastaldo, and Thomas Row, eds. *The Columbus People: Perspectives in Italian Immigration to the Americas and Australia*. Staten Island, NY: Center for Migration Studies, 1994.

Véliz, Claudio. *The New World of the Gothic Fox: Culture and Economy in English and Spanish America*. Berkeley: University of California Press, 1994.

1995

Berger, Mark T. *Under Northern Eyes: Latin American Studies and U.S. Hegemony in the Americas, 1898-1990*. Bloomington: Indiana University Press, 1995.

Couillard, Marie, and Patrick Imbert, eds. *Les Discours du Nouveau Monde au XIXe siècle au Canada français et en Amérique Latine*. New York: Legas, 1995.

Field, Ron. *African Peoples of the Americas: From Slavery to Civil Rights*. New York: Cambridge University Press, 1995.

Guarneri, Carl J. "Reconsidering C. Vann Woodward's *The Comparative Approach to American History*." *Reviews in American History* 23.3 (September 1995): 552-563.

Kupperman, Karen Ordahl, ed. *America in European Consciousness, 1493-1750*. Chapel Hill: University of North Carolina Press, 1995.

Moore, Carlos, ed. *African Presence in the Americas*. Trenton, NJ: Africa World Press, 1995.

Native Americas. (Journal.)

"North American Art, Themeless." *The Economist*, March 4-10, 1995, 85.

Pagden, Anthony. *Lords of All the World: Ideologies of Empire in Spain, Britain, and France, 1492-1830*. New Haven: Yale University Press, 1995.

Palmer, Colin. *The First Passage — Blacks in the Americas, 1509-1617*. New York: Oxford University Press, 1995.

Smith, Peter H., ed. *Latin America in Comparative Perspective: New Approaches to Methods and Analysis*. Boulder, CO: Westview Press, 1995.

1996

Bryan, Anthony T., and Andrés Serbin, eds. *Distant Cousins: The Caribbean-Latin American Relationship*. Miami: North-South Center, University of Miami,1996.

Cooper, Frederick. "Race, Ideology, and the Perils of Comparative History." *American Historical Review* 101 (1996): 1122-1139.

Hall, Gwendolyn M. *Social Control in Slave Plantation Societies: A Comparison of St. Domingue and Cuba*. Baton Rouge: Louisiana State University Press, 1996.

Hill, Jonathan D. *History, Power, and Identity: Ethnogenesis in the Americas, 1492-1992*. Iowa City: University of Iowa Press, 1996.

Langley, Lester D. *The Americas in the Age of Revolution, 1750-1850*. New Haven: Yale University Press, 1996.

Mace, Gordon, and Jean-Philippe Thérien, eds. *Foreign Policy and Regionalism in the Americas*. Boulder, CO: Lynne Rienner, 1996.

Magaro Rubin, Amy. "Trying to Revive a 3-Way Collaboration." *The Chronicle of Higher Education* 42 (May 17, 1996): A43, A46.

Marx, Jennifer. *Gold in the Americas*. Dallas, TX: Ram Publishing, 1996.

Polzer, Charles, S.J. "As I See It: Historian's View." *Company: A Magazine of the American Jesuits* 13 (1996): 26-27. (Comparative study of the historical role of the Jesuits in Canada, Mexico and the United States.)

Trigger, Bruce, et al., eds. *The Cambridge History of the Native Peoples of the Americas*. 3 Vols. New York: Cambridge University Press, 1996.

Walker, William O. III, ed. *Drugs in the Western Hemisphere: An Odyssey of Cultures in Conflict*. Jaguar Books on Latin America no. 12, Wilmington, DE: Scholarly Resource's, 1996.

Williams, Meyers, A. J. "Slavery, Rebellion, and Revolution in the Americas: A Historiographical Scenario on the Theses of Genovese and Others." *Journal of Black Studies* 26 (March 1996): 381-400.

1997

Blackburn, Robin. *The Making of New World Slavery: From the Baroque to the Modern, 1492-1800*. London: Verso, 1997.

Carroll, Anne W. *Christ and the Americas*. Rockford, IL: Tan Books, 1997.

Dickason, Olive P. *The Myth of the Savage and the Beginnings of French Colonialism in the Americas*. Edmonton: University of Alberta Press, 1997.

Guarneri, Carl J. *America Compared: American History in International Perspective*. 2 vols. Boston: Houghton Mifflin, 1997.

——. "Out of Its Shell: Internationalizing the Teaching of United States History." *Perspectives* 35.2 (February 1997): 1, 5-8.

Harrison, Lawrence E. *The Pan-American Dream: Do Latin America's Cultural Values Discourage True Partnership with the United States and Canada?* New York: Basic Books, 1997.

Jenkins, Everett. *Pan-Africa Chronology: A Comprehensive Reference to the Black Quest for Freedom in Africa, The Americas, Europe, and Asia, 1865-1915*. Jefferson, NC: McFarland, 1997.

Schwartz, Marion. *A History of Dogs in the Early Americas*. New Haven: Yale University Press, 1997.

Slatta, Richard W. *Comparing Cowboys and Frontiers*. Norman: University of Oklahoma Press, 1997.

Weber, David J. "Conflicts and Accommodations: Hispanic and Anglo-American Borders in Historical Perspective, 1670-1853." *Journal of the Southwest* 39 (1997): 1-32.

Wood, Gordon S. "Doing the Continental." *The New York Review of Books* 44.18 (November 20, 1997): 51-54.

Woodward, C. Vann. *A Comparative Approach to American History*. Repr. New York: Oxford University Press, 1997.

1998

Guy, Donna J., and Thomas E. Sheridan, eds. *Contested Ground: Comparative Frontiers on the Northern and Southern Edges of the Spanish Empire*. Tucson: University of Arizona Press, 1998.

Lane, Kris E. *Pillaging the Empire: Piracy in the Americas, 1500-1750*. Armonk, NY: M. E. Sharpe, 1998.

Magnaghi, Russell M. *Indian Slavery, Labor, Evangelization, and Captivity in the Americas: An Annotated Bibliography*. Lanham, MD: Scarecrow Press, 1998.

Bibliography

PRIMARY SOURCES

Bancroft Library, University of California, Berkeley.
Bentley Library, University of Michigan, Ann Arbor.
California State University at San Francisco, Archives.
Central Upper Peninsula and University Archives, Northern Michigan University, Marquette.
Columbus Memorial Library, Organization of American States, Washington, DC.
Georgia State Archives and History Department, Atlanta.
Henry Huntington Library, San Marino, California.
Library of Congress, Rare Book Room, Washington, DC.
McGill University Archives, Montreal, Quebec, Canada.
National Archives, Washington, DC.
Queen's University Archives, Kingston, Ontario, Canada.
St. Louis University, University Archives, St. Louis, Missouri.
Smith College, College Archives, Northampton, Massachusetts.
Stanford University, University Archives, Stanford, California.
Tulane University, University Archives, New Orleans, Louisiana.
University of Arizona, Special Collections, Tucson.
University of San Francisco Archives, Gleason Library, San Francisco, California.
University of Texas, Austin, American History Center.
University of Toronto Archives, Toronto, Ontario, Canada.

SECONDARY SOURCES

Aguilar, Alonso. *Pan-Americanism from Monroe to the Present: A View from the Other Side*. Trans. Asa Zatz. New York: Monthly Review Press, 1968.
Aguilar Vidal, Oscar. *Don Diego Barros Arana*. Santiago de Chile: Imprenta Universitaria, 1930.

Alcedo, Antonio de. *El diccionario geográfico histórico de las Indias Occidentales o América.* 5 vols. Madrid: Imprenta de B. Cano, 1786-1789. Repr. Madrid: Ediciones Atlas, 1967.

———. *The Geographical and Historical Dictionary of America and the West Indies Containing an Entire Translation of the Spanish Work of Colonel Don Antinio de Alcedo with Large Additions and Compilations from Modern Voyages and Travels and from Original and Authentic Information.* Trans. G. A. Thompson. 5 vols. London: J. Carpenter, 1812-1815. Repr. New York: Burt Franklin, 1970.

"All Aboard! American Republics at the New York World's Fair." *Bulletin of the Pan-American Union* 73.7 (July 1939): 387-412.

Alvarez Barret, Luis, and Antonio Rangel. *Historia de América.* México, DF: Talleres de "El Nacional," 1938.

Alvord, Clarence W. "A Critical Analysis of the Works of Reuben Gold Thwaites." Mississippi Valley Historical Association, *Proceedings for the Year 1913-1914* 7 (1914): 321-333.

"American Council of Learned Societies and the Newberry Library." *Latin American Studies in the United States.* Chicago: ACLS, 1958.

"An American Exposition." *Outlook* 67 (April 13, 1901): 850-851.

Anonymous. *A General History of North and South America.* London: Mayhew, Isaac and Co., 1834.

Annual Report, 1959-1960, of the John Carter Brown Library. Providence, RI: Brown University, 1962.

Announcement of Courses, 1920-1921. Berkeley: University of California Press, 1920.

Applebaum, Stanley. *The New York World's Fair, 1939-1940.* New York: Dover, 1977.

Appleby, Joyce. "Recovering America's Historic Diversity: Beyond Exceptionalism." *Journal of American History* 79.2 (September 1992): 419-431.

Arciniegas, Germán. *America in Europe: A History of the New World in Reverse.* Trans. Gabriela Arciniegas and R. Victoria Arana. San Diego: Harcourt Brace Jovanovich, 1986.

———. *Caribbean: Sea of the New World.* Trans. Harriet de Onís. New York: Knopf, 1946.

———. "Las cuatro Américas." *Cuadernos* 60 (1962): 1-9.

———. "The Four Americas." *Trans. Helen Delpar.* In *Do the Americas Have a Common History? A Critique of the Bolton Theory,* 235-249. Ed. Lewis Hanke. New York: Knopf, 1964.

———. "Have the Americas a Common History? A South American View." *Canadian Historical Review* 23 (1942): 148-156.

———. "Latin America at the San Francisco Exposition." *Bulletin of the Pan-American Union* 73.10 (October 1939): 549-561.

Armillas, Pedro. *A Program of the History of the New World Coordinator's Summary Reports.* Vol. 1, *The Native Period in the History of the New World.* Trans. Glenda Crevenna and Theo Crevenna. Publication no. 108. México, DF: Instituto Panamericano de Geografía e Historia, Comisión de Historia, 1962.

Armstrong, Christopher, and H. V. Nelles. *Southern Exposure: Canadian Promoters in Latin America and the Caribbean, 1896-1930.* Toronto: University of Toronto Press, 1988.

The Articulate Traveler: Johann Georg Kohl, Chronicler of the American Continents. A Library of Congress Exhibition. Madison Building Foyer, March 24-June 27,

1993. Washington, DC: Library of Congress, 1993.

"Arts on Parade." *Time* 35 (June 24, 1940): 69.

Ausubel, Herman. *Historians and Their Craft: A Study of the Presidential Addresses of the American Historical Association, 1884-1945.* New York: Columbia University Press, 1950.

Axtell, James. "A North American Perspective for Colonial History." *History Teacher* 12.4 (1979): 549-562.

Bailey, Thomas A. *The American Pageant Revisited: Recollections of a Stanford Historian.* Stanford, CA: Hoover Institution Press, 1982.

Bakewell, Peter. "Conversación sobre historia: Peter Bakewell entrevista a Silvio Zavala." *Memoria de El Colegio Nacional* 10 (1982): 13-28.

———. "An Interview with Silvio Zavala." Trans. Dolores Gutiérrez Mills. *Hispanic American Historical Review* 62 (1982): 553-568.

Ballesteros y Beretta, Antonio. *Historia de América y de los pueblos Americanos.* 2 vols. Barcelona: Salvat, 1936.

Bancroft, Hubert Howe. *Literary Industries: A Memoir.* New York: Harper. 1891.

Bandelier, Adolph. "America." In *Catholic Encyclopedia* 1 (1907): 409-416.

Bannon, John Francis, S.J. *Colonial North America – A Short History.* St. Louis: St. Louis University Press, 1946.

———. *The Department of History, St. Louis University, 1925-1973: An Historical Sketch.* St. Louis: n.p., 1980.

———. *Herbert E. Bolton: The Historian and the Man, 1870-1953.* Tucson: University of Arizona Press, 1978.

———. "Herbert Eugene Bolton – Western Historian." *Western Historical Quarterly* 2 (1971): 261-282.

———. *History of the Americas.* 2 vols. 1952. 2nd ed. New York: McGraw-Hill, 1963.

———. *The Spanish Borderlands Frontier, 1513-1821.* New York: Holt, Rinehart and Winston, 1970.

———. "A Western Historian – How He Got That Way." *Western Historical Quarterly* 1 (1970): 243-248.

———, ed. *Bolton and the Spanish Borderlands.* Norman: University of Oklahoma Press, 1964.

Barros Arana, Diego. *Compendio de historia de América.* 2 vols. Santiago, Chile: Imprenta del Ferrocarril, 1865.

———. *Compendio elemental de historia de América.* Santiago, Chile: Imprenta del Ferrocarril, 1865.

Batllori, Miguel. "Silvio Zavala en mis recuerdos." *Historia Mexicana* 39.1 (1989): 3-6.

Becker, Carl L. *Beginnings of the American People.* Boston: Houghton Mifflin, 1915.

Bellot, H. Hale. *American History and American Historians: A Review of Recent Contributions to the Interpretation of the History of the United States.* Norman: University of Oklahoma Press, 1952.

Bender, Thomas. "Public Culture: Inclusion and Synthesis in American History." In *Historical Literacy: The Case for History in American Education,* 188-202. Ed. Paul Gagnon and the Bradley Commission on History in Schools. New York: Macmillan, 1989.

———. "Wholes and Parts: The Need for Synthesis in American History." *Journal of American History* 73 (June 1986): 120-136.

Bendix, Reinhard. "Concepts in Comparative Historical Analysis." In *Comparative Research Across Cultures and Nations, 67-81.* Ed. Stein Rokkan. Paris: International Social Science Council, and The Hague: Mouton, 1968.

Berger, Carl. *The Writing of Canadian History: Aspects of English-Canadian Historical Writing Since 1900.* 2nd ed. Toronto: University of Toronto Press, 1986.

Berger, Mark T. *Under Northern Eyes: Latin American Studies and U.S. Hegemony in the Americas, 1898-1990.* Bloomington: Indiana University Press, 1995.

Berkhofer, Robert F., Jr. *A Behavioral Approach to Historical Analysis.* New York: Free Press, 1969.

——. *Beyond the Great Story: History as Text and Discourse.* Cambridge, MA: Harvard University Press, 1995.

Berman, Milton. *John Fiske: The Evolution of a Popularizer.* Cambridge, MA: Harvard University Press, 1961.

Bernstein, Harry. *Making an Inter-American Mind.* Gainesville: University of Florida Press, 1961.

Bertelson, Cynthia D. "Lewis Hanke: Historian and Propagandist." Thesis, University of Wisconsin, White Water, 1975.

Billington, Ray Allen. Frederick Jackson Turner: Historian, Scholar, Teacher. New York: Oxford University Press, 1973.

Binkley, William C. "Have the Americas a Common History?: A United States View." *Canadian Historical Review* 23 (1942): 125-132.

Bibliotheca Americana, Being Choice Collection of Books Relating to North and South America and the West Indies. Paris: Paul Renouard, 1831.

Biobibliografía de Silvio Zavala. México, DF: El Colegio Nacional, 1993.

Black, John B. *The Art of History; A Study of Four Great Historians of the Eighteenth Century.* New York: Crofts & Co., 1926. Repr. New York: Russell & Russell, 1965.

Blackmar, Frank W. *Spanish Institutions of the Southwest.* Baltimore: Johns Hopkins University Press, 1891.

Blair, Emma Helen, and James Alexander Robertson, eds. *The Philippine Islands, 1493-1803.* 55 vols. Cleveland: Arthur Clark, 1903-1909.

Blakemore, Harold. *Latin American Studies in British Universities: Progress and Prospects.* London: Hispanic and Luso-Brazilian Councils, 1971.

Bloch, Marc. "Pour une Histoire comparée des sociétiés européenes." *Revue de Synthèse Historique* (Paris) 46 (1928): 15-50.

——. "Toward a Comparative History of European Societies." In *Enterprise and Secular Change: Readings in Economic History. 494-521.* Trans. Jelle C. Riemersma. Ed. Frederic C. Lane and Jelle C. Riemersma. Homewood, IL: Irwin, 1953.

Bolton, Frederick. "Random Memories of an Admiring Brother." *Arizona and the West* 4 (1961): 72-83.

Bolton, Herbert E. *The Bolton Collection — Manuscript Materials for the History of the Pacific Coast and the Southwest.* Berkeley: Bancroft Library, 1951.

——. "The Confessions of a Wayward Professor." *The Americas* 6 (1950): 359-362.

——. "Cultural Coöperation with Latin America." *National Educational Association Journal* 29 (1940): 1-4.

——. "Defensive Spanish Expansion and the Significance of the Borderlands."

In *The Trans-Mississippi West: Papers Read at a Conference Held at the University of Colorado, June 18-June 21, 1929*, 1-42. Ed. James Field Willard and Colin Brummitt Goodykoontz. Boulder: University of Colorado Press, 1930.

————. "The Epic of Greater America." *American Historical Review* 38 (1933): 448-474.

————. *La epopeya de la máxima América*. Trans. Carmen Alessio Robles. Publication no. 30. México, DF: Instituto Panamericano de Geografía e Historia, 1937.

————. *Guide to Materials for the History of the United States in the Principal Archives of Mexico*. Washington, DC: Carnegie Institution of Washington, 1913. Repr. New York: Kraus, 1965.

————. *History of the Americas: A Syllabus with Maps*. 1928. 2nd ed. Boston: Ginn, 1935.

————. "An Introductory Course in American History." *Historical Outlook* 15.1 (1924): 17-20.

————. "The Mission as a Frontier Institution in the Spanish-American Colonies." *American Historical Review* 23 (1917): 42-61.

————. "The Place of American History in the High-School Course." *School Review: A Journal of Secondary Education* 9 (1901): 516-525.

————. "Some Materials for Southwestern History in the Archivo General de Mexico." Texas State Historical Association, *Quarterly* 6 (October 1902): 103-112; 7 (January 1904): 196-213.

————. *The Spanish Borderlands: A Chronicle of Old Florida and the Southwest.* "Chronicles of America" series, vol. 23. New Haven: Yale University Press, 1921.

————. "Tienda de Cuervo's Ynspección of Laredo, 1757." Texas State Historical Association, *Quarterly* 6 (January 1903): 187-203.

————. "'Turner, as I Remember Him.'" Ed. Wilbur R. Jacobs. *Mid-America* 36 (1954): 54-61.

————. *Wider Horizons of American History*. New York: Appleton-Century, 1939. Repr. Notre Dame, IN: University of Notre Dame Press, 1967.

Bolton, Herbert E., and Thomas Maitland Marshall. *The Colonization of North America, 1492-1783*. New York: Macmillan, 1920.

Bonnell, Victoria E. "The Uses of Theory: Concepts and Comparison in Historical Sociology." *Comparative Studies in Society and History* 22 (1980): 156-173.

Borah, Woodrow W. Review of *Do the Americas Have a Common History?*, by Lewis Hanke. *Hispanic American Historical Review* 45 (1965): 101-03.

————. Review of *The Native Period in the History of the New World*, by Pedro Armillas. *American Historical Review* 69 (1964): 851-852.

Botting, Douglas. *Humboldt and the Cosmos*. New York: Harper, 1973.

Bourne, Edward G. *Spain in America, 1450-1580*. New York: Harper, 1904.

————. "The Relation of American History to Other Fields of Historical Study." In *Congress of Arts and Science, Universal Exposition, St. Louis, 1904*. Ed. Howard J. Rogers. 2 vols. Boston: Houghton Mifflin, 1906.

Boyd, Julian, et al., eds. *The Papers of Thomas Jefferson*. 27 vols. to date. Princeton: Princeton University Press, 1950-1997.

Brebner, John B. *The Explorers of North America, 1492-1806*. New York: Macmillan, 1937.

————. *The Neutral Yankees of Nova Scotia: A Marginal Colony During the Revolu-*

tionary Years. New York: Columbia University Press, 1937.

———. *New England's Outpost: Acadia before the Conquest of Canada.* New York: Columbia University Press, 1927.

———. *North Atlantic Triangle: The Interplay of Canada, the United States, and Great Britain.* New Haven: Yale University Press, 1945.

Brooks, Philip C. "Do the Americas Share a Common History?" *Revista de historia de América* 33 (1952): 75-83.

Brown, Everett S. "Freshman History at the University of California." *History Teacher's Magazine* 7 (1916): 268-269.

Brown, George W., ed. "Have the Americas a Common History?" *Canadian Historical Review* 23 (1942): 125-156.

———. "Have the Americas a Common History?: A Canadian View." *Canadian Historical Review* 23 (1942): 132-138.

———. Review of *The Coming of the White Man, 1492-1848,* by Herbert I. Priestley. *Canadian Historical Review* 12 (1931): 69.

Brown, George W., J.M.S. Careless, Gerald M. Craig, and Eldon Ray, eds. *Canada and the Americas.* Toronto: J. M. Dent, 1953.

Brown, Richard Maxwell. "Western Violence: Structure, Values, Myth." *Western Historical Quarterly* 24 (1993): 5-20.

Buffington, Arthur H. "British and French Imperialism in North America." *History Teacher's Magazine* 10 (1919): 489-496.

Bulletin of the University of Texas. Austin: University of Texas Press. April 1, 1902; June 1, 1904; June 1, 1905; April 1, 1906; February 15, 1908.

Burke, Edmund. *An Account of the European Settlements in America.* 2 vols. London: R & J Dodsley, 1757.

Burke, Peter, ed. *New Perspectives on History Writing.* University Park: Pennsylvania State University Press, 1991.

Burkholder, Mark A., and Lyman L. Johnson. *Colonial Latin America.* New York: Oxford University Press, 1990.

Burmester, Luis Germán. *Historia Americana.* Vol. 1. Buenos Aires: n.p., 1939.

Burns, E. Bradford. *Latin America: A Concise Interpretative History.* 6th ed. Englewood Cliffs, NJ: Prentice-Hall, 1994.

Burrage, Henry S., ed. *Early English and French Voyages, Chiefly from Hakluyt, 1534-1608.* New York: Scribner's, 1906.

Bushnell, David, and Lyle N. McAlister. "An Interview with Lewis Hanke." *Hispanic American Historical Review* 68 (1988): 653-674.

Bynum, Caroline Walker. "The Last Eurocentric Generation." *Perspectives* 34.2 (February 1996): 3-4.

Calderón, Quijano, José Antonio. *El Americanismo en Seville, 1900-1980.* Seville: Escuela de Estudios Hispano-Americanos de Seville, 1987.

Calendar of the Faculty of Arts, Queen's University, Kingston, Ontario. Kingston, ON: Jackson Press, 1922.

Calendar of the Faculty of Arts, 1933-1934, Queen's University. Kingston, ON: Jackson Press, 1933.

Carroll, John Alexander. "Dedication to Herbert Eugene Bolton." *Arizona and the West* 1 (1959): 102-104.

Cassani, Juan E. "Disertación del director del Instituto de Didáctica." *II° Congreso Internacional de Historia de América.* Buenos Aires: Academia Nacional de la

Historia, 1938.

Castañeda, Carlos E., and Jack Autry Dabbs. *Guide to the Latin American Manuscripts in the University of Texas Library*. Cambridge, MA: Harvard University Press, 1939.

Caughey, John Walton. "Herbert Eugene Bolton." *Pacific Historical Review* 9 (1953): 108-112.

——. "Herbert Eugene Bolton." *Turner, Bolton, Webb: Three Historians of the West*, 41-74. By Wilbur R. Jacobs, John W. Caughey, and Joe Franz. Seattle: University of Washington Press, 1965.

——. "Hubert Howe Bancroft: Historican of Western America." *American Historical Review* 50 (1945): 461-470.

Chapman, Charles E. *Colonial Hispanic America: A History*. New York: Macmillan, 1923.

——. "The Founding of the Review." *Hispanic American Historical Review* 1 (1918): 8-23.

——. "A Producing Class in Hispanic-American History." *History Teacher's Magazine* 9 (1918): 84-86.

——. *Republican Hispanic America: A History*. New York: Macmillan, 1937.

Chapman, Gerald W. *Edmund Burke: The Practical Imagination*. Cambridge, MA: Harvard University Press, 1967.

Chase, Lew Allen. "How the Furs Came Down from the North Country." *History Teacher's Magazine* 7 (February 1916): 44-46.

——. "The Last American Frontier." *History Teacher's Magazine* 6 (February 1915): 37-46.

Chaunu, Pierre. *Les Amériques, 16ᵉ, 17ᵉ, 18ᵉ siècles*. Paris: A. Colin, 1976.

Chavolla, Arturo. *La idea de América en el pensamiento europeo de Fernández de Oviedo a Hegel*. Guadalajara: Universidad de Guadalajara, 1993.

Chevalier, François. "Silvio Zavala, primer historiador de la América hispano-indígena. El caso del trabajo de la tierra." *Historia Mexicana* 39 (1989): 21-32.

Christman, Florence. The Romance of Balboa Park. San Diego: San Diego Historical Society, 1985.

The Civilization of the Americas: Lectures Arranged by the University of California at Los Angeles, Committee on International Relations, Delivered in the Spring of 1938. Berkeley: University of California Press, 1938.

Clark, Edith M. "The History Curriculum Since 1850." *History Teacher's Magazine* 11 (February 1920): 58-68.

Clark, John Spencer. *The Life and Letters of John Fiske*. 2 vols. Boston: Houghton Mifflin, 1917.

Clementi, Hebe. *La frontera en América: Una clave interpretativa de la historia americana*. 4 vols. Buenos Aires: Editorial Leviatán, 1985.

Cleven, N. Andrew N. "Latin American History in Our Secondary Schools." *History Teacher's Magazine* 8 (1917): 219-222.

Cline, Howard F., ed. *Latin American History: Essays on Its Study and Teaching, 1898-1965*. 2 vols. Austin: University of Texas Press, 1967.

——, comp. *Latin American Studies in the United States, Proceedings of a Meeting [of the American Council of Learned Societies Devoted to Humanistic Studies] Held in Chicago, November 6-8, 1958*. Washington, DC: Hispanic Foundation, Reference Department, Library of Congress, 1958.

Comas, Juan. *Cien años de congresos internacionales de americanistas: Ensayo histórico-crítico y bibliográfico*. México, DF: Instituto de Investigaciones Históricas, 1974.

Compagnoni, Giuseppe. *Storia dell' America, in continuazione del compendio della storia universale del Sig. conte di Segur....* 28 vols. Milan: Fusi, Stella e Com., 1820-1822.

"Compendio de la historia de América, por don Diego Barros Arana. Noticia sobre esta obra." *Anales de la Universidad* 22 (May 1865): 634.

Cone, Carl B. *Burke and the Nature of Politics*, 2nd ed. 2 vols. 1957. Lexington: University of Kentucky Press, 1964.

Conference on Canadian-American Affairs. Canton, NJ: St. Lawrence University Press, 1935; Kingston, ON: Queen's University Press, 1937; Canton, NJ: St. Lawrence University Press, 1939; Kingston, ON: Queen's University Press, 1941.

Contreras, Remedios. *Catálogo de la colección de manuscritos sobre America de la Real Academia de la Historia*. Badajoz: Real Academia de la Historia, Institución "Pedro Valencia," 1978.

Cooke, Jacob E., ed. *Encyclopedia of the North American Colonies*. 3 vols. New York: Scribner's, 1993.

Cooper, Frederick. "Race, Ideology, and the Perils of Comparative History." *American Historical Review* 101 (1996): 1122-1139.

Cooper, William J. "Berkeley Public Schools — Courses in History." *History Teacher's Magazine* 6 (1915): 328-330.

Corbett, Percy E. "Canada and Pan Americanism." *Quarterly Journal of Inter-American Relations* 1.4 (1939): 30-34.

Cotterill, Robert S. *A Short History of the Americas*. 1939. Revised ed. New York: Prentice-Hall, 1945.

Couillard, Marie, and Patrick Imbert, eds. *Les discours du Nouveau Monde au XIXe siècle au Canada français et en Amérique Latine*. New York: Legas, 1995.

Cox, Isaac J. "Courses in Hispanic American History." *Hispanic American Historical Review* 2 (1919): 399-403.

———. "The European Background for the History Course in American History." *History Teacher's Magazine* 7 (1916): 163-169.

———. Review of *The Coming of the White Man, 1492-1848*, by Herbert I. Priestley. *American Historical Review* 35 (1930): 374.

———. "Syllabi of Courses: The History of Hispanic America." *Hispanic American Historical Review* 2 (1919): 419-430.

Craven, Wesley F. *The Colonies in Transition, 1660-1713*. New York: Harper & Row, 1968.

Cronan, William, George Miles, and Jay Gitlin, eds. *Under an Open Sky: Rethinking America's Western Past*. New York: Norton, 1992.

Curiel, Gustavo, Renato González Mello, and Juana Gutiérrez Haces, eds. *Arte, historia, e identidad en América: Visiones comparativas*. XVII Coloquio Internacional de Historia del Arte. 4 vols. México, DF: Instituto de Investigaciones Estéticas, Universidad Nacional Autónoma de México, 1994.

Curtin, Philip D. "Depth, Span, and Relevance." *American Historical Review* 89 (1984): 1-9.

Dambrosio, Monica. *The Americas in the Colonial Era*. Trans. Mary Di Ianni. Austin, TX: Raintree Steck-Vaughn, 1992.

Daudelin, Jean, and Edgar J. Dosman, eds. *Beyond Mexico*. Ottawa: Carleton University Press, 1995.

Davenport, Frances G., ed. *Treaties Bearing on the History of the United States and Its Dependencies*. 4 vols. Washington, DC: Government Printing Office, 1914.

Davis, Harold E. *The Americas in History*. New York: Ronald Press, 1953.

———. "Three Interpretations of America in History." *The Americas* 10 (1953): 131-140.

Davis, Natalie Zemon. "Who Owns History? History in the Profession." *Perspectives* 34.8 (November 1996): 1, 4-6.

"A Decade of History Teaching [1909-1919]." *History Teacher's Magazine* 10 (December 1919): 497-511.

DeConde, Alexander. *Herbert Hoover's Latin American Policy*. Stanford, CA: Stanford University Press, 1951.

Delgado-Gómez, Angel. *Spanish Historical Writing About the New World, 1493-1700*. Providence, RI: The John Carter Brown Library, 1992.

Delpar, Helen. *The Enormous Vogue of Things Mexican: Cultural Relations Between the United States and Mexico, 1920-1935*. Tuscaloosa: University of Alabama Press, 1992.

De Terra, Helmut. *Humboldt: The Life and Times of Alexander von Humboldt, 1769-1859*. New York: Knopf, 1955.

Dickerson, O. M. Review of *The Coming of the White Man, 1492-1848*, by Herbert I. Priestley. *Mississippi Valley Historical Review* 16 (1930): 565.

"Diego Rivera: His Amazing New Mural Depicts Pan-American Unity." *Life* 10 (March 3, 1941): 52-56.

Directory of Canadian Scholars Interested in Latin American and Caribbean Studies. 4th ed. Ottawa: Canadian Association of Latin American and Caribbean Studies, 1982.

Donoso, Ricardo. *Diego Barros Arana*. México, DF: Instituto Panamericano de Geografía e Historia, 1967.

Doyle, Henry G. "Spanish Studies in the United States." *Bulletin of the Pan-American Union* 60 (March 1926): 223-234.

Dufour, Ronald P. *Colonial America*. St. Paul, MN: West, 1994.

Duggan, Stephen. *The Two Americas: An Interpretation*. New York: Scribner's, 1934.

Dunn, William Edward. "Portrait of a Teacher: Herbert E. Bolton." *The Alcalde* (University of Texas Press) 42 (1953): 54-56.

Dunne, Peter M., S. J. "The Americas and the Jesuits." *San Francisco Quarterly* 3 (1937): 1-15.

Eastlack, Charles L. "Herbert Eugene Bolton (1870-1953): His Ideas and Practice as a Historian of the Americas." Thesis, University of Texas, Austin, 1958.

Eccles, W. J. *The Canadian Frontier, 1534-1760*. New York: Holt, Rinehart & Winston, 1972. Rev. ed. Albuquerque: University of New Mexico Press, 1983.

———. *France in America*. 1972. 2nd ed. East Lansing: Michigan State University Press, 1992.

Eisenstadt, S. N. "Culture, Religions and Development in North American and Latin American Civilizations." *International Social Science Journal* 34 (1992): 593-603.

———. "Social Institutions: Comparative Study." *International Encyclopedia of the Social Sciences* 14 (1968): 421-428.

Emery, Edwin. "Bolton of California." *California Monthly* 47 (1941): 12-13, 39-43.

Espinosa, J. Manuel. "Bolton: History of the Americas." *Historial Bulletin* (St. Louis University) 14 (1936): 81-82.

——. *Inter-American Beginnings of U.S. Cultural Diplomacy, 1936-1948.* Historical Studies no. 2. Washington, DC: U.S. Department of State, Bureau of Educational and Cultural Affairs, 1976.

Etulain, Richard W., ed. *Writing Western History: Essays on Major Western Historians.* Albuquerque: University of New Mexico Press, 1991.

Everett, Alexander H. *America: Or a General Survey of the Political Situation of the Several Powers of the Western Continent with Conjectures on Their Future Prospects.* Philadelphia: H. C. Carey and I. Lea, 1827.

Everett, Edward. *The Discovery and Colonization of America, and Immigration to the United States.* Boston: Little, Brown, 1853.

Ewing, Russell C. "Our Cultural Contact with Latin America." *Arizona Quarterly* 3.3 (Autumn 1946): 47-56.

——. "Southwestern Chronicle: Modern Histories and Historians of the Spanish Southwest." *Arizona Quarterly* 4.1 (1947): 71-82.

Etzioni, Amitai, and F. Dubow, eds. *Comparative Perspectives: Theories and Methods.* Boston: Little, Brown, 1970.

Fell, Marie Léonone. *The Foundations of Nativism in American Textbooks, 1783-1860.* Washington, DC: Catholic University of America Press, 1941.

Fifer, Valerie. *United States Perceptions of Latin America, 1850-1930: A "New West" South of Capricorn?* Manchester: Manchester University Press, 1991.

"Fifth Columnists Beware." *Time* 37.1 (January 6, 1944): 32-33.

Fink, Carole. *Marc Bloch: A Life in History.* New York: Cambridge University Press, 1989.

"The First Annual Meeting." *Hispania* 1 (1918): 15.

Fiske, John. *The Discovery of America, with Some Account of Ancient America and the Spanish Conquest.* Boston: Houghton, 1892.

FitzGerald, Frances. *America Revisited: History Schoolbooks in the Twentieth Century.* New York: Vintage, 1980.

Fleener, Charles J. "John Francis Bannon, S.J. (1905-1986)." *Hispanic American Historical Review* 67 (1987): 139-142.

The Foreign Student in America. New York: Association Press, 1925.

"Forum: 'Why the West Is Lost.'" *The William and Mary Quarterly* 51.4 (October 1994): 717-754.

Fredrickson, George M. "Comparative History." In *The Past Before Us: Contemporary Historical Writing in the United States,* 457-473. Ed. Michael Kammen. Ithaca, NY: Cornell University Press, 1980.

——. "Giving a Comparative Dimension to American History: Problems and Opportunities." *Journal of Interdisciplinary History* 16 (1985): 108-110.

Funes, Gregorio. "Review of *Ensayo de la historia civil del Paraguay, Buenos Aires y Tucuman." North American Review and Miscellaneous Journal* 3 (1821): 432-443.

Gabriel, Ralph H., and Arthur B. Darling. *The Yale Course of Home Study Based on the Chronicles of America.* New Haven: Yale University Press, 1924.

Gagnon, Paul and the Bradley Commission on History in Schools, eds. *Historical Legacy: The Case for History in American Education.* New York: Macmillan, 1989.

Gandía, Enrique de. "El panamericanismo en la historia." *Boletín de la Academia Nacional de la Historia* (Buenos Aires) 5 (1942): 383-393.

———. "Pan-Americanism in History." In *Do the Americas Have a Common History?* Ed. Lewis Hanke. New York: Knopf, 1964.

General Catalogue...1940-41. Berkeley: University of California Press, 1940.

General Catalogue...1942-43. Berkeley: University of California Press, 1942.

Genovese, Eugene D. "The Comparative Focus in Latin American History." *Journal of Inter-American Studies and World Affairs and World Affairs* 12 (1970): 317-327.

Geyer, Michael, and Charles Bright. "History in the Global Age." *American Historical Review* 100 (1995): 1034-1060.

Gibson, A. H., and John S. Whitehead. *Yankees in Paradise: The Pacific Basin Frontier.* Albuquerque: University of New Mexico Press, 1993.

Gibson, Charles. "Latin America and the Americas." In *The Past Before Us: Contemporary Historical Writing in the United States,* 187-202. Ed. Michael Kammen. Ithaca, NY: Cornell University Press, 1980.

———. "Pan-American Institute of Geography and History." *Hispanic American Historical Review* 37 (1957): 146-149.

———. *Spain in America.* New York: Harper & Row, 1966.

———, ed. *The Spanish Tradition in America.* New York: Harper & Row, 1968.

Gibson, Charles, and Benjamin Keen. "Trends of United States Studies in Latin American History." *American Historical Review* 62 (1957): 855-877.

Gilderhus, Mark T. *Pan-American Visions: Woodrow Wilson in the Western Hemisphere, 1913-1921.* Tucson: University of Arizona Press, 1986.

Goetz, Delia, and Varian Fry. *The Good Neighbors: The Story of the Two Americas.* New York: Foreign Policy Association, 1939.

Goldsmith, Peter H. *The Next Steps in Interamerican Relations.* International Conciliation, Pan-American Division, Bulletin no. 14. New York: American Association of International Conciliation, Pan-American Division, 1917.

Goodrich, Samuel G. *North America: Or the United States and the Adjacent Countries.* Louisville, KY: Morton and Griswold, 1847.

———. *Peter Parley's Pictorial History of North and South America.* Hartford, CT: Peter Parley Publishing, 1858.

———. *Peter Parley's Tales About South America.* Baltimore: J. Jewett, 1832.

———. *A Pictorial History of America: Embracing Both the Northern and Southern Portions of the New World.* Hartford, CT: House and Brown, 1852.

Gordon, Amy Glassner. "Confronting Cultures: The Effect of Discoveries on Sixteenth-Century French Thought." *Terrae Incognitae* 8 (1976): 45-56.

Grant, William L. *History of Canada.* 1919. Rev. ed. London: Heinemann, 1924.

Grew, Raymond. "The Case for Comparing Histories." *American Historical Review* 85 (1980): 763-778.

———. "The Comparative Weakness of American History." *Journal of Interdisciplinary History* 16 (1986): 87-101.

Griffin, Charles C. "Problems of the National Period." *Revista de Historia de América* 34 (1952): 470-476.

———. "Unity and Variety in American History." Trans. Anna Macias. In *Do the Americas Have a Common History? A Critique of the Bolton Theory,* 250-269. Ed. Lewis Hanke. New York: Knopf, 1964.

Griffith, William J. "Herbert Eugene Bolton." *Mississippi Valley Historical Review* 41 (1953): 185-186.

Guarneri, Carl J. *America Compared: American History in International Perspective*. 2 vols. Boston: Houghton Mifflin, 1997.

———. "Out of Its Shell: Internationalizing the Teaching of United States History." *Perspectives* 35.2 (February 1997): 1, 5-8.

———. "Reconsidering C. Vann Woodward's *The Comparative Approach to American History*." *Reviews in American History* 23.3 (September 1995): 552-563.

Haar, Jerry, and Edgar J. Dosman, eds. *A Dynamic Partnership: Canada's Changing Role in the Americas*. New Brunswick, NJ: Transaction, 1993.

Hacker, Andrew. "'Diversity' and Its Dangers." *New York Review of Books* 7 (October 7, 1993): 21-25.

Hakluyt, Richard. *Divers Voyages Touching the Discouerie of America and the Ilands Adiacent vnto the Same, Made First of all by Our Englishmen and Afterward by the Frenchmen and Britons*. London: Thomas Woodcocke, 1582.

———. *Virginia Richly Valued...of Don Fernando de Soto...by a Portugall Gentleman of Elvas*. London: F. Kyngston, 1609.

Hale, Charles A. "The History of Ideas: Substantive and Methodological Aspects of the Thought of Leopoldo Zea." *Journal of Latin American Studies* 3 (1971): 59-70.

Hamill, Hugh M., Jr. "Charles Carroll Griffin (1902-1976)." *Hispanic American Historical Review* 57 (1977): 691-694.

Hammel, E. A. "The Comparative Method in Anthropological Perspective." *Comparative Studies in Society and History* 22 (1980): 145-155.

Hammond, George Peter. "In Memoriam: Herbert Eugene Bolton." *The Americas* 9 (1953): 391-398.

Hammond, George Peter, Charles W. Hackett, J. Lloyd Mecham, William C. Binkley, Cardinal Goodwin, and J. Fred Rippy, eds. *New Spain and the Anglo-American West: Historical Contributions to Herbert Eugene Bolton*. 2 vols. Los Angeles: privately published, 1932.

Hammond, George P., Lawrence Kinnaird, James King, and Engel Sluiter. "Herbert Eugene Bolton." *Hispanic American Historical Review* 33 (1953): 184-186.

Hanke, Lewis. "The Development of Latin American Studies in the United States, 1939-1945." *The Americas* 4 (1947): 32-64.

———. Review of *Greater America: Essays in Honor of Herbert Eugene Bolton*, edited by Adele Ogden and Engel Sluiter. *American Historical Review* 52 (1946): 205.

———. *Selected Writings of Lewis Hanke on the History of Latin America*. Tempe: Arizona State University, Center for Latin American Studies, 1979.

———. ed. *Do the Americas Have a Common History? A Critique of the Bolton Theory*. New York: Knopf, 1964.

Haring, Clarence H. *South America Looks at the United States*. New York: Macmillan, 1928.

———. *The Spanish Empire in America*. New York: Harcourt, Brace & World, 1947.

Hart, Estellita, comp. *Courses on Latin America in Institutions of Higher Education in the United States, 1948-1949*. Washington, DC: Pan-American Union, Division of Education, Department of Cultural Affairs, 1949.

Hartz, Louis. "American Historiography and Comparative Analysis." *Comparative Studies in Society and History* 5 (1962): 365-377.

Harvey, Gordon E. "'Without Conscious Hypocrisy': Woodrow Wilson's Mobile Address of 1913." *Gulf Coast Historical Review* 10 (1995): 25-46.

Hayes, Carlton J. H. "The American Frontier—Frontier of What?" *American Historical Review* 51 (1946): 199-216.

Headley, Phineas C., ed. *The History of Two Americas.* Chicago: A.S.L. Coburn & Co., 1878.

Healey, Miriam. "Great Historical Sketches: Herbert Eugene Bolton." *Pacific Historian* 13 (1969): 76-78.

Hennessy, Alistair. *The Frontier in Latin American History.* Albuquerque: University of New Mexico Press, 1978.

Hernández Sánchez-Barba, Mario. *Historia de América.* Madrid: Universidad Nacional de Educación a Distancia, Departamento de Historia, 1982.

———. *Historia universal de América.* 2 vols. Madrid: Guadarrama, 1963.

Higham, John. "The Future of American History." *Journal of American History* 80 (1994): 1289-1309.

———. *History.* Englewood Cliffs, NJ: Prentice Hall, 1965.

———. "Multiculturalism and Universalism: A History and Critique." *American Quarterly* 45 (1993): 195-219.

Hijiya, James. "Why the West Is Lost." *The William and Mary Quarterly* 51.2 (April 1994): 276-292.

Hill, Alette Olin, and Boyd H. Hill, Jr. "Marc Bloch and Comparative History: AHR Forum." *American Historical Review* 85 (1980): 828-857.

Hilton, Ronald. *Los estudios hispánicos en los Estados Unidos.* Trans. Lino Gómez Canedo, O.F.M. Madrid: Ediciones Cultura Hispánica, 1957.

Hilton, Sylvia L. *El americanismo en España: Bibliografía, 1988-1989.* Madrid: Centro de Estudios Históricos, Departamento de Historia de América, Consejo Superior de Investigaciones Científicos, 1989.

Holmes, Vera Brown. *A History of the Americas.* 2 vols. New York: Ronald Press, 1950-1964.

Hoover, Herbert. *The Memoirs of Herbert Hoover: The Cabinet and the Presidency, 1920-1933.* New York: Macmillan, 1952.

Horsman, Reginald. *Race and Manifest Destiny: The Origins of American Racial Anglo-Saxonism.* Cambridge, MA: Harvard University Press, 1981.

Hull, William I. "International Interpretation of United States History." *History Teacher's Magazine* 5 (1914): 135-139.

Humboldt, Alexander. *Voyage de Humboldt et Bonpland.* 23 vols. Paris: F. Schoell, 1805-1834.

Humphreys, John P. *The Inter-American System—A Canadian View.* Toronto: Macmillan, 1942.

Humphreys, R. A. *William Robertson and His "History of America."* London: Hispanic and Luso-Brazilian Councils, 1954.

Hurtado, Albert L. "Herbert E. Bolton, Racism, and American History." *Pacific Historical Review* 42 (1993): 127-142.

———. "Parkmanizing the Spanish Borderlands: Bolton, Turner, and the Historians' World." *Western Historical Quarterly* 26.2 (1995): 149-168.

Les Institutions coloniales dans les Amériques au XVIIIᵉ siècle: Colloque / Colonial Institutions in the Americas of the 18th Century: Seminar. Organized by the Canadian section of the historical commission of the Pan-American Institute of Geography and History. Laval University, March 6-10, 1972 (Mexico: L'Institut, 1974).

"Inter-American Notes." *The Americas* 1 (July 1944): 111.

Jacobs, Wilbur J. *The Historical World of Frederick Jackson Turner, with Selections from His Correspondence.* New Haven: Yale University Press, 1968.

Jacobs, Wilbur R., John W. Caughey and Joe B. Frantz. *Turner, Bolton, and Webb: Three Historians of the American Frontier.* Seattle: University of Washington Press, 1963.

Jacobsen, Jerome V. "Herbert E. Bolton." *Mid-America* 24 (1953): 75-80.

Jameson, J. Franklin. "A New Historical Journal." *Hispanic American Historical Review* 1 (1918): 2-7.

Kammen, Michael G. "The Problem of American Exceptionalism: A Reconsideration." *American Quarterly* 45 (1993): 12-43.

Kammen, Michael G., ed. *The Past Before Us: Contemporary Historical Writing in the United States:* Ithaca, NY: Cornell University Press, 1980.

Keen, Benjamin. *The History of Latin America.* 4th ed. Boston: Houghton Mifflin, 1992.

Kellner, Lotte. *Alexander von Humboldt.* New York: Oxford University Press, 1963.

Kinnaird, Lawrence. "Bolton of California." *California Historical Society Quarterly* 32 (1953): 97-103.

———. "Herbert Eugene Bolton: Historian of the Americas." *Andean Quarterly* (Santiago, Chile) Christmas iss. (1942): 3-5.

———. "Our Distinguished Faculty: Professor Herbert E. Bolton." *California Monthly* 41 (1951): 16, 30-31.

Kirk, Russell. *Edmund Burke: A Genius Reconsidered.* Peru, IL: Sherwood Sugden, 1988.

Koch, Hans-Albrecht, Margrit B. Knewson, and John A. Wolter, eds. *Progress of Discovery: Johann Georg Kohl.* Graz, Austria: Akademisch Druck, 1993.

Kolchin, Peter. "Comparing American History." *Reviews in American History* 10 (1982): 64-81.

Kottenkamp, Franz J. *Geschichte der Colonisation Amerika's.* 2 vols. Frankfurt: Literarische Anstalt, 1850.

Krause, Michael, and Davis D. Joyce. *The Writing of American History.* 1937. Rev. ed. Norman: University of Oklahoma Press, 1985.

Kupperman, Karen Ordahl, ed. *America in European Consciousness, 1493-1750.* Chapel Hill: University of North Carolina Press, 1995.

Latin American Studies in American Institutions of Higher Learning, Academic Year, 1935-36. Washington, DC: Pan-American Union, Division of Intellectual Cooperation, 1936.

Latin American Studies in the Universities of the United Kingdom, 1977-1978. London: University of London, Institute of Latin American Studies, 1978.

Laudonnière, René Goulaine de. "Narrative of Ribault's Whole and True Discovery of Terra Florida, as Far North as 36 Degrees, and the Founding of the First Settlement of French Protestants in America, 1562." In *The Genesis of South Carolina, 1562-1670.* Ed. William A. Courtenay. Columbia, SC: Privately printed by the State Company, 1907.

Laves, Walter H. C., ed. *Inter-American Solidarity.* Chicago: University of Chicago Press, 1941.

Leiken, Robert S., ed. *A New Moment in the Americas.* New Brunswick, NJ: Transaction, 1994.

Lemonich, M. D. "Coming to America." *Time* 141.18 (May 3, 1993): 60-62.

León, Pedro R. *Los estudios sobre iberoamérica en el Canada.* Toronto: Scarborough College, University of Toronto, 1974.

Levene, Ricardo. *Historia de América.* 15 vols. Buenos Aires: W.M. Jackson, 1940-1951.

Levy, Jim, and Peter Ross. "A Common History?: Two Latin Americans View the Writing of US History in Hemispheric Perspective." *Australasian Journal of American Studies* 12 (1993): 3-25.

Libby, O. G. Review of *The Colonization of North America*, by Herbert E. Bolton and Thomas M. Marshall. *Mississippi Valley Historical Review* 7 (1921): 397-399.

Library of Congress. *Hispanic Foundation.* Departmental and Divisional Manual no. 12. Washington, DC: Library of Congress, 1950.

Lippy, Charles H., Robert Choquette, and Stafford Poole. *Christianity Comes to America, 1492-1776.* New York: Paragon House, 1992.

Lockwood, Frank. "Adventurous Scholarship—Dr. Herbert E. Bolton." *Catholic World* 138 (1933): 185-194.

Lowery, Woodbury. *The Spanish Settlements Within the Present Limits of the United States, 1513-1561.* New York: G. P. Putnam's, 1901.

Lucas, Charles P. "The ABC of West Indian History." *History Teacher's Magazine* 6 (1913): 183-187.

———. *History of Canada: The History from the Discoveries to 1763.* 2nd ed. Oxford: Clarendon Press, 1931.

Mable, H. W. "Spirit of the New World as Interpreted by the Exposition." *Outlook* 68 (July 6, 1901): 529-547.

MacCormac, John. *Canada: America's Problem.* New York: Viking, 1940.

MacGregor, John. *The Progress of America: From the Discovery by Columbus to the Year 1846.* 2 vols. London: Whittaker and Co., 1847.

Maciel, David. R. "An Interview With Leopoldo Zea." *Hispanic American Historical Review* 65.1 (1985): 1-20.

Mackenzie, Robert. *America and Her Army.* London: Thomas Nelson, 1865.

———. *America: A History.* 1882. Repr. New York: Thomas Nelson, 1894.

———. *The Nineteenth Century.* 1880. Repr. London: Thomas Nelson, 1895.

———. *The United States of America: A History.* London: Thomas Nelson, 1870.

Madsen, William. Review of *The Native Period in the History of the New World*, by Pedro Armillas. *Hispanic American Historical Review* 44 (1964): 405-407.

Magaro Rubin, Amy. "Trying to Revive a 3-Way Collaboration. *Chronicle of Higher Education* 42 (May 17, 1996): A43, A46.

Magnaghi, Russell M. "Herbert E. Bolton and Sources of American Indian Studies." *Western Historical Quarterly* 6 (1975): 33-46.

———. *The History of the Americas at Two Jesuit Universities: St. Louis University and the University of San Francisco.* Marquette, MI: Belle Fontaine Press, 1994.

Maltby, William S. *The Black Legend in England: The Development of Anti-Spanish Sentiment, 1558-1660.* Durham, NC: Duke University Press, 1971.

Maltin, Leonard. *The Disney Films.* 1973. Rev. ed. New York: Popular Library, 1978.

Marshall, Thomas M. "Present Tendencies in High School History Teaching." *History Teacher's Magazine* 5 (1914): 179-181.

Martiniere, Guy. "La escuela de los Annales y las Américas Latinas (1929-1949)." *Estudios Latinoamericanos* (Warsaw) 4 (1980): 133-153.

McCormick, Richard P. "The Comparative Method: Its Application to American History." *Mid-America* 56 (1974): 231-247.

———. "The New York Meeting, 1954." *American Historical Review* 60 (1955): 720-751.

McGerr, Michael. "The Price of the 'New Transnational History.'" *American Historical Review* 96 (1991): 1056-1067.

McGill Calendar, 1926-1927. Montreal: McGill University, 1926.

McNeill, William H. *The Global Connection: Conquerors, Catastrophes, and Community*. Princeton: Princeton University Press, 1992.

"The Meeting of the AHA at Buffalo and Ithaca [December 27-30, 1911]." *Annual Report of the AHA for the Year 1911*. 2 vols. Washington, DC: Government Printing Office, 1913.

Mesa-Lago, Carmelo, Sandra E. Miller, and Shirley A. Kregar. *Latin American Studies in Europe*. Pittsburgh: Center for Latin American Studies, 1979.

Mesa y Leopart, José. *Compendio de la historia de América desde su descubrimiento hasta nuestros días*. 2 vols. Paris: Rosa y Bourte, 1870.

Meyer, Jean, coord. *Egohistorias. El amor a Clío*. México, DF: Centre d'Études Mexicaines et Centraméricaines, 1993.

Millán, José R. *Compendio de historia americana*. Buenos Aires: A. Kapelusz, 1932.

Moore, J. Preston. Review of *The Colonial Period in the History of the New World*, by Silvio Zavala. *Hispanic American Historical Review* 43 (1963): 546-547.

Morehouse, Frances. "Broadening the Historical Background." *Historical Outlook* 14 (1923): 220-222.

Morison, Samuel Eliot. *The European Discovery of America: The Southern Voyages, A.D. 1492-1616*. New York: Oxford University Press, 1974.

Mörner, Magnus, Julia Fawaz de Viñuela, and John D. French. "Comparative Approaches to Latin American History." *Latin American Research Review* 17 (1982): 55-89.

Morón, Guillermo. "Informe sobre proyecto de historia general de América." *Revista de historia de América* 90 (1980): 61-66.

Morris, William A. "The Origin and Authorship of the Bancroft Pacific States Publication: A History of a History." *Oregon Historical Society Quarterly* 4 (1903): 287-364.

———. "Proceedings of the Tenth Annual Meeting of the Pacific Coast Branch of the American Historical Association." In *Annual Report of the AHA for the Year 1913*. 2 vols. Washington, DC: Government Printing Office, 1913.

———. "Report of the Proceedings of the 13th Annual Meeting of the Pacific Coast Branch of the American Historical Association." In *Annual Report of the American Historical Association for the Year 1916*. 2 vols. Washington, DC: Government Printing Office, 1919.

Moses, Bernard. *The Establishment of Spanish Rule in America: An Introduction to the History and Politics of Spanish America*. New York: G. P. Putnam's, 1898.

———. "The Neglected Half of American History." *University Chronicle* (Berkeley) 1 (1898): 120-126.

Mosk, Sanford A. "Latin America Versus the United States." *American Economic Association, Papers and Proceedings* 40 (1951): 367-383.

Münster, Sebastian. *A Treatyse of the Newe India*. Trans. Richard Eden. London: Edward Sutton, 1553.

Nasatir, A. P. Review of *Herbert Eugene Bolton: The Historian and the Man, 1870-1953,* by John F. Bannon. *Hispanic American Historical Review* 50 (1979): 499.

Nash, Gerald D. *Creating the West: Historical Interpretations, 1890-1990.* Albuquerque: University of New Mexico Press, 1991.

Navarro García, Luis, coord. *Historia de las Américas.* 4 vols. Madrid: Alhambra Longman, 1991.

Nichols, Roy F. "A United States Historian's Appraisal." *Revista de historia de América* 43 (1957): 144-158.

Nicholson, Norman L. *Canada in the American Community.* Princeton: Van Nostrand, 1963.

"North American Art—Themeless." *The Economist* 334 (March 4-10, 1995): 85.

North-South Center, University of Miami. Coral Gables, FL: North-South Center, 1996.

Northrop, Filmer S. C. *The Meeting of East and West: An Inquiry Concerning World Understanding.* New York: Macmillan, 1946.

"Obituaries, Vera Brown Holmes." *Smith Alumnae Quarterly* 72.2 (1981), 51-52.

Ocampo, Victoria, ed. *Is America a Continent? A Round Table Discussion.* Trans. Angel Flores. Points of View no. 2. Washington, DC: Division of Intellectual Cooperation, Pan-American Union, 1941.

Official Catalogue and Guide Book to the Pan-American Exposition. Buffalo: Charles Ahrahart, 1901.

Ogden, Adele, and Engel Sluiter, eds. *Greater America: Essays in Honor of Herbert Eugene Bolton.* Berkeley: University of California Press, 1945.

Ogelsby, J.C.M. *Gringos from the Far North: Essays in the History of Canadian-Latin American Relations, 1866-1968.* Toronto: Macmillan, 1976.

———. "Latin American Studies in Canada, 1866-1981." *Inter-American Review of Bibliography* 32 (1982): 347-355.

O'Gorman, Edmundo. *Do the Americas Have a Common History?* Trans. Angel Flores. Points of View no. 3. Washington, DC: Pan-American Union, Division of Intellectual Cooperation, 1941.

———. "Do the Americas Have a Common History?" In *Do the Americas Have a Common History?: A Critique of the Bolton Theory,* 103-111. Ed. Lewis Hanke. New York: Knopf, 1964.

———. *Fundamentos de la historia de América.* México, DF: Universitaria, 1942.

———. "Have the Americas a Common History? A Mexican View." *Canadian Historical Review* 23 (1942): 139-148.

———. "Hegel y el moderno panamericanismo." *Universidad de la Habana* 8 (1939): 61-74.

Oliveira Lima, Manuel de. *The Evolution of Brazil Compared with That of Spanish and Anglo-Saxon America.* Stanford, CA: Stanford University Press, 1914. Repr. New York: Russell & Russell, 1966.

Onís, José de. "The Americas of Herbert E. Bolton." *The Americas* 12 (1955): 157-168.

———. "Out of its Shell: Internationalizing the Teaching of United States History." *Perspectives* 35.2 (February 1997): 1, 5-8.

Padover, S. K., ed. *The Complete Madison.* New York: Harper, 1953.

Páez, J. R. "Don Antonio de Alcedo y su biblioteca americana." *Boletín de la Academia Nacional de la Historia* (Quito) 37 (1937): 90-91.

Painter, Sidney. "The Washington Meeting, 1952." *American Historical Review* 58 (1953): 742-765.

Palmer, Colin A. "Distant Neighbors: Teaching about the Caribbean." *Perspectives* 33.2 (February 1995): 1, 7-8, 10.

Parks, George Bruner. *Richard Hakluyt and the English Voyages*. Ed. James A. Williamson. 1928. New York: Frederick Ungar, 1961.

Parry, John H., and Robert G. Keith, eds. *New Iberian World: A Documentary History of the Discovery and Settlement of Latin America to the Early 17th Century*. 5 vols. New York: Time Books, 1984.

Peixoto, Afranio. *Pequeña historia de las Américas*. Trans. Pedro Gonzáles-Blanco. México, DF: Botas 1946.

Pereyrea, Carlos. *Breve historia de América*. 2 vols. 1939. Rev. ed. Santiago, Chile: Zig-Zag, 1946.

Perkins, Dexter. Review of *The National Period in the History of the New World*, by Charles C. Griffin. *American Historical Review* 69 (1964): 467-468.

"Personal—Recent Deaths." [John B. Brebner.] *American Historical Review* 63 (1958): 859.

Pike, Frederick B. *The United States and Latin America: Myths and Stereotypes of Civilization and Nature*. Austin: University of Texas Press, 1992.

Pomfret, John E. *Founding of the American Colonies, 1583-1660*. New York: Harper & Row, 1970.

Popelinière, Lancelot du Voisin, Sieur de La. *Les Trois Mondes*. Paris: Pierre L'Huillier, 1582.

Prado, Eduardo. *A ilusão americana*. 2nd ed. Paris: A. Colin, 1895.

Priestley, Herbert I. *The Coming of the White Man, 1492-1848*. New York: Macmillan, 1929.

Purchas, Samuel. *Hakluytus Posthumus or Purchas His Pilgrimes*. 4 vols. London: William Stansby/Henry Fetherstone, 1625.

Quijano, Aníbal, and Immanuel Wallerstein. "Americanity as a Concept, or The Americas in the Modern World-System." *International Social Science Journal* 34 (1992): 549-557.

Quinn, David B. *North America from Earliest Discovery to First Settlements: The Norse Voyages to 1612*. New York: Harper & Row, 1977.

———, ed. *The Hakluyt Handbook*. 2 vols. London: The Hakluyt Society, 1974.

———, ed. *New American World: A Documentary History of North America to 1612*. 5 vols. New York: Arno Press, 1979.

———, ed. *North American Discovery, Circa 1000-1612*. New York: Harper & Row, 1971.

Quintanilla, Luis. *A Latin American Speaks*. New York: Macmillan, 1943.

Redlich, Fritz. "Toward Comparative Historiography: Background and Problems." *Kyklos. International Review for the Social Sciences* (Basle) 11 (1958): 362-389.

"Règlement de la Société des Américanistes de Paris." *Journal de la Société des Américanistes de Paris* 1 (1895-1896): 1-2.

Report of the Committee on Latin American Studies. London: Her Majesty's Stationery Office, 1965.

"Review of *Wider Horizons of American History*, by Herbert E. Bolton." *Pacific Historical Review* 8 (1939): 361.

Rippy, J. Fred. *Bygones I Cannot Help Recalling: The Memoirs of a Mobile Scholar*.

Austin, TX: Steck-Vaughn, 1966.

―――. "Herbert Eugene Bolton: A Recollection." *Southwest Review* 39 (1954): 166-177.

―――. *Historical Evolution of Hispanic America*. Oxford: Basil Blackwell, 1936.

―――. *South America and Hemisphere Defense*. Baton Rouge: Louisiana State University Press, 1941.

Rivale, Pascal. "L'Américanisme français à la veille de la fondation de la Société des Américanistes." *Journal de la Société des Américanistes de Paris* 81 (1995): 207-231.

Rivera, Diego, with Gladys March. *My Art. My Life: An Autobiography*. New York: Citadel Press, 1960. Repr. New York: Dover, 1991.

Robertson, James A., ed. "A Symposium on the Teaching of the History of Hispanic America in Educational Institutions of the United States." *Hispanic American Historical Review* 2 (1919): 397-446.

Robertson, William. *The History of the Discovery and Settlement of America*. 2 vols. Dublin: Messrs. Whitestone, 1777; Edinburgh: W. Strahan, 1777.

―――. *The History of America*. New York: S. Campbell, 1798.

―――. *The History of America*. 2 vols. Philadelphia: Johnson & Warner, 1812.

―――. *The History of the Reign of the Emperor, Charles V*. 3 vols. London: W. Strahan, 1769.

―――. *The Works of William Robertson*. 8 vols. London: Talboys and Wheeler, 1825.

Robertson, William Spence. *History of the Latin-American Nations*. New York: D. Appleton, 1922.

Robinson, Geroid. "Changing Emphasis in European History in the High Schools of California." *History Teacher's Magazine* 8 (1917): 85-88.

Robinson, Nicholas K. *Edmund Burke: A Life in Caricature*. New Haven: Yale University Press, 1996.

Rochlin, James. *Discovering the Americas: The Evolution of Canadian Foreign Policy Towards Latin America*. Vancouver: University of British Columbia Press, 1994.

―――. "The Evolution of Canada as an Actor in Inter-American Affairs." *Millennium* 19 (1990): 229-248.

Rodriques, Celso, ed. "The Writings of Lewis Hanke." *Inter-American Review of Bibliography* 36 (1986): 427-451.

Rogers, Howard J., ed. *Congress of Arts and Sciences, Universal Exposition, St. Louis, 1904*. 2 vols. Boston: Houghton Mifflin, 1906.

Rokkan, Stein, ed. *Comparative Research Across Cultures and Nations*. Paris: International Social Science Council, and The Hague: Mouton, 1968.

Root, Elihu. *Speeches Incident to the Visit of Secretary Root to South America*. Washington, DC: Government Printing Office, 1906.

Roussin, Marcel. *Le Canada et le système interaméricain*. Ottawa: University of Ottawa Press, 1959.

Ruprecht, Alvina, ed. *The Reordering of Culture: Latin America, the Caribbean, and Canada in the Hood*. Ottawa: Carleton University Press, 1995.

Rydell, Robert W. *All the World's a Fair: Visions of Empire at American International Expositions, 1876-1916*. Chicago: University of Chicago Press, 1984.

Sachse, William L. "Echoes from Chicago." *American Historical Review* 47 (1942): 481-482.

Sage, Walter N. Review of *History of the Americas*, by Herbert E. Bolton. *Canadian*

Historical Review 10 (1929): 70-71.

——. "Some Aspects of the Frontier in Canadian History." *Canadian Historical Association Report* 6 (1928): 62-72.

Sampablo, Raúl, dir. *América, que hermosa eres.* 3 vols. Barcelona: Editorial Mateu, 1974.

Sánchez, Luis Alberto. *América desde la revolución emancipadora hasta nuestros días.* Madrid: EDAF, 1975.

——. *Historia general de América.* 2 vols. Santiago de Chile: Ediciones Ercilla, 1942.

——. "A New Interpretation of the History of America." *Hispanic American Historical Review* 23 (1943): 441-456.

——. *The Presence of Tradition.* Points of View no. 4. Washington, DC: Pan-American Union, 1941.

Sarmiento, Domingo. *North and South America: Discourse Delivered Before the Rhode Island Historical Society, December 27, 1865.* Providence: Rhode Island Historical Society, 1865.

Sater, William F. "Joining the Mainstream: Integrating Latin America into the Teaching of World History." *Perspectives* 33.5 (1995): 19-22, 37.

Sauer, Carl O. "Herbert Eugene Bolton (1870-1953)." *American Philosophical Society Yearbook, 1953* (Philadelphia: APS, 1954): 321.

Schlesinger, Arthur M. "The History Situation in Colleges and Universities, 1919-20." *History Teacher's Magazine* 11 (1920): 103-106.

Schlesinger, Arthur M., Jr. *The Disuniting of America: Reflections on a Multicultural Society.* New York: Norton, 1991.

Scobel, Albert. *Nordamerika, Mexico, Mittelamerika und Westindien kommerziell, politisch und statistich.* Leipzig: Metzger & Wittig, 1882.

Second General Assembly of the Pan-American Institute of Geography and History, Washington, October 14-19, 1935. Washington, DC: Pan-American Union, 1935.

Sewell, William H., Jr. "Marc Bloch and the Logic of Comparative History." *History and Theory* 6 (1967): 208-218.

Shaw, Albert, ed. *President Wilson's State Papers and Addresses.* New York: George H. Doran, 1918.

Shepherd, William R. "The Contribution of the Romance Nations to the History of the Americas." In *Annual Report of the American Historical Association for the Year 1909*, 221-227. Washington, DC: Government Printing Office, 1910.

Simonds, Frank H. "Hoover, South Americanus." *Review of Reviews* 79 (February 1929): 67.

Sivirichi, Atilio. *Historia de América.* Lima: D. Miranda, 1939.

Sjoberg, Gideon. "The Comparative Method in the Social Sciences." In *Comparative Perspectives: Theories and Methods.* Ed. Amitai Etzioni and F. Dubow. Boston: Little, Brown, 1970.

Slatta, Richard W. *Cowboys of the Americas.* New Haven: Yale University Press, 1990.

Soward, F. H., and A. M. Macaulay. *Canada and the Pan-American System.* Toronto: Ryerson, 1948.

Spell, J. R. "Spanish Teaching in the United States." *Hispania* 10 (May 1927): 141-159.

Stabb, Martin S. "Obituary: Harold Eugene Davis (1902-1988)." *Hispanic American*

Historical Review 69 (1989): 331-332.

Stearns, W. N. "Canadian History Next?" *History Teacher's Magazine* 6 (November 1915): 294.

Stein, Stanley J. Review of *The Colonial Period in the History of the New World*, by Silvio Zavala. *American Historical Review* 68 (1963): 757-758.

Stephens, H. Morse. "Courses in History in the Junior Colleges." *History Teacher's Magazine* 4 (1913): 153-155.

Stephens, H. Morse, and Herbert E. Bolton, eds. *The Pacific Ocean in History*. New York: Macmillan, 1917.

Stephens, Leslie, and Sidney Lee, eds. *The Dictionary of National Biography*. 34 vols. Oxford: Oxford University Press, 1925-1986.

Stewart, Dugald. *Account of the Life and Writings of William Robertson*. London: T. Cadell, Jr., & W. Davies, 1801.

———. *Biographical Memoir of Adam Smith, LL.D., of William Robertson, D.D., and of Thomas Reid, D. D.* Edinburgh: G. Ramsay & Co. 1811.

Sullivan, Mark. "With Hoover in Latin America." *Review of Reviews* 79 (February 1929): 53-54.

Sweet, William W. *A History of Latin America*. New York: Abington, 1929.

Swigart, Beulah H. "The Americas as Revealed in the Encyclopédie." Diss., University of Illinois, Urbana, 1939.

Tanzi, Héctor José. "Historiografía americana." *Revista de historia de América* 104 (1987): 65-112.

TePaske, John J. "An Interview with Irving A. Leonard." *Hispanic American Historical Review* 63 (1983): 233-53.

Thevet, André. *André Thevet's North America: A Sixteenth Century View*. Ed. and trans. Roger Schlesinger and Arthur P. Stabler. Kingston, ON: Queen's University Press; Montreal: McGill University Press, 1986.

———. *The New Found Worlde or Antarctike*. London: Henry Bynneman, 1568.

Thompson, Wallace. *The Civilization of the Americas*. Berkeley: University of California Press, 1938.

———. *Greater America: An Interpretation of Latin America in Relation to Anglo-Saxon America*. New York: E. P. Dutton, 1932.

Thorning, Joseph F. "The Place of the American Republics and Canada in the New World Order." *The Americas* 3 (1946): 161-167.

Thwaites, Reuben G. *The Colonies, 1492-1750*. New York: Longman's, Green, & Co., 1897.

"Toward the Internationalization of American History: A Round Table." *Journal of American History* 79.2 (September 1992): 432-532.

Treutlein, Theodore E. "Deceased: Herbert Eugene Bolton." *American Historical Review* 58 (1953): 791-792.

———. "Necrologías: Herbert Eugene Bolton (1870-1953)." *Revista de historia de América* 37-38 (1954): 299-302.

Trotter, Reginald G. *Canadian History: A Syllabus and Guide to Reading*. Toronto: Macmillan, 1934.

———. "Canadian History in the Universities of the United States." *Canadian Historical Review* 8 (1927): 190-207.

———. "Canadian Interest in the History of the United States." *Queen's Quarterly* 36 (1929): 98.

————. *Conference on Canadian-American Affairs*. Canton, NY: St. Lawrence University Press, 1935; Kingston, ON: Queen's University Press, 1937; Canton, NY: St. Lawrence University Press, 1939; Kingston, ON: Queen's University Press, 1941.

————. "More on Canada and Pan-Americanism, A Reply to Professor Corbett." *Inter-American Quarterly* 2 (1940): 5-10.

————. "Some American Influences upon the Canadian Federation Movement." *Canadian Historical Review* 5 (1924): 213-227.

Tulchin, Joseph. *The Aftermath of War: World War I and U.S. Policy Toward Latin America*. New York: New York University Press, 1971.

Turner, Frederick J. "Problems in American History." In *Congress of Arts and Science, Universal Exposition, St. Louis, 1904*. Ed. Howard J. Rogers. 2 vols. Boston: Houghton Mifflin, 1906.

————. *Reuben Gold Thwaites, Memorial Address*. Madison: Wisconsin State Historical Society, 1914.

————. "The Significance of the Frontier in American History." American Historical Association. *Annual Report for the Year 1893*, 197-227. Washington, DC: Government Printing Office, 1894.

Turner, Ralph E. "Comments on the Project on the History of America." *Revista de historia de América* 34 (1952): 486-489.

Tyrrell, Ian. "American Exceptionalism in an Age of International History." *American Historical Review* 96 (1991): 1031-1055.

Ullrick, Laura F. "Latin American History in the High School: An Experiment." *History Teacher's Magazine* 8 (1917): 296.

Unsigned Review of *Wider Horizons of American History* by Herbert E. Bolton. *Pacific Historical Review* 9 (1939): 361.

The University as a Factor in American Relations. International Conciliation, Pan-American Division, Bulletin no. 9. New York: American Association for International Conciliation, Pan-American Division, 1916.

Van Den Braembussche, A. A. "Historical Explanation and Comparative Method: Towards a Theory of the History of Society." *History and Theory* 28 (1989): 1-24.

Vargas Martínez, Gustavo, comp. *Bibliografía de Leopoldo Zea*. México, DF: Fondo de Cultura Económica, 1992.

Vianna, Hélio. "Bases sociológicas de formação americana." *Espelho* (Rio de Janeiro) 8 (November 1935): 14+.

————. *Estudos de história colonial*. São Paulo: Companhia Editora Nacional, 1948.

Warden, David Baille. *Chronologie historique de l'Amérique*. 10 vols. Paris: A. Dupont et Roret, 1826-1844.

Ware, Edith E. ed. *The Study of International Relations in the United States, Survey for 1934*. New York: Columbia University Press, 1935.

————. *The Study of International Relations in the United States, Survey for 1937*. New York: Columbia University Press, 1938.

Watson, James E. "Bernard Moses: Pioneer in Latin American Scholarship." *Hispanic American Historical Review* 42 (1962): 212-216.

Webb, Victor L. Edna Fay, and William L. Nida. *The New World, Past and Present: A Unified Course in History and Geography for Elementary Schools*. Chicago: Scott Foresman, 1938.

Weber, David J. "Conflicts and Accommodations: Hispanic and Anglo-American

Borders in Historical Perspective, 1670-1853." *Journal of the Southwest* 39 (1997): 1-32.

——. *The Mexican Frontier, 1821-1846: The American Southwest Under Mexico.* Albuquerque: University of New Mexico Press, 1982.

——. Our Hispanic Past: A Fuzzy View Persists." *The Chronical of High Education* 10 (March 1993): A44.

——. *The Spanish Frontier in North America.* New Haven: Yale University Press, 1992.

——. "Turner, the Boltonians, and the Borderlands." *American Historical Review* 91 (1986): 66-81.

Westergaard, Waldemar. "American Interest in the West Indies." *History Teacher's Magazine* 8 (1917): 249-253.

Whitaker, Arthur P. "The Americas in the Atlantic Triangle." In *Ensayos sobre la historia del Nuevo Mundo*, 69-96. Ed. Edgar McInnis. México, DF: Pan-American Institute of Geography and History, 1951.

——. "Introduction to the Project for a History of America." *Revista de historia de América* 43 (1957): 141-144.

——. Review of *The Coming of the White Man, 1492-1848*, by Herbert I. Priestley. *Hispanic American Historical Review* 10 (1930): 63.

——. Review of *Wider Horizons of American History*, by Herbert E. Bolton. *Mississippi Valley Historical Review* 26 (1939): 458-460.

——. *The United States and the Independence of Latin America, 1800-1830.* Baltimore: Johns Hopkins University Press, 1941.

——. *The Western Hemisphere Idea: Its Rise and Decline.* Ithaca, NY: Cornell University Press, 1954.

Wilgus, A. Curtis. *The Historiography of Latin America: A Guide to Historical Writing, 1500-1800.* Metuchen, NJ: Scarecrow, 1975.

Williams, Mary W. *The Peoples and Politics of Latin America: A History.* Boston: Ginn, 1930.

Wilson, Samuel K. *American History.* Chicago: Loyola University Press, 1929.

Wilson, Woodrow. Speech. *Congressional Record*, 64th Cong., 1st sess., December 7, 1916. 53: 95-96.

Winsor, Justin, ed. *A Narrative and Critical History of America.* 8 vols. Boston: Houghton Mifflin, 1884-1889.

Winterbotham, William. *American Historical, Geographical, Commercial and Philosophical Views of the American United States and of the European Settlements in America and the West-Indies.* 4 vols. London: J. Ridgway, 1795.

Wish, Harvey. *The American Historian: A Social-Intellectual History of the Writing of the American Past.* New York: Oxford University Press, 1960.

Wittke, Carl. "Canada—Our Neglected Neighbor." *History Teacher's Magazine* 10 (1919): 485-488.

Wolfe, Bertram D. *The Fabulous Life of Diego Rivera.* New York: Stein & Day, 1963.

Woll, Allen. "For God or Country: History Textbooks and the Secularization of Chilean Society, 1840-1890." *Journal of Latin American Studies* 7 (1975): 23-43.

——. *A Functional Past: The Uses of History in Nineteenth Century Chile.* Baton Rouge: Louisiana State University Press, 1982.

Wood, Gordon S. "Doing the Continental." *The New York Review of Books* 44.18 (November 20, 1997): 51-54.

Woodward, C. Vann. "The Comparability of American History." In *The Comparative Approach to American History*. Ed. C. Vann Woodward. New York: Basic Books, 1968. Repr. New York: Oxford University Press, 1997.

——, ed. *The Comparative Approach to American History*. New York: Basic Books, 1968.

Worcester, Donald E. Review of *The National Period in the History of the New World*, by Charles C. Griffin. *Hispanic American Historical Review* 43 (1963): 144-145.

Young, W. A. *The History of North and South America, with an Account of the First Discovery of the New World, the Customs, Genius, and Persons of the Original Inhabitants, and a Particular Description [of] Air, Soil, Natural Products, Manufactures and Commerce of Each Settlement Including a Geographical, Commercial and Historical Survey of the British Settlements, from the Earliest Times to the Present Period, with an Account of the West Indies and American Islands, to Which Is Added an Impartial Enquiry into the Present American Dispute*. 2 vols. London: for J. Whitaker, 1776.

——. *The History of North and South America, with an Account of the West Indies and American Islands, to Which Is Prefixed a Candid and Impartial Enquiry into the Present Disputes*. 2 vols. London: W. Lane, 1776.

Zabre, Teja. *Dinámica de la historia y frontera intramericana*. México, DF: Botas, 1947.

Zavala, Silvio. "Colaboración internacional en torno de la historia de América." *Revista de historia de América* 35-36 (1953): 209-226.

——. "The Commission on History of the Pan-American Institute of Geography and History." *The Americas* 6 (1950): 489.

——. "International Collaboration in the History of America." *Comparative Studies in Society and History* 1 (1959): 284-287.

——. *El mundo americano en la época colonial*. 2 vols. México, DF: Instituto Panamericano de Geografía e Historia, 1962. Repr. México, DF: Editorial Porrúa, 1990.

——. *A Program of the History of the New World Coordinator's Summary Reports*. Abr. ed. Vol. 2, *The Colonial Period in the History of the New World*. Trans. Max Savelle. Publication no. 102. 1962. Westport, CT: Greenwood Press, 1983.

——. Review of *La epopeya de la máxima América*, by Herbert E. Bolton. *Revista de historia de América* 1 (1938): 81.

Zavala, Silvio, Francisco Monterde, and Felipe Teixidor, eds. "Propósitos." *Revista de historia de América* 1 (1938): v-vi.

Zea, Leopoldo. *América en la historia*. México, DF: Fondo de Cultura Económica, 1957.

——. "The Interpretation of the Ibero-American and North American Cultures." *Philosophy and Phenomenological Research* 9 (1949): 538-543.

——. *The Role of the Americas in History*. Ed. Amy A. Oliver, trans. Sonja Karsen. Savage, MD: Rowman & Littlefield, 1992.

Zoltvany, Yves F., ed. *The French Tradition in America*. New York: Harper & Row, 1969.

Index

About the Author

RUSSELL M. MAGNAGHI is Professor of History and University Historian at Northern Michigan University. He also serves as Director for the Center for Upper Peninsula Studies.